WORLDS
of
WONDER

Elwin Street would like to extend their grateful thanks to the contributors:

John Batchelor, Catherine Butler, David Colmer, Nicola Daly, Sara K. Day, Julia Eccleshare, Marianne Eloise, Joseph Farrell, Alison Fincher, Alison Flood, Rosemary Goring, Daniel Hahn, Robert Holden, Kat Howard, Simon Hubbert, Jon Hughes, Peter Hunt, Rosemary Johnston, Sam Jordison, Reyes Lazaro, Emily Lethbridge, Antonia Lloyd-Jones, Sarah Mesle, Laura Miller, Mahvesh Murad, Abigail Nussbaum, Margaret J. Oakes, Stephanie Owen Reeder, Jess Payn, Eric Rabkin, Kim Reynolds, Maria Russo, Elena Sheppard, Jared Shurin, Drew Smith, Michelle Smith, Maureen Speller, Björn Sundmark, John Sutherland, John Stephens, Francesca Tancini, Phoebe Taplin, James Thurgill, Anja Tröger, Nicholas Tucker, Lisa Tuttle, Kiera Vaclavik, Derong Xu.

For more about the contributors, see page 248

First published by Princeton University Press in 2025 in North America and the United Kingdom
41 William Street, Princeton, NJ 08540, USA
99 Banbury Road, Oxford, OX2 6JX, UK
press.princeton.edu

Copyright © 2025 by Elwin Street Productions Limited
Conceived and produced by Elwin Street Productions Limited
10 Elwin Street, London, E2 7BU, UK
www.elwinstreet.com

Cover design by Haley Jin Mee Chung
Cover image: illustration by John Tenniel for the first edition of *Alice's Adventures in Wonderland*
Picture credits: page 256

Every effort has been made to trace copyright holders and to obtain their permission for the use of copyrighted material. The publisher apologizes for any errors or omissions in the following list and would be grateful if notified of any corrections that should be incorporated in future reprints or editions of this book.

All rights reserved. No part of this book may be used or reproduced in any manner whatsoever without written permission from the publisher except in the case of brief quotations embodied in critical articles or reviews.

ISBN 978-0-691-27463-8

Library of Congress Control Number: 2024952027
British Library Cataloging-in-Publication Data is available

10 9 8 7 6 5 4 3 2 1

Printed in Dubai

FSC is a non-profit international organization established to promote the responsible management of the world's forests. Products carrying the FSC label are independently certified to assure consumers that they come from forests that are managed to meet the social, economic, and ecological needs of present and future generations, and other controlled sources.

Overleaf: Liesel discovers the mayor's library, illustration by Alexis Deacon for the 2024 Folio Society edition of *The Book Thief*.

WORLDS of WONDER

Celebrating
the Great Classics *of*
Children's Literature

Daniel Hahn, General Editor
Foreword by Julia Eccleshare

Princeton University Press
Princeton and Oxford

CONTENTS

FOREWORD: Julia Eccleshare   10

INTRODUCTION: Daniel Hahn   12

 1837–1929

1   THE FIRST GOLDEN AGE

HANS CHRISTIAN ANDERSEN   18
The Little Mermaid, 1837

LEWIS CARROLL   21
Alice's Adventures in Wonderland, 1865

LOUISA MAY ALCOTT   26
Little Women, 1868

OUIDA   30
A Dog of Flanders, 1872

MARK TWAIN   32
The Adventures of Tom Sawyer, 1876

ANNA SEWELL   34
Black Beauty, 1877

HECTOR MALOT   36
Nobody's Boy, 1878

JOHANNA SPYRI   39
Heidi, 1880

CARLO COLLODI   42
The Adventures of Pinocchio, 1883

ROBERT LOUIS STEVENSON   44
Treasure Island, 1883

ETHEL TURNER   47
Seven Little Australians, 1894

RUDYARD KIPLING   50
The Jungle Book, 1894

L. FRANK BAUM   52
The Wonderful Wizard of Oz, 1900

E. NESBIT   56
Five Children and It, 1902

BEATRIX POTTER   58
The Tale of Peter Rabbit, 1902

SELMA LAGERLÖF   62
The Wonderful Adventures of Nils, 1906

LUCY MAUD MONTGOMERY   64
Anne of Green Gables, 1908

KENNETH GRAHAME   68
The Wind in the Willows, 1908

FRANCES HODGSON BURNETT   72
The Secret Garden, 1911

J. M. BARRIE   75
Peter and Wendy, 1911

A. A. MILNE   80
Winnie-the-Pooh, 1926

ERICH KÄSTNER   84
Emil and the Detectives, 1929

2 NEW HORIZONS

1930–1959

ANDRÉ MAUROIS	88	ASTRID LINDGREN	113
Fattypuffs and Thinifers, 1930		*Pippi Longstocking*, 1945	
KENJI MIYAZAWA	90	TOVE JANSSON	115
Night on the Galactic Railroad, 1934		*The Moomins and the Great Flood*, 1945	
P. L. TRAVERS	94	C. S. LEWIS	118
Mary Poppins, 1934		*The Lion, the Witch, and the Wardrobe*, 1950	
NOEL STREATFEILD	97	E. B. WHITE	124
Ballet Shoes, 1936		*Charlotte's Web*, 1952	
J. R. R. TOLKIEN	99	RUSKIN BOND	126
The Hobbit, 1937		*The Room on the Roof*, 1956	
T. H. WHITE	102	DODIE SMITH	128
The Sword in the Stone, 1938		*The Hundred and One Dalmatians*, 1956	
HERGÉ	104	MICHAEL BOND	130
The Adventures of Tintin: The Secret of the Unicorn, 1942		*A Bear Called Paddington*, 1958	
ENID BLYTON	108	JAMES VANCE MARSHALL	132
The Magic Faraway Tree, 1943		*Walkabout*, 1959	
ANTOINE DE SAINT-EXUPERY	110		
The Little Prince, 1943			

3. Modern Narratives

1960–1984

RENÉ GOSCINNY & ALBERT UDERZO *Asterix the Gaul*, 1961	136
NORTON JUSTER *The Phantom Tollbooth*, 1961	138
MADELEINE L'ENGLE *A Wrinkle in Time*, 1962	142
TONKE DRAGT *The Letter for the King*, 1962	144
GIANNI RODARI *Telephone Tales*, 1962	146
CLIVE KING *Stig of the Dump*, 1963	150
JOAN AIKEN *The Wolves of Willoughby Chase*, 1963	152
ROALD DAHL *Charlie and the Chocolate Factory*, 1964	155
RUSSELL HOBAN *The Mouse and His Child*, 1967	160
MARIAN ORŁOŃ *Detective Nosegoode and the Music Box Mystery*, 1967	162
URSULA K. LE GUIN *A Wizard of Earthsea*, 1968	164
ANNIE M. G. SCHMIDT *The Cat Who Came in off the Roof*, 1970	168
JUDY BLUME *Are You There God? It's Me, Margaret*, 1970	170
RICHARD ADAMS *Watership Down*, 1972	172
SUSAN COOPER *The Dark Is Rising*, 1973	176
MARGARET MAHY *The Great Piratical Rumbustification*, 1978	178
MAURICE GEE *Under the Mountain*, 1979	181
MICHAEL ENDE *The Neverending Story*, 1979	184
MICHAEL MORPURGO *War Horse*, 1982	186
DICK KING-SMITH *The Sheep-Pig*, 1983	188

4 Contemporary Classics

EIKO KADONO *Kiki's Delivery Service, 1985*	192	CORNELIA FUNKE *Inkheart, 2003*	225
DIANA WYNNE JONES *Howl's Moving Castle, 1986*	194	MORRIS GLEITZMAN *Once, 2003*	228
WITI IHIMAERA *The Whale Rider, 1987*	198	CAO WENXUAN *Bronze and Sunflower, 2005*	230
SALMAN RUSHDIE *Haroun and the Sea of Stories, 1990*	200	MARKUS ZUSAK *The Book Thief, 2005*	232
PHILIP PULLMAN *The Golden Compass, 1995*	204	SHAUN TAN *The Arrival, 2006*	234
LUIS SEPÚLVEDA *The Story of a Seagull and the Cat Who Taught Her to Fly, 1996*	206	JUAN VILLORO *The Wild Book, 2008*	236
J. K. ROWLING *Harry Potter and the Sorcerer's Stone, 1997*	208	SACHIKO KASHIWABA *Temple Alley Summer, 2011*	239
HANS MAGNUS ENZENSBERGER *The Number Devil, 1997*	214	PATRICK NESS *A Monster Calls, 2011*	241
MALORIE BLACKMAN *Pig-Heart Boy, 1997*	216	R. J. PALACIO *Wonder, 2012*	244
LEMONY SNICKET *The Bad Beginning, 1999*	218		
ANDRI SNÆR MAGNASON *The Story of the Blue Planet, 2000*	220	About the Contributors	248
		Index	252
PHILIP REEVE *Mortal Engines, 2001*	222	Picture Credits	256

Foreword

by Julia Eccleshare

In childhood, most is unknown and much is strange; wonder is commonplace because so much is new. Fiction set in wonderlands is merely an extension of that novelty. Narnia, Neverland, the Enchanted Wood, Hogwarts, Svalbard as imagined by Philip Pullman; such richly imagined worlds provide perfect playgrounds in which unspoiled children can exist; or, imperfect, bruising worlds in which they must play heroic roles in order to create a better world.

In many works of children's fiction, social norms are set aside, allowing children unusual freedoms and powers. They enable children to retain their sense of the fantastical and their belief in it—a kind of bulwark against the rationalism of growing up. Exploring these places is a rich experience, providing children with the ultimate opportunity to test their reserves of courage, loyalty, kindness, and much more. Worlds of wonder can also be places in which the reality that children are innocent or ignorant is upended so that they may be wise in a world where others are fools—as in *Alice's Adventures in Wonderland* where Alice takes on the traditionally most revered adults: royalty and lawyers.

Where these literary worlds lie in relation to our own world and how they are reached is an integral part of the imagination. Some take place entirely in a wholly invented world, without humans, and the separateness of the world makes it a place to discard human characteristics on entry and enjoy the vast-scale mythical quests and battles. Other worlds of wonder co-exist alongside our own in a secondary world whose charm is enhanced by its unorthodox entry: a rabbit hole, the back of a wardrobe, through special openings carefully cut with a knife, or via Platform 9¾ at King's Cross station. In these, the journey and the arrival begin a process that

> *"Stories are wild creatures, the monster said. When you let them loose, who knows what havoc they might wreak?"*
>
> *A Monster Calls*, Patrick Ness (2011)

leads to the wonderland being in direct contrast to the real one from which the children arrive; the completeness of the fantasy world once entered makes it a perfect escape.

These landscapes offer the most fertile opportunities for children to reinvent themselves and take on characteristics they might like or hope for in adulthood. They are a place where children can imagine themselves in various adult roles, roles which they may either be eager to embrace or, just as typically, scared of encountering for fear that they might fail in them.

Other kinds of wonderlands run within the real world. The arrival of something—or often someone—magical or different, alters the possibilities of ordinary life. Thus in P. L. Travers' *Mary Poppins*, as soon as the eponymous nanny arrives, the lives of the Banks children are suddenly confronted by the unusual and magical. Or sometimes, it is the nostalgic reimagining of the author's own childhood that creates a certain kind of magic, as in Louisa May Alcott's *Little Women*, whose characters and their exploits were inspired by her own siblings.

Whether imagined or remembered, *Worlds of Wonder* showcases beloved children's literature from around the world in which a sprinkle of some kind of magic lets us see the world anew, enabling unimpeded play, heroic feats, and quests of unusually bold proportions to be enjoyed by all.

Introduction

by Daniel Hahn

Children's literature has been around for a long time, and today it's to be found in most cultures where there are printed books. In other words, there's a lot of it, and it's happening in a lot of languages. Which makes working on a book of this kind a delight—so many riches to explore and to celebrate! But also, frankly, a bit of a nightmare—how on earth are we supposed to choose?

This volume covers nearly two hundred years, starting with *The Little Mermaid* by the great Hans Christian Andersen, followed by *Alice's Adventures in Wonderland*, which is not the first book for children but certainly among the first of its kind (entertainment without too much explicit didacticism), and running all the way up to R. J. Palacio's *Wonder*, published in 2012. Spread across all the decades in between, we have selected seventy seven other books, many of them from around the English-speaking world but also including books written in other languages, by writers from some twenty different countries.

To determine our books for inclusion we needed some ground rules. First of all, we are mostly talking about stories that first circulated in print, so you won't find folk tales here. With very few exceptions, the books we've chosen aren't just works that happen to appeal to young readers but that were written expressly *for* them—that's important. We were looking at fiction rather than non-fiction work; and when we say it's fiction "for children," this means that we're mostly avoiding the teen/YA end of the scale. We're also not including picture books for the very young but only longer narratives, especially leaning towards selecting mostly those that a child might have the pleasure of reading independently. (Otherwise my most beloved *Where the Wild Things Are* would have pride of place.)

And—as important as any of our other criteria—every book here is immensely well *loved*. We're interested not only in significant landmark texts in the history of children's literature; we're also interested in what it is that these books mean to us readers, in our relationship to them. As a reader yourself, you might encounter some things that are new to you, and be tempted to go out and read and discover; but I hope that you will also be reminded of books that were important to you once, and you might suddenly feel the urge to be reunited with them. The entries I wrote myself were largely for books I loved forty years ago and still love today (rereading my old Tintin books *for work*!); and you'll find plenty of that enthusiasm in the entries that follow. Our contributors are experts in children's literature and in literature more widely, they are great readers and critics—but they are also enthusiasts, writing about stories that had an impact on their own childhoods, sharing things that they love and that we hope you will, too.

The books range across the world, written originally in twelve languages—and all available in great English translations—but we do need to acknowledge that the very conspicuous Anglophone bias that grips our publishing market is inevitably reflected here. We've tried to include some favorites from beyond the older traditional Anglophone/European centers of global publishing power where we could, but our market has historically paid little attention to translations from Asia; and the whole continent of Africa is a shameful blind-spot. Certainly the more recently published titles are culturally and linguistically more diverse, and we've also included several authors like Tonke Dragt, Gianni Rodari, and Annie M. G. Schmidt, whose books are many decades old but are only finding their belated way to English-language children now—which is to say, I suppose, that things are slowly improving. Some parts of children's publishing might at last be widening their horizons. A future edition of this volume might, I hope, reflect those wider cultural improvements.

Every book is a thrilling act of imaginative storytelling, and world-building, but as Julia Eccleshare points out in her foreword, the wonderlands we experience in our books can just as easily be worlds that are built—imaginatively *re*-built—to resemble our own. Some of the worlds that these writers have created for us are too vast to be contained within this one planet; others are small, domestic, interior—the richly realized places experienced by Judy Blume's Margaret or Louisa May Alcott's March sisters. Yes, we have the astonishing inventiveness of the fantasy creations of Madeleine L'Engle or Michael Ende or Philip Reeve; or those that draw some fantasy out of our world (just meet this talking spider, just step into this chocolate factory, just open this book); but real worlds, realistic ones, need to be re-made in books, too. Anne Shirley's Prince Edward Island and Emil's Berlin are expertly conjured by L. M. Montgomery and Erich Kästner, even though Prince Edward Island and Berlin existed long before them.

The boundaries for others are much blurrier: the Hundred Acre Wood created by A. A. Milne and E. H. Shepard is a real forest in the south of England, but also it isn't. The Gaul that's home to Asterix is the real France, but that's not quite true either. Joan Aiken's England in *The Wolves of Willoughby Chase* is a real England given a counterfactual history—it's not a fantasy place, but it's ruled over by James III, a nineteenth-century king who never was. And Mississippi is a real place and the 1840s were a real time, but a very long way both literally and temporally from my childhood; so when I was invited to engage imaginatively with the world of Tom Sawyer, as it was skillfully constructed by Mark Twain, it might as well have been fantasy. Every book is, in its own way, an invitation into a world, the writers' imaginations activating our own.

With the newest of these books more than a decade old, and the oldest more than a hundred and eighty years old, we can get a sense not just of them in themselves, but of their afterlives, too—buffeted by changing sensibilities, exploited by corporations and producers of merchandise, but each in their way enduring, and often influencing others. Because among the enthusiastic readers who have loved these books there have been many who became great writers in turn, so that many of these books helped to shape and teach those that came after them. Yes, these books are all original, but they're also part of a family. So you might track all sorts of lineages through this volume, some obvious and easy to spot, others more surprising. I don't know how widely people read T. H. White's *The Sword in the Stone* these days—they should!—but something of it survives in the work of Cornelia Funke. (*The Once and Future King*, of which *The Sword in the Stone* is the first part, is her favorite book.) The entry on *The Sheep-Pig* compares it to *Charlotte's Web*, and to *Alice*. As a child, Norton Juster read his way through the Oz books by L. Frank Baum and Ruth Plumly Thompson; and one day, these books would influence his own *The Phantom Tollbooth*. And Baum's Oz also evolved into a famous movie, of course, which was described by Salman Rushdie as "my first literary influence" when he discovered it, growing up in the fifties in Bombay —and there are traces of Oz in Rushdie's *Haroun and the Sea of Stories* unquestionably. Ursula K. Le Guin used to talk about the enabling influence of Tolkien; he showed her, she said, what it was possible to do with fantasy; and in turn Le Guin's fantasy books begat pretty much every subsequent generation.

Emily Lethbridge's piece on *Haroun and the Sea of Stories* begins with our young hero's big question: "What's the use of stories that aren't even true?" Perhaps many adults have forgotten the answer to that question. But we all knew it as children. I hope you'll find this book full of delightful reminders.

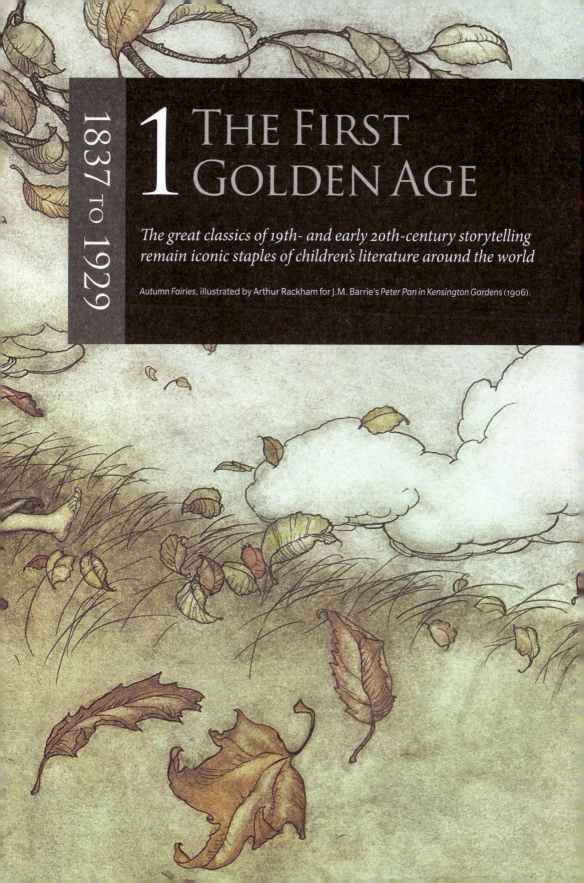

1 The First Golden Age

1837 to 1929

The great classics of 19th- and early 20th-century storytelling remain iconic staples of children's literature around the world

Autumn Fairies, illustrated by Arthur Rackham for J.M. Barrie's *Peter Pan in Kensington Gardens* (1906).

HANS CHRISTIAN ANDERSEN

The Little Mermaid (1837)

The master storyteller sets the standard for others to follow with the fabled story of the young princess from the deep.

Translated by Naomi Lewis (1981); Montague Rhodes James (1930).

Hans Christian Andersen (1805–1875) worked as a weaver, tailor and actor before turning to writing. He published his first work, "The Ghost at Palnatoke's Grave", in 1822 at the age of just 17.

There have been numerous movie adaptations including Disney's animated *The Little Mermaid* in 1989, and the 2023 live-action adaptation.

The Hans Christian Andersen Award, sometimes called the "Nobel Prize for children's literature", is presented biennially by the International Board on Books for Young People to recognize a living author's "lasting contribution to children's literature".

It is easy to imagine *The Little Mermaid* being read out loud to a family dining room in a dark Danish 19th century winter- no one listening or daring to move as the colour and vision of a world beneath the sea comes to life.

The story has one of the greatest bargains in literature, a villainous witch for the ages, an operatic crescendo and a psycho romance that might not be out of place in a modern-day drama.

Andersen is a extraordinary storyteller. Barely a word is out of place. He lets out his tale carefully, a sailor with an anchor. For a short story of just nine thousand words, it has, and still retains, the heft of a grand novel. In the 1930s translation by Montague Rhodes James, who had his own reputation as a writer of ghost stories, it has a poetic lyricism. From the first lines the tempo is melodic:

Far out to sea the water is as blue as the petals of the loveliest of cornflowers, and as clear as the clearest of glass…

Deep down in the ocean, "deep as many church steeples stacked one on top of each other" stands the sea king's palace built in coral and amber with a roof of living mussels opening and closing their shells as the water moves. But there is a sadness about.

The king is a widower, his six beautiful daughters looked after by their wise and all-knowing grandmother. The old queen tells stories of the human world above where the flowers do not just look pretty but smell beautiful, where the birds, unlike the fish, can sing.

When each of the princesses is fifteen years old she will be allowed to rise up to the surface and see the sun and moon for herself. Five princesses swim to the surface in turn. The first marvels at the sound of the church bells; the second princess is enthralled by the sun going down, the third princess is enchanted by the sight of children. The next year the princess stays out at sea to play with dolphins and whales while the fifth princess goes in winter and finds huge icebergs shimmering "in strange shapes, like diamonds."

Now you must not think for a moment that there is only a bare white sandy bottom there; no, no: there the most extraordinary trees and plants grow, which have stems and leaves so supple that they stir at the slightest movement of the water, as if they were alive…

The sixth princess is the most beautiful amd thoughtful of all the sisters, the one who has had to listen to these stories of the wonderful world above the sea, growing more impatient to see for herself. Finally, her day arrives. The old queen dresses her with a wreath of lilies and pearls and a skirt of oyster shells to hide her tail.

She swims to the surface. The sun is going down, "the clouds still glowing like gold and roses". On board a ship nearby she hears dancing and singing. She swims closer, and then spies the handsome young prince with black eyes.

But the sea starts to murmur and get restless.

"The ship dived down like a swan between the tall billows, and rose again over the heaving waters. To the little mermaid it seemed just a pleasant jaunt, but not so to the sailors. The ship creaked and cracked, the stout planks bent with the mighty blows."

The tempest savages the ship throwing everyone into the sea, but the mermaid saves her prince and takes him to the beach. She knows she can never keep him with her under the sea. Her grandmother has told her: Humans only have a short life before their souls go to heaven, where mermaids live for three hundred years, but they have no soul nor life after death. The only way for a mermaid to attain eternal life is if a human loves her enough to share his soul with her.

And so we come to the bargain. The mermaid finds a sea witch who gives her a potion that will let her walk on the land but every step she takes will be painful, like walking on knifes. The witch promises that she will still be able to dance more gracefully than any earth-dweller and so seduce her prince and win his heart and attain a soul.

The Little Mermaid has always invited different critical interpretations—Shakespearian pathos, Faustian overtones, Christian symbolism and pagan hubris, a feminist quest for emancipation, but it is also a tale of a little girl who wants to go the stars.

The ending is as sharp as the dagger the sisters will give their sister, but not to be spoiled here. Much better for young readers and old to return what is one of literature's great masterpieces.

Previous page: The Little Mermaid diving for treasure, in an illustration by Edmund Dulac for a 1910 edition of *Stories from Hans Andersen*.

LEWIS CARROLL (CHARLES LUTWIDGE DODGSON)

ALICE'S ADVENTURES IN WONDERLAND (1865)

A classic of nonsense fantasy and the curiosities it contains; a rabbit with a pocket watch, the Mad Hatter, the Cheshire Cat, the tyrannical Queen of Hearts and, of course, Alice.

Charles Lutwidge Dodgson, pen name Lewis Carroll, famously wrote *Alice's Adventures in Wonderland* specifically for a colleague's three little girls: Ina, Alice, and Edith Liddell, whom he used to take on outings on summer days to the river. He would entertain them, as adults traditionally do with the children under their charge, by "telling them stories." Luckily for the Liddell girls, he was one of the greatest (if strangest) storytellers of all time. Alice in Wonderland is, as the title suggests, principally directed at one of the little Liddells, but the trio makes its appearance, as lovers of the book will recall, in the tale within a tale told by the Dormouse:

> "Once upon a time there were three little sisters," the Dormouse began in a great hurry; "and their names were Elsie, Lacie, and Tillie; and they lived at the bottom of a well . . ."

Alice's Adventures in Wonderland commemorates a bachelor's kindness to three well-behaved and charming little girls. But, having created it, should that be the total audience? Should the Revd Dodgson publish it? A novelist staying with him at his college, Henry Kingsley (brother of the better-known Charles, author of *The Water-Babies*), was strongly of the opinion that Alice should be given to the world at large.

A perplexed Dodgson sent it to George MacDonald (who would publish his own children's adventure, *At the Back of the North Wind*, in 1871), who agreed with Kingsley. The unworldly Dodgson first thought of Oxford University Press, and for the text to be illustrated with his own drawings. The Press rejected the manuscript as not suitable for their learned list, and further it was intimated that it would do him no good academically to publish such a work under his own name.

Eventually Dodgson was persuaded to submit the work to Macmillan, Kingsley's publisher, with illustrations by John Tenniel. Dodgson came up with a pen name that suited him and his witty tale, "Lewis Carroll." It was a

Reverend Charles Lutwidge Dodgson (1832–1898) was a mathematics don at Christ Church College in Oxford University, England.

Alice's Adventures in Wonderland has been translated into 175 languages and has never been out of print.

A stickler for perfection, the book's original illustrator, John Tenniel, insisted the first edition of two thousand copies be pulped because his exquisite designs were imperfectly reproduced.

"Oh my ears and whiskers how late it's getting!" The White Rabbit checks his pocket watch, illustrated by John Tenniel.

Pevious page, left: "At this the whole pack rose up into the air, and came flying down upon her". Illustration by Arthur Rackham for the 1907 edition.

Previous page, right: Arthur Rackham's illustration of the Mad Hatter's Tea Party for the 1907 edition.

Opposite: "How do you know I'm mad?" said Alice. "You must be," said the Cat, "or you wouldn't have come here." Alice meets the Cheshire Cat in an illustration by Tenniel.

pun, inevitably—and one that his colleagues at the high table at Christ Church College doubtless had a high time puzzling out (Lewis is etymologically linked, via Latin, to "Lutwidge;" Carroll, likewise, to "Charles").

The two "Alice books" (the successor to *Wonderland* took the little girl *Through the Looking-Glass, and What Alice Found There*) are unusual among children's literature in appealing also to adult readers. This broad appeal is due in part to the author's rejection of the moral didacticism that had defined the era of children's literature arguably brought to a close by *Alice*'s success. Instead, Dodgson's tale is suffused with symbolism, wordplay and nonsense intended simultaneously to delight and challenge young readers.

Alice, in the first volume, is discovered reading under a tree in high summer. She sees a white rabbit rush by, feverishly consulting a watch:

There was nothing so very remarkable in that; nor did Alice think it so very much out of the way to hear the Rabbit say to itself, "Oh dear! Oh dear! I shall be late" (when she thought it over afterwards, it occurred to her that she ought to have wondered at this, but at the time it all seemed quite natural); but when the Rabbit actually took a watch out of its waistcoat-pocket, and looked at it, and then hurried on, Alice started to her feet, for it flashed across her mind that she had never before seen a rabbit with either a waistcoat-pocket, or a watch to take out of it, and burning with curiosity, she ran across the field after it, and fortunately was just in time to see it pop down a large rabbit-hole under the hedge.

Alice follows, and, after falling down a hole she finds herself in a room faced with a tiny door. The ever-obedient Alice drinks from a bottle labelled "drink me", causing her to shrink to "only ten inches high," conveniently "the right size for going through the little door."

And so begins Alice's adventure in Wonderland, comprising a cascade of transformations in size, generally brought on by one or another kind of consumption, and an array of iconic characters. She encounters mythical creatures like the Gryphon, extinct creatures like the Dodo (often read as a cariacature of Dodgson himself), toothy, but smiling, creatures like the Cheshire Cat. She is interrogated by a hookah-smoking caterpillar, breaks in on the Mad Hatter's tea party, and is finally sentenced to be beheaded by the irascible Queen of Hearts.

As the queen's playing card entourage falls on her, with decapitation in mind, Alice wakes with dead leaves brushing her face. It was spring, and now is autumn. The little girl is growing up.

LOUISA MAY ALCOTT

LITTLE WOMEN (1868)

Following the lives of the four March sisters, Meg, Jo, Beth, and Amy, Louisa May Alcott called her novel a "domestic drama" and it is; but it is also a classic of American literature, and a story beloved by generations of readers.

Louisa May Alcott (1832–1888) wrote *Little Women* in less than three months. She used her own family as inspiration for the story and the sisters. In the place of Meg, Jo, Beth, and Amy in real life the Alcott sisters were Anna, Louisa, Lizzie, and May.

Despite Alcott initially being reluctant to write children's literature, calling it "moral pap for the young," *Little Women* has never been out of print, selling more than 1.5 million copies and being translated into more than 50 languages. It was originally published in two installments, titled *Little Women* and *Good Wives*.

There is timelessness to *Little Women*; a quality that changing centuries, changing customs, and changing technologies has not dulled. As Louisa May Alcott guides readers through the growing up of the four March sisters, she details their interior and exterior lives with such consideration, patience, and humanity that it feels safe to say *Little Women* will remain a beloved coming-of-age story for as long as books are made and stories are told.

The novel opens in early 1860s Massachusetts, with the March family living in genteel poverty. Mr. March is off serving as a chaplain in the Civil War, and at home remain his wife and their four girls—Meg, sixteen, beautiful and maternal; Jo, fifteen, bookish and ambitious; Beth, thirteen, feeble but endlessly kind; and Amy, twelve, the consummate baby of the family, vain and adored. Next door live a well-to-do older gentleman and his grandson Laurie. It is within that neighborly dynamic that you find the centrality of the book's main characters.

As for what happens in *Little Women*, the plot is often the goings-on-of-the-day—sewing, embroidery, cleaning, singing. Some days are more dramatic than others, but Alcott herself called the novel, "Not a bit sensational, but simple and true." The day's drama is often nothing more than a skating sister falling through the ice or jelly preserves that refuse to congeal. That quotidian pace is makes the book so comforting and quiet—the backbone of the plot is not a mystery, or something fantastical, or even terribly adventurous. The backbone is love, the backbone is life.

Alcott penned the novel at the urging of her publisher, who wanted a "girls' story." She wrote in her journal of the writing of *Little Women*, "I plod away, though I don't enjoy this sort of thing. Never liked girls or knew many, except my sisters; but our queer plays and experiences may prove interesting, though I doubt it." But they did prove interesting, and there is value in that—children, like all of us, find joy in reading about the everyday. And little girls deserved stories geared toward them just as much as little boys did. *Little Women*'s first printing, in 1868–1869, of 2,000 copies sold out in just two weeks. Alcott wrote in her journal that some young girls who read early

"'You'll come and meet me as usual, girls?' Laurie said, as he put the sisters into the carriage." Illustration by Frank T. Merrill for the 1880 edition of *Little Women*.

copies of the book called it "splendid!" It's been in print ever since.

That first edition of the novel was released in two installments. Part one introduces readers to the March sisters firmly in the home of their girlhood; part two brings us along with the young women as they leave that home, traveling from quiet Concord, Massachusetts, to great cities like New York, London, Paris, and Nice.

When we meet the March sisters they are young enough to still share a bedroom. Their grown-up lives still so far in the future that the girls refer to their fantasy adulthoods as "castles in the air." The early chapters are cozy and nearly entirely domestic, with most of the action occurring in and around the March's house—their world only growing slightly wider as they befriend "the Laurence boy" next door. As readers we follow along quietly and chronologically with the little women as they go from making mud pies and playing dolls, to getting married and having children. The drama does include one (now quite famous) death, but in many respects we readers experience their growth in such a slow, quotidian way that it's easily understandable why so many people consider *Little Women* a comfort read. Structurally, the first part of the book is imbued with the romps of childhood—plays, songs, and make-believe are written out in full. As the girls grow up, those childhood games are replaced by the more mature letters and poems.

It is impossible to talk about *Little Women* without mentioning the importance of Jo. When readers are introduced to Jo, she is instantly identified as headstrong and a bit rebellious. "I hate to think I've got to grow up, and be Miss March, and wear long gowns, and look as prim as a China Aster!" Jo says. "It's bad enough to be a girl, anyway, when I like boy's games

and work and manners!" Generations of girls have fallen in love with Jo, the character loosely based on Alcott herself, being drawn to her intellect and independence and literary ambition and heart. The ambitions of Jo as a writer have also been cited by many famous female writers as an inspiration. Susan Sontag credited Jo with her becoming a writer; Simone de Beauvoir said that in her own girlhood she'd often pretend to be Jo.

Opposite: "Meg goes to Vanity Fair." Jo, Beth, and Amy help Meg pack for her trip, illustrated by British artist Harold Copping for the 1912 edition.

Jo more than any of the other March sisters pushes back against the fact of her maturing. When she is scolded for romping around when she should be acting like a lady, Jo replies that she won't stop: "Never till I'm stiff and old and have to use a crutch. Don't try to make me grow up before my time, Meg. It's hard enough to have you change all of a sudden. Let me be a little girl as long as I can." When Meg is to be married, Jo is the sister most devastated by the nuclear family's dissolution. "I just wish I could marry Meg myself, and keep her safe in the family," she says.

We do stay with the little women until they start their own families, but Alcott was much less interested in their happy endings than in their every day. "Girls write to ask who the little women marry," she wrote in her journal. "As if that was the only end and aim of a woman's life." Alcott herself never married, and made a point of not concluding the marriage plots of the March sisters in a way that anyone expected. "I won't marry Jo to Laurie to please anyone," Alcott wrote, knowing that her editors would demand Jo marry someone. The choice of partner for the beloved heroine has been debated ever since.

> I'll try and be what he loves to call me, 'a little woman,' and not be rough and wild; but do my duty here instead of wanting to be somewhere else.

With such a lasting runaway success, it's no surprise that *Little Women* has been adapted every which way: plays, radio dramatizations, films (both talkies and silent), television adaptations. The sisterly bond created by Alcott grasps at something universal, simple, and true.

The world of the March sisters is vivid, even now more than when it was first created. As Jo says to her mother about her younger sister Beth, "She is growing up, and so begins to dream dreams, and have hopes and fears and fidgets, without knowing why or being able to explain them. Why, Mother, Beth's eighteen, but we don't realize it, and treat her like a child, forgetting she's a woman." The journey of *Little Women* truly is in experiencing that transition from girlhood to womanhood along with Meg, Jo, Beth, and Amy—and perhaps that is exactly why the novel is so timeless. Growing up is growing up, no matter when it happens.

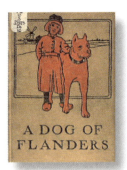

OUIDA (MARIE LOUISE DE LA RAMÉ)

A Dog of Flanders (1872)

The heart-wrenching tale of the unbreakable bond between a loyal dog and an orphan boy in search of a great artistic vision.

Marie Louise de la Ramé (1839–1908) was a best-selling English author, widely read and admired for her popular novels of adventure and romance from the 1850s and well into the 1920s. She wrote as Ouida, a pen name derived from her own childish pronunciation of her given name, "Louise."

The author had many dogs throughout her life, often rescues, and apparently preferred them to people. Some scenes in *A Dog of Flanders* are depicted through the dog's puzzled, sympathetic eyes.

Marie Louise de la Ramé, writing as Ouida, would likely be forgotten now, except for this story, first published as part of a collection titled *A Leaf in the Storm: A Dog of Flanders and Other Stories*. Popular with readers of all ages, it is the tale of the unbreakable bond between a poor orphan and his loyal dog. She wrote it as a plea for kindness and protest against cruelty to animals, five years before Anna Sewell's famous *Black Beauty*.

It is set in Flanders (now Belgium), in a rural area a few miles from Antwerp. According to the author, although good for farming, "it is not a lovely land . . . a characterless plain [where] there is no change, no variety, no beauty anywhere." Here orphaned Nello is raised by his loving but impoverished grandfather who scrapes a bare living by pulling a cart to make milk deliveries. They rescue a dog who was abandoned on the brink of death by his cruel master, and nurse him back to health. The dog, Patrasche, having been trained to the harness, is eager to reward their kindness by pulling the milk cart, and becomes like a brother to Nello.

The child dreams of being an artist. He has never been taught, and can't afford to buy paints, but his charcoal drawings reveal his natural talent. He often walks into Antwerp, where the great artist Peter Paul Rubens lived, where "the greatness of the mighty Master still rests upon Antwerp, and wherever we turn in its narrow streets his glory lies therein, so that all mean things are thereby transfigured."

Nello can see some of Rubens's work, but the two masterpieces in the cathedral—*The Elevation of the Cross* and *The Descent from the Cross*—are only shown to those who can afford to pay. Nello thinks: "If I could only see them, I would be content to die."

After a series of unhappy events, including the death of his grandfather leaving him homeless, Nello trudges through the snow to Antwerp, late on Christmas Eve, and finds the door to the cathedral has been left open. He finally sees those two paintings illuminated by moonlight. Happy at last, he

There was only Patrasche out in the cruel cold—old and famished and full of pain, but with the strength and the patience of a great love to sustain him in his search.

Illustration of Nello and Patrasche by Edmund H. Garrett for the 1893 edition.

curls up beside Patrasche and falls asleep. In the morning, the boy and dog are found huddled together, dead.

Five Hollywood movies have been made based on the story, including a silent film produced in 1924 as a vehicle for nine-year-old child star Jackie Coogan, titled *A Boy of Flanders*, and remakes in 1960 and 1999, all family-friendly films with happy endings. The Japanese animated film in 1997 kept the original ending

Although translated into Flemish in 1878, the book was almost unknown in Belgium. Only when thousands of international tourists began arriving in Antwerp hoping to find connections to the fictional boy and dog did that change. In 1985, a statue sculpted by Yvonne Bastiaans, was erected in Hoboken—presumed to have been the site of grandfather's small hut. Later, a marble statue by Batist Vermeulen, depicting the boy and his dog beneath a cobblestone coverlet, was sited on Antwerp's Handschoenmarkt, in front of the Cathedral of Our Lady.

The First Golden Age

MARK TWAIN (SAMUEL LANGHORNE CLEMENS)

The Adventures of Tom Sawyer (1876)

The classic American novel of two childhoods: Tom Sawyer's and America's. As Ernest Hemingway said of The Adventures of Huckleberry Finn, *all modern American literature starts here.*

Samuel Langhorne Clemens (1835–1910) based his pen name, Mark Twain, on the calls used to signal when a craft had two fathoms of water below it after spending time amongst the steamboat pilots of the Mississippi River

The Adventures of Tom Sawyer did not sell well on first publication. There was particular resistance from public librarians and the teaching profession appalled by Tom's "sass" and bad grammar.

Testament to the author's lasting influence, US President Harry S. Truman had on his desk the salty Twainism: "Always do Right. It will please some People and Astonish the Rest." Twain rarely fails to astonish.

There are few writers whose greatness can be summed up in a single word. Mark Twain is an exception. "I am not an American" he allegedly claimed, "I am *the* American."

The Adventures of Tom Sawyer (1876), his first published novel, is primal to Twain's achievement; particularly when read in tandem with its sequel *Adventures of Huckleberry Finn* (1885). The partnering boyhood sagas have a core of autofiction. Both are set in fictional "St. Petersburg, Missouri," actually Hannibal, Missouri. The real town is nowadays a site of literary pilgrimage.

When Tom Sawyer and Mark Twain (born Samuel Langhorne Clemens in 1835) were growing up there, Hannibal/St. Petersburg was a small port town along the Mississippi River dealing principally in the transit of baled cotton. The river was young Sam Clemens's earliest and longest love. His chosen pen name was the steamboat pilot's regular yell indicating two fathoms water ahead and safe to navigate.

The mighty Mississippi, like the historically later interstate railroads and freeways, served to knit continental America together. The other great unifier was the Civil War (1861–1865). Twain is careful in his short preface to date Tom Sawyer's action around the late 1840s, early 1850s. As presented it is, like childhood, an age of innocence. America's childhood as well as Tom's.

The novel is set in summertime when, as the song says, the living is easy. White children of Tom's lower-middle class will be shoeless except for school and Sunday school attendance. Come winter they will remain for a month or two in their underclothes. Tom's home has a house slave, as did Samuel Clemens's. One notes that Aunt Polly's boy-slave Jim repeatedly calls the hero "Mars Tom"—Master Tom. The master/slave theme is touched on lightly in Tom Sawyer's story and at greater depth in Huck's.

Mark Twain is studiously vague about the exact date in *Tom Sawyer* to give himself a decade's "elasticity" to have Tom variously, as the scene demands, a pre-teen, teenager, or near adult (Clemens left Hannibal at age seventeen). Without that elasticity the "marriage" scenes between Tom and Becky would make uncomfortable reading.

Illustration by Edward W. Kemble showing Tom and his 'gang', including Huck. Illustration from *The Adventures of Huckleberry Finn* (1884), the sequel and companion novel to *The Adventures of Tom Sawyer*.

Tom's parents have died. Of what we are never told. The hero, nonetheless, has literary paternity in Dickens's Artful Dodger in *Oliver Twist*. There are important differences. The Dodger is an apprentice criminal. Tom, by contrast, is a master of the art of the deal. The novel opens with a one word sentence "Tom!". Tom has been raiding the jam jar.

His guardian Aunt Polly, when she finally catches up with him, toys with corporal punishment, the "switch" (cane), before deciding on hard labor. Tom must paint the yard fence. By cunning swaps of prize possessions (trinkets, marbles, curios) Tom tricks passing kids to do the work the for him. The result is a better-painted fence than he could ever have done by himself. Smart or what?

The novel has three parts. The first records the childhood joys of summer in the American South—somewhat marred when Tom nearly dies of measles. He plays truant, swims, fishes, and plays pranks on luckless teachers. He falls in love with Judge Thatcher's higher born daughter Becky and "licks" (beats) a rival lover. He fantasizes "adventures" when he grows up, infatuated as he is by "Dime Novel" tales of cowboys and Indians, Robin Hood, and above all—pirates. A few nights' sojourn on Jackson's Island, however, suggests the freebooter's life might be harder than his favorite fiction describes it.

In the novel's last adventure Tom and Becky find themselves trapped in McDougal's Cave in search of hidden pirate treasure. Tom, in the life-and-death crisis that ensues, proves himself truly heroic. And rich, since he finds the treasure. Twain promised to follow Tom and Huck into later life but never quite got around to it.

The First Golden Age

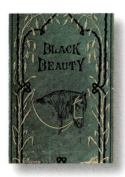

ANNA SEWELL

BLACK BEAUTY (1877)

The story of handsome Black Beauty sees him narrate in the first person his own difficult life, from a prized carriage horse to working all day dragging cabs in London, and would change attitudes to animal welfare.

Although Anna Sewell (1820-1878) was born to Mary Wright Sewell, a contemporarily popular poet and author of children's books, the success of *Black Beauty* has seen Mary's fame eclipsed by that of her daughter.

Black Beauty has become one of the best selling books of all time, selling 50 million copies worldwide and being translated into more than fifty languages.

Sewell received a single payment of £40 for *Black Beauty*. A longtime sufferer of poor health, she died on April 25, 1878, just five months after the novel's publication.

"The first place that I can well remember was a large pleasant meadow with a pond of clear water in it. Some shady trees leaned over it, and rushes and water-lilies grew at the deep end."

The narrator of *Black Beauty* is a high-born, spirited young horse, warned early on by his mother not to mix with the humbler cart-horse colts in the adjoining meadow. Growing up and finally broken in, he dislikes his new bridle and saddle and particularly that "nasty hard thing," the bit. As he explains in his perfect English, "Those who have never had a bit in their mouths, cannot think how bad it feels." But as a cherished carriage horse owned by the kindly local squire, life for him is still agreeable enough until a series of mishaps drag him down. Stories featuring horses at that time usually concentrated on their privileged lives as valued hunters. Anna Sewell chose instead to describe the harsh conditions suffered by everyday working horses.

Sold on after to another wealthy landowner, Black Beauty has his first encounter with the hated bearing rein, a device for keeping horses' heads artificially high. While this look was considered stylish by the lady of the house it was torture for the animal. Badly injuring his knees after a fall and no longer handsome enough for the home stables, Black Beauty ends up working as a humble cab horse. His great friend Ginger is not so lucky, dropping down dead one day in the street worn out from over-work. Fortunately, Black Beauty is then bought by an appreciative former owner and returns to light work and life in the meadow.

Chronically lame herself and never in good health, Anna Sewell identified with horses so often experiencing the pain and distress she also knew from her own life. Dependent on them for pulling her around in her small cart, she soon learned to love as well as understand them. Realizing she was dying, she wrote this story at intervals while she still could during her last five years, hoping it would lead to much needed change. She never lived to see its enormous success, with the hated bearing rein eventually banned. Given its large cast of horses and owners, the story appealed to all classes at home and abroad. In America, 70,000 copies were given to drivers and stablemen. One

"I shall never forget the first train that ran by."
Illustration by Cecil Aldin for the 1938 edition.

Texas cowpuncher arraigned for ill-treating his pony would be sentenced to one month's imprisonment where he was required to read the story three times. In Britain it was distributed by campaigners for animal rights as well as booksellers, both parties extolling its informed understanding of how best to treat horses, from what they should eat to common ailments to look out for.

Black Beauty was also hugely influential in encouraging increased kindness to all animals as well as horses at a time when this was much needed. But Anna's story is far more than a self-improving tract for its time. Beautifully written, vividly descriptive, and stuffed with memorable detail, it still reads as freshly now as it did on first publication in 1877.

HECTOR MALOT

NOBODY'S BOY (SANS FAMILLE) (1878)

Orphaned Rémi treks across Europe as a traveling street musician, discovering life-changing revelations about his past and his real family.

Translated by Florence Crewe-Jones (1916).

Hector-Henri Malot (1830–1907) originally trained as a lawyer before quitting against his family's wishes to pursue a literary calling. He partially sustained himself in the early years of his career by writing articles on botany for *Le Journal Pour Tous*.

Sans Famille was published in 1878 and was reportedly inspired by Italian street musicians. Music plays an important part in the plot and the book ends with the score of a Neapolitan song.

The story has served as the basis for many adaptations, including an anime television series by Tokyo Movie Shinsha.

Even after the Franco-Prussian War of 1870–1871 and the devastating loss of Alsace-Lorraine, France remained a vast and highly varied country. Vastness and heft are perhaps also what first strike the reader of Hector Malot's two-volume *Nobody's Boy*, which sees child hero Rémi repeatedly crisscrossing France and other neighboring lands.

A foundling quest narrative blending melodrama and social realism, it is widely hailed as a French classic, with a host of famous readers from Simone de Beauvoir to Annie Ernaux. Far more cosmopolitan than many children's books thanks to its varied settings and nationalities, it has enjoyed international circulation—121 Japanese editions of the work appeared between 1903 and 1986 alone. Yet it is now little known in the English-speaking world.

Nobody's Boy was first published in installments in an adult newspaper that had previously published such acclaimed works as Dumas's *Three Musketeers*, but it was always intended for children. Malot read his drafts aloud every evening to his own daughter, nine-year-old Lucie, using her responses to shape the work. When it appeared in volume form, it was dedicated to her and published by Jules Verne's publisher, Hetzel, with arresting and atmospheric illustrations by artist Émile Bayard. Known for his illustrations of Victor Hugo's *Les Misérables*, Bayard was an eminently suitable choice.

Rémi's journey begins when his foster father sells him to a traveling musician. Initially a matter of survival, his travels are later motivated by service, affection, and self-discovery. Unwanted and homeless, Rémi navigates his way through the very lowest strata of society. Given that he ends up working in a mine and surviving a deadly mining accident—seven years before Zola's *Germinal* portrayed a similar episode—this journey through the depths is literal as well as metaphorical. Eventually, though, after visits to Paris, the squalid East End of London, and finally Switzerland, he discovers the very different, much more elevated, truth of his identity.

In the course of his travels, there are key moments of respite when Rémi puts down some roots, but the story is basically one of relentless forward

Rémi, Vitalis, and Capi in a woodcut print designed by French illustrator Émile Bayard for the 1880 edition.

movement. Rémi has the plucky resourcefulness, self-reliance, and determination common to nineteenth-century adventure-story heroes. Drawing heavily on the educational and philosophical principles of Jean-Jacques Rousseau, it's a story about getting out there and directly experiencing the world. Rémi gains a varied education, growing strong in body and mind and gaining literacy with people and music as well as with books. Malot combines melodrama, romance, and idealism with gritty social realism. Through Rémi's varied encounters, he presents the reader with a diverse range of social groups and environments. Travel is rarely fun, and life—it is quickly established—is a battle. Malot constantly pulls on the heartstrings in

The First Golden Age 37

Again I had to tramp behind my master with the harp strapped to my shoulder, through the rain, the sun, the dust, and the mud.

Print by Émile Bayard for the 1880 edition.

this highly emotive work. Despite his poverty, what Rémi ceaselessly hankers after is not material wealth but love. In the end, the reward for his dogged efforts and goodness is . . .

Overall, *Nobody's Boy* never fundamentally rocks the boat of bourgeoisie values of the newly established French Third Republic. It is entirely based on strongly gendered roles that link masculinity with dynamism, movement, and action, and femininity with care, comfort, and staying put. It does, though, encourage a certain questioning of appearances and understanding for life's mishaps and misadventures. A street performer turns out to be a talented opera singer; impoverished Rémi is really an English aristocrat. What, Malot asks, might any person in a position of precarity—overlooked and mistreated—actually be?

JOHANNA SPYRI

HEIDI (1880)

A paean to the power and beauty of the mountains and a simple life in nature, as our heroine is sent to live with her reclusive grandfather, high in the Swiss Alps.

Orphaned Heidi is five years old when her aunt Dete decides she's had enough of looking after her, and hauls her up the mountainside to palm her off on her grandfather, who is known as the Alm-Uncle. To a modern eye, this young girl has been through quite a lot: her parents died in disturbing ways when she was very small. Her father Tobias is killed when a beam falls on him while he is working. His body is carried home, and when Heidi's mother "saw the poor disfigured body of her husband she was so overcome with horror and grief that she fell into a fever from which she never recovered." Now, the only mother she has known, Dete, is handing her over to another carer as if she were nothing more than a package. And not just any carer, but the father of Tobias, who has turned away from God after his son's death, and grown "only more wrathful and obdurate" ever since.

Thrown into this new situation, Heidi is quick to make the best of it, removing her Sunday best to run through the fresh green grass; immediately captivating the heart of her irascible, lonely grandfather as she delights in the simple, wholesome world he can offer her. No bed, but an attic where she can sleep on the straw, and listen to the wind in the trees. No fancy meals, but the most delicious milk she's ever tasted, from her grandfather's goats. No school, but days spent taking the goats up the mountain with local goatherd Peter—and seeing sunsets so beautiful that Heidi is quite transfixed.

Translated by Marion Edwards (1884)

Johanna Spyri (1827–1901) is said to have been inspired by the village of Maienfeld in the Bündner Herrschaft region of Graubünden in Switzerland. Today, the region benefits from Heidi tourism, with a Heidi House, a Heidi Village, and a Heidi trail on offer for fans.

Movie adaptations of *Heidi* include a 1937 English-language version starring Shirley Temple as the titular character.

Sequels to *Heidi* were published from 1933, after Spyri's death, including *Heidi Grows Up* and *Heidi's Children* (in which Heidi marries her goatherd friend Peter). They were by Spyri's French translator, Charles Tritten.

> Heidi was again sitting on the ground, silently gazing at the blue bell-shaped flowers, as they glistened in the evening sun, for a golden light lay on the grass and flowers, and the rocks above were beginning to shine and glow. All at once she sprang to her feet, "Peter! Peter! everything is on fire! All the rocks are burning, and the great snow mountain and the sky! O look, look! the high rock up there is red with flame! O the beautiful, fiery snow! Stand up, Peter! See, the fire has reached the great bird's nest! look at the rocks! look at the fir trees! Everything, everything is on fire!"

Johanna Spyri found inspiration for her story while visiting a childhood friend in the beautiful mountains in Maienfeld. According to historian Georg Thürer, it was after a walk that Spyri said she had "the basis for a new story," with locals saying she was inspired by a neighborhood girl with a happy and cheerful manner.

The carefree happiness of Heidi's days on the mountain are contrasted with the confined, miserable life she is transported to when she is sent to Frankfurt (by Dete, who unexpectedly returns for her) to be the companion for a sickly little girl, Clara. Heidi can't fit into this new world of rules, and learning to read, and buildings. There is no nature, no beauty, and she starts to pine away for lack of her beloved mountains.

Thankfully, the adults around her eventually realize what's going on and send her home, where she makes a triumphant return and delights all those who love her. She has even learned to read, so can bring joy to the heart of Peter's blind grandmother, who has been longing to hear the hymns she can no longer read aloud.

Spyri could easily have fallen into the trap of making Heidi a saccharine and unbearable little goody-goody, but her story still works today precisely because Heidi isn't. She is determined, and fierce, and, at heart, a wild child of the mountains who needs them to survive.

A strong element of religiosity runs through the book, increasing as the story progresses. Heidi herself, longing to return to the mountains, stops praying because God doesn't listen to her; Clara's grandmother explains that God "knows better than we do what is good for us." Heidi, persuaded by this line of argument, turns the face of the Alm-Uncle back to God so we can have our happy ending.

Heidi remains perennially popular, translated into more than fifty languages and adapted time and again. Spyri's celebration of the joys of sunshine, snow, flowers, and mountains (along with that goat's milk, of course) remains undimmed by time, as does her clear-sighted vision into the mind of a child. As the book's subtitle puts it so well, this is a book "for children and those who love children."

Opposite: "Heidi introduced each in turn by its name to her friend Clara." Illustrated by Jessie Willcox Smith for the 1922 edition.

> The happiest of all things is when an old friend comes and greets us as in former times; the heart is comforted with the assurance that some day everything that we have loved will be given back.

CARLO COLLODI

The Adventures of Pinocchio
(Le Avventure di Pinocchio) (1883)

The morality tales behind one of literature's most iconic characters were designed as lessons for the newly unified country of Italy.

Translated by M. A. Murray (1892).

Carlo Collodi (1826–1890) began his literary career as a journalist during the Italian Wars of Independence, founding the satirical newspaper *Il Lampione* in 1853.

The Adventures of Pinocchio has been translated into 240 languages, making it the world's third most translated book behind the Bible and *The Little Prince* by Antoine de Saint-Exupéry.

Spawning more than 60 movie adaptations, the best known is undoubtedly the 1940 Disney retelling. The film, however, differs significantly from Collodi's original, offering a far more optimistic take on the tale.

Carlo Collodi lived a somewhat irregular life. He was a supporter of the Risorgimento, the armed movement for Italian Unification that resulted in the creation of the Kingdom of Italy in 1861, and even served in the Tuscan army under Giuseppe Garibaldi, a central figure in the fight for Italian independence.

Pinocchio was not originally conceived as a novel and Collodi did not start with an overall structure, plot, or direction in mind. In fact, he wrote to provide income for his gambling and alcohol addictions and he was trying to stave off poverty when he sent the early chapters to the *Giornale per i bambini* (*Children's Newspaper*) in 1881. In 1883, when *The Adventures of Pinocchio* was published as a single book by Felice Paggi, it met with immediate success and has gone on to sell eighty million or more copies and, most famously, been adapted into an animated Disney movie.

The storyline offers an episodic tale that develops at breakneck speed in a series of entertaining incidents. If Collodi's storytelling skill makes the book highly engaging, there is a more serious layer under the fantasy adventures; this being the moral guidance (even imperatives) on how to behave and become worthy citizens in the new Italian Republic as it emerged from the Risorgimento.

Pinocchio comes to life in the workshop of a carpenter, Geppetto, who while carving a puppet is taken aback when the piece of wood in his hand protests that the chisel strokes are hurting him. Geppetto, who has always wanted a son, is immediately enamored of his creation and teaches him to walk, only to see him run off. Things take a turn for the worse for Geppetto when he is accused of mistreating Pinocchio, arrested and imprisoned. Without Geppetto to watch over him, Pinocchio is now released on the world to face the most varied escapades and to meet some fabulous characters, some kindly but some scoundrels. He himself is good-hearted but fickle, a naughty boy incapable of resisting temptation. He has an innate rebellious streak that will also not allow him to accept the poverty into which he was born.

The plot takes the classic form of a journey, physical and mental, with Pinocchio repeatedly proving overly trusting, easily tempted, and incapable

Pinocchio and Figaro, (Geppetto's pet cat) in the 1940 Walt Disney adaptation of the novel.

of taking the good advice given him. He learns the hard way that not all the people he meets are good and honest. His journey is also moral, both in the fantasyland he inhabits and, by extension, in the new Italy being created at the time Collodi was writing. There are punishments for misdeeds, the most dramatic of which sees Pinocchio hanged from a tree and only rescued in the nick of time by the good Fairy who becomes his mother figure.

Arguably the most famous aspect of the story is Pinocchio's unconscious physical reaction to telling lies. When, after being deceived into giving up his gold coins by the sinister Cat and Wolf, he is rescued by the Fairy. He tells one lie after another to explain the missing coins to his mother figure, causing his nose to grow and grow. She shows him no pity because, she says, "telling lies is the most nasty vice a boy can have." In this passage, as in many other parts of the narrative, Pinocchio is being taught the need for a conscience if he is to become a good boy and, by extension, a good citizen. The result of this moral education is that, at the story's conclusion, by which point he has proved himself reformed, the Fairy rewards Pinocchio by transforming him into a real boy.

Though Pinocchio was written for children, it has, like *Alice in Wonderland*, intrigued adult critics who have interpreted the story in accordance with their own psychological, political, or philosophical beliefs. It is this, in tandem with its perpetual popularity with children, that has made *The Adventures of Pinocchio* into one of the most widely known and best-loved works of children's literature.

Below: Illustration by Attilio Mussino for the first color edition of Pinocchio (1926).

The First Golden Age

ROBERT LOUIS STEVENSON

Treasure Island (1883)

The sometimes dark but timeless tale of pirates, mutiny, and buried treasure has proven to be as enduring as it is engrossing.

Born in Edinburgh, Scotland, to a family of lighthouse designers, Robert Louis Stevenson (1850–1894) spent much of his life travelling in search of warmer climates to ease his ill-health. In December 1889, Stevenson relocated to the Pacific Island nation of Samoa with his wife, where he took on the title of Tusitala—meaning "Teller of Stories"—and worked on translations of local stories until his death.

Treasure Island was serialized in *Young Folks* magazine in 1881, credited to Captain George North (see above for the first US edition, published by Roberts Brothers in 1884). The original manuscript is lost—having been auctioned by his family during World War I.

Take a poll of the greatest adventure stories ever written and the odds are that this rattling pirate tale will appear very high on the list. Robert Louis Stevenson—"Louis," as friends and family called him—was no longer a young man when he finally wrote what in later life he proclaimed to be "my first book." Stevenson and his new wife, Fanny, had returned from California to Louis's native Edinburgh for the summer of 1880. Fanny, previously married, brought to the marriage an eleven-year-old son, Lloyd. Back in his hometown Louis was reunited with an old comrade, W. E. Henley. The two men had earlier met in a hospital where Louis was being treated for his weak lungs and Henley had just had a leg amputated. Henley is today remembered for his poem "Invictus," with its rousing final lines: "I am the master of my fate/I am the captain of my soul." The character he inspired, however, has long been accepted into the collective memory.

As Stevenson admitted to Henley, after the publication of *Treasure Island*: "It was the sight of your maimed strength and masterfulness that begot [the novel's central villain] Long John Silver . . . the idea of the maimed man, ruling and dreaded by the sound, was entirely taken from you." Wooden legs were more usually associated in the nineteenth century, not with poets, but with sea-going men. At sea, if your leg was injured, in battle or even accidentally, immediate amputation was the surest remedy. Ships had no hospital facilities and cutting the damaged limb off at once and cauterizing the wound in boiling tar was the only protection against gangrene. Often the ship's cook performed the operation using kitchen knives. A piece of timber was strapped on after the wound had healed. If a hand was lost, one of the meat hooks in the ship's galley would serve as a replacement. (Captain Hook in *Peter and Wendy*, 1911, was directly inspired, as J. M. Barrie acknowledged, by Long John Silver.)

Doctors pronounced Edinburgh—known as "auld reekie" because of its smog-filled air—hazardous for Stevenson's health. Fanny and Louis did not have the funds to wander far and rented a cottage in Braemar in the Highlands.

The pirate Blind Pew is run down by tax collectors on horseback, illustrated by George Roux for the 1885 illustrated edition.

The weather was "absolutely and consistently vile" and the family was confined to the house. One day, in an effort to entertain Lloyd, Stevenson painted a map of an island.

> it was elaborately and (I thought) beautifully colored; the shape of it took my fancy beyond expression; it contained harbors that pleased me like sonnets . . . as I paused on my map of "Treasure Island," the future character of the book began to appear there visibly among imaginary woods. . . . The next thing I knew I had some papers before me and was writing out a list of chapters.

The tale sprang from Stevenson's pen at the rate of a chapter every morning. Other chores were suspended. At this stage it was entirely a domestic enterprise. Luckily, for literature and for Stevenson's career, a visitor,

Dr. Alexander Hay Japp, was invited to listen to the ongoing tale. One should imagine Stevenson's thrilling, Scots-accented voice as the first paragraph was read out:

> I remember him as if it were yesterday, as he came plodding to the inn door, his sea-chest following behind him in a hand-barrow—a tall, strong, heavy, nut-brown man, his tarry pigtail falling over the shoulder of his soiled blue coat, his hands ragged and scarred, with black, broken nails, and the saber cut across one cheek, a dirty, livid white.

As luck would have it, Japp was closely connected with the editor of the popular weekly comic *Young Folks*. Based in London, the editor-proprietor was James Henderson, a fellow Scot. Why not, Japp suggested, publish the tale in *Young Folks*? It would make a welcome handful of "jingling guineas" for the author (who was, as it happened, in dire need of funds).

Stevenson completed the history of Jim Hawkins and *Treasure Island* was duly serialized, earning its author a little under £50, and Stevenson went on to make a small fortune from subsequent reprints. *Treasure Island* also heralded the arrival of a major new talent in British fiction. The story that had begun as a domestic entertainment, recited by the fireside to while away tedious days and nights, became a classic. One cannot imagine English fiction without it.

Astonishingly, given its later popularity, *Treasure Island* was not a great success in *Young Folks*. Arguably Stevenson's story was too complex, psychologically, for the paper's juvenile readership. And perhaps, more significantly, *Treasure Island* was rather too disturbing for young readers. The murder of Tom Redruth, for example, goes well beyond the routinely spilled gore relished by Victorian children. Silver has failed to recruit the Squire's loyal man to the mutineers' cause. It is Tom's death sentence. On witnessing the brutal homicide, described gruesomely, Jim faints. And the reader, whether adult or child, also finds it hard to restrain a shudder—not least at the thought of Silver surviving, unpunished for this callous crime and rewarded with ill-gotten gold, to crack further spines that may happen to raise his ire. Whatever happened to the poetic justice that is the stock in trade of children's fiction?

Treasure Island is a richly complex work of imagination. And where did the novel's imagined world begin? With a wooden leg, bad weather, and the chance visit of a stranger.

ETHEL TURNER

Seven Little Australians (1894)

The first Australian family saga set in the bushy suburbs of Sydney set the tone for generations of outback literature.

On January 24, 1893, her twenty-third birthday, Ethel Turner wrote a brief note in the diary she was to keep for more than sixty years: "Seven L. Aust.—sketched it out." A few days later she wrote: "Night started a new story that I shall call Seven Little Australians. . . . I'll see if I can get it published in book form."

It did not take her very long. Turner's book was published in 1894 by Ward Lock & Bowden. The first editions sold out within weeks. By 1994 it was the only book by an Australian author to have been continuously in print for more than 100 years

Seven Little Australians is set in the bushy suburbs of late-nineteenth-century Sydney and tells the story of gruff Captain Woolcot and his large family; six children by his late first wife, and a baby son with his new wife Esther. The timing of its publication in 1894 (just over 100 years since the penal colony had been established in New South Wales) helps signify the book's cultural and social significance. It appeared when the states were loosely connected but just before they federated to become the nation of Australia in 1901.

From the start, Turner invokes a keen sense of distinctive Australian nationhood in her narrative, a focus on difference that was to become so pervasive in the stories that Australia both told of itself to others and told of itself to itself.

Ethel Turner (1870–1958) was born in Yorkshire, England, and migrated to Australia with her mother and sister in 1879. In September 1891, her family moved from inner-city Sydney to a rural suburb known today as Killara.

After finishing school, Ethel and her sister Lilian co-founded *Parthenon*, a sixpenny monthly magazine, to which she contributed children's and romance stories.

The book has sold more than 2 million copies in the English language and been translated into at least 13 other languages.

> Before you fairly start this story I should like to give you just a word of warning. If you imagine you are going to read of model children, with perhaps; a naughtily inclined one to point a moral, you had better lay down the book immediately and betake yourself to "Sandford and Merton" or similar standard juvenile works. Not one of the seven is really good, for the very excellent reason that Australian children never are. . . . There is a lurking sparkle of joyousness and rebellion and mischief in nature here, and therefore in children.

The First Golden Age

Seven Little Australians is a story about individual children at very different stages of their development: a teenage girl (Meg, sixteen) struggling in her first relationships with boys, her brother (Pip, fourteen) clever but rebellious, beginning to clash with his father, the stern Captain Woolcot, and Judy (thirteen), the real hero of the story, an outspoken leader, who is sent away to boarding school as a punishment by her father. The other three children—Nell (ten), Bunty (six), and Baby (four)—were very young when their mother died; the children's stepmother, Esther, is only twenty and has had a baby boy they call "The General," whom they all love, but she cannot control the children. This is a story about family life, and about a terrible tragedy that occurs through love and loyalty but that cannot be easily accepted in the pious Victorian tradition of its time; it is fought against, desperately.

Seven Little Australians is a family fiction and the children are not perfect and the family is not perfect. The setting is the rural outskirts of Sydney but the isolation and distances of pastoral life are glimpsed during a visit to Esther's father's property at Yarrahappini, where the trees are tall and heavy and dangerous, and where the tragedy happens.

Turner's original version included a controversial story about an Indigenous man, Tettawonga:

> "Once . . . upon a time," said Mr. Gillet, "when this young land was still younger, and incomparably more beautiful, when Tettawonga's ancestors were brave and strong and happy as careless children, when their worst nightmare had never shown them so evil a time as the white man would bring their race, when . . . , in short, an early Golden Age wrapped the land in its sunshine, a young kukuburra and its mate spread their wings and set off toward the purple mountains beyond the gum trees. . . ."

This story was omitted from subsequent editions but reinstated in the centenary edition in 1994. The omission reflects community social attitudes avoiding issues related to Indigenous Australians of the time but it is significant that Turner's original intention was to include rather than exclude.

Both celebrated and criticized over time, *Seven Little Australians* has always remained hugely popular. It is an important part of literary history, and also an important part of the Australian national story.

Opposite: "Everyone fetched some offering to lay at Judy's shrine for a keepsake." Illustration by John Macfarlane for the 1912 illustrated edition.

RUDYARD KIPLING

The Jungle Book (1894)

Kipling's celebrated account of an Indian boy who loses his parents and is adopted by a family of wolves became world famous and helped to consolidate his reputation as a writer of startling originality.

Rudyard Kipling (1865–1936) was born in Bombay (now Mumbai), India to British parents. His time in India inspired a lifelong passion for its life, religions, traditions and nature that greatly influenced his work.

The Jungle Book became a bestseller upon publication and has never been out of print, with more than 500 print editions. The book was adapted by Walt Disney into a hugely successful animated movie for children in 1967 and a live action movie in 2016.

Many of the striking illustrations for the original edition were by Lockwood Kipling, Rudyard's father, who was director of the School of Art in Bombay.

There are two volumes to what we now call Kipling's *Jungle Book*. They appeared together in a single volume called *The Two Jungle Books* in 1924. The original *Jungle Book* of 1894, though, is complete in itself, and has seven chapters, the first three of which concern Mowgli while the final four chapters have different animal stories. It is the stories of Mowgli, the Indian boy adopted by a pack of wolves in conflict with Shere Khan that form the dramatic spine of the wolf-boy narrative and rightly made the book so famously memorable.

The Jungle Book was written at a time when India was part of the British Empire. Kipling suggests that the location of the jungle is near Seeonee (Seoni) City, which is in Madhya Pradesh State, though this is not actually a rain forest. The stories are related by an omniscient third person narrator, having access to the consciousness of both animals and humans, and were among a growing number of children's books in the late Victorian and Edwardian eras that focused on talking animals, alongside, for example, *The Wind in the Willows* and *Five Children and It*.

The story starts with the baby Mowgli, a human child, escaping from Shere Khan, the tiger, who claims him as his prey, and wandering into the Wolves' cave. The wolves are won over. They treat him as one of their own cubs, and protect him from the tiger. The moral training of a human orphan is one of the themes of this book. Mowgli allows himself to be kidnapped by the "Bandar log," the monkey people, in defiance of Baloo the bear and Bagheera the panther—the two creatures who are training Mowgli to survive in the jungle— and for this act of disobedience Mowgli is severely punished by his animal tutors. The monkeys are dealt with by Kaa, the great rock snake, who can mesmerize the monkeys and then kill them. This last is a particularly chilling scene, dramatized vividly in a chapter entitled "Kaa's Hunting."

The final chapter about Mowgli concerns Mowgli's defense of the wolf pack from Shere Khan. Mowgli visits an Indian settlement and steals Red Flower (fire) and uses this judiciously to defeat Shere Khan. We learn from the close of the narrative that Mowgli will later leave his wolf-pack, return to human civilization and marry.

Still from the 1967 Disney animated adaptation of *The Jungle Book*, depicting Mowgli and the bear Baloo.

A modern reader will discern that Mowgli's animal world comes to be ruled by the "man-child" as the colonies were dominated by their imperialist masters, but a poignant theme of the Mowgli stories is abandonment and fostering. The young Kipling, born in Bombay (now Mumbai), was happiest as a child in India, reportedly learning Hindi with his Ayah (nurse) before the English language, and enjoying the kindness and freedom afforded by his Indian home. However, his parents sent the five-year-old Kipling and his younger sister back to England to stay with two strangers, Captain and Mrs. Holloway. He wrote of Mrs. Holloway's cruelty and neglect later in one of his short stories, "Baa Baa, Black Sheep" and in his autobiography *Something of Myself*.

The Mowgli stories represent two worlds: one is the kindly world of the wolves where children are protected by the wolf family and educated firmly but kindly by Bagheera and Baloo, and the other world hinted at is the hostile world of humans, which Mowgli chooses not to return to until he is a man with the strength and wisdom to deal with it. In this way the Mowgli stories can be seen as a reparative wish for something the young Kipling never had.

Although there had been talking animal stories published before, *The Jungle Book* was startling in the vividness of a human child being adopted by animals. It helped the young journalist develop a reputation as a writer and poet. Kipling received the Nobel Prize for Literature 1907.

The First Golden Age

L. FRANK BAUM

The Wonderful Wizard of Oz (1900)

The ageless morality tale of Dorothy, Toto, the Scarecrow, the Tin Woodman, and the Cowardly Lion continues to captivate readers young and old.

Having always disliked his first name, Lyman, L. Frank Baum (1856–1919) shortened it early in his childhood, a choice he kept throughout his various careers as a poultry farmer, actor, and journalist.

Baum recalled taking the name for his magical kingdom from a filing cabinet in which his papers "O–Z" were stored.

On finishing the work, Baum knew instinctively that he had created something remarkable. After writing the last page he had his pencil framed and placed over his desk. By the time *The Wonderful Wizard of Oz* entered the public domain in 1956, it had sold more than 3 million copies.

L. Frank Baum (the L. stands for Lyman) was born in New York State, the son of a merchant enriched by the oil business. Baum went into journalism and published his first book for children in 1897. In 1900, together with the illustrator W. W. Denslow (1856–1915), he produced *The Wonderful Wizard of Oz* (first entitled "The Emerald City"). Baum later spun off a series of "Oz" sequels and was one of the first generation of American writers to adapt his work for the screen, moving himself and his family to Hollywood to do so.

Now more people have seen *The Wizard of Oz* than have read it. MGM's epoch-making movie of 1939 is fairly faithful to what Baum wrote and Denslow pictured. The book was conceived and published during one of the recurrent depressions in American commercial life, and one of the points that Baum makes in his 1900 preface is that his story is "modernized"—set in the uncomfortable present.

The narrative opens on an impoverished farm, in a bleak landscape of the "great Kansas prairies." An orphan, Dorothy is cared for by her Uncle Henry and Auntie Em. The description of Dorothy's home is of a humble, dusty place, setting up a stark comparison to the glittering world she is to discover.

And sure enough, a cyclone does come. It carries away the rackety old house, Dorothy and her faithful dog Toto inside, transporting it to the land of the dwarfish Munchkins in the republic of Oz. From there Dorothy and Toto set off along the yellow brick road for the Emerald City, where, she understands, she will find a wizard who can help her get home to Kansas. On the way she meets up with her famous three companions: a Scarecrow, a Tin-Woodman, and a Cowardly Lion.

After various adventures along the way, the quartet arrives at the magnificent city and is ushered into the chamber of the Great Wizard. Quickly, though, they discover him to be a fraud and a "humbug," fed up with his pretences and dreaming of his previous life as a circus clown. The Emerald City, too, is nothing but an illusion produced by the green spectacles worn by everyone who visits. The moral is clear. Help yourself—the traditional American remedy of self-improvement, which Dorothy and her companions

> "That proves you are unusual," returned the Scarecrow; "and I am convinced that the only people worthy of consideration in this world are the unusual ones. For the common folks are like the leaves of a tree, and live and die unnoticed."

eventually manage with some aid from the Good Witch of the South. And too, by her own efforts, Dorothy gets back to Kansas, realizing that however poor it is, she loves her humble home.

Since *The Wonderful Wizard of Oz* has become one of the best-known stories in the world, scholars have gone to work on it. No longer is it a text for children of all ages, but evidence for the inquisitive social scientist and historian. Baum, as has been said, was writing about a period of severe economic depression and he had been very impressed, in 1894, by a hunger march on the White House by "Coxey's Army," named after the political organizer, Jacob Coxey. The unemployed, in their hundreds and sometimes thousands, marched across America to the capital. Eventually their demonstration was broken up in Washington and the leaders arrested on charges of "trespassing on the White House lawn."

As such, some have interpreted the phony Wizard of Oz as representing the all-talk-and-no-action President of the United States, William McKinley. And, on their epic march up the yellow brick road (taken to be an allusion to the gold standard, which Coxey and other populists wanted to get rid of), Dorothy, the farm girl, represents the decent working classes; the Scarecrow represents the rural poor; and the Tin Man represents the toiling masses in the factories. The Lion is harder to fit in, although various "cowardly" leaders of the people have been proposed. It's intriguing stuff—but not, in the end, particularly nourishing.

While many things can be read into this much-loved tale of the real and unreal, the dream and nightmare, in the end they are incidental—although they do add to the charm of this perennially fascinating work of imagination.

Opposite: "The Monkeys caught Dorothy in their arms and flew away with her." Illustration by Baum's friend and collaborator W.W. Denslow for the original publication.

Previous page: Dorothy, the Tin Woodman, the Scarecrow, and the Cowardly Lion make their way to the Emerald City in MGM's legendary 1939 movie.

"There were big yellow and white and blue and purple blossoms, besides great clusters of scarlet poppies, which were so brilliant in color they almost dazzled Dorothy's eyes." Illustration by W. W. Denslow.

E. NESBIT

FIVE CHILDREN AND IT (1902)

When five children on vacation in the countryside discover a sand fairy living in a quarry, he unwillingly grants them one wish a day, leading to unforgettable adventures and unexpected trouble.

Born in England, Edith Nesbit (1858–1924) was prominent socialist and a founding member of the Fabian Society, a precursor to the UK Labour Party.

Originally published in installments in *Strand Magazine* with the title *The Psammead, or the Gifts*, *Five Children and It*, Nesbit's book was first published as an expanded novel later that same year.

The Psammead's name was coined by Nesbit from the Greek word *psámmos*, meaning sand, following the naming pattern of nymphs in Greek mythology, such as dryads, naiads, and oreads.

Edith Nesbit always saw herself as a writer for adults, with her many children's stories dashed off when money was short and her family still growing. Regularly asking her children or visitors for new ideas she would then get to work as quickly as possible before joining in with whatever was going on in her hectic, unconventional home life. But no one could ever notice signs of carelessness, for Nesbit was a brilliant writer at whatever speed, with an abiding love and understanding of children. Not always happy herself when young, she set out to entertain future generations while also slipping in some of her own strongly held views on social justice.

This story starts with mother and father both called away from their new home in the countryside, with the five children, Robert, Anthea, Cyril, Jane, and the baby left with a cook and an over-worked nursemaid. Digging in a nearby gravel pit they discover a sand-fairy, also known as a *psammead*, with long horns like a snail's eyes and a tubby body covered in thick fur. Sammyadd, as the children call him, speaks perfect English and is unwillingly able to grant wishes lasting one day. Seizing their chance the children embark on the first of many adventures. In the process they learn that what is most wished for may not always turn out for the best.

Their first unwise escapade, courtesy of the increasingly grumpy sand-fairy, is to wish they were all as beautiful as the day. But when this transformation happens their baby brother starts howling, no longer recognizing them. Returning home they are turned away as strangers and have to wait till sunset before the effects finally wear off. Their next wish, to be rich beyond their wildest dreams, is equally unsuccessful, with the children suspected of robbery by the inhabitants of the nearby village once they produce the gold sovereigns that had come their way. Taken to a police station they are returned home in disgrace when all their new money happily disappears again at sunset. Future wishes, like being able to fly, also turn bad when alarmed by their huge new wings no one wants to have anything to do with them. There is also a near fatal visit to a formerly beleaguered castle, with the children just escaping advancing

> Grown-up people find it very difficult to believe really wonderful things, unless they have what they call proof.

"It burrowed, and disappeared, scratching fiercely to the last."
Illustration for the first edition by Scottish artist H. R. Millar.

medieval soldiers out to get them. Any idea that warfare at any stage of history could actually be fun is now gone forever.

Nesbit used the idea of more lightning visits to the past in this book's two sequels, *The Phoenix and the Carpet* and *The Story of the Amulet*. That way her characters could also witness ancient injustices first hand, with the author cleverly making the point that some of the worst practices still remain close to what was happening in the United Kingdom at their own time. But she always avoided overtly preaching to her readers.

Her stories instead offer continuous fun, packed with jokes, odd historical facts, quick conversational asides, and plenty of dialogue between family members who, despite getting on well, still occasionally quarrel and sulk. Nesbit's language is equally lively, as in "Cyril merely observed that his sister must have gone off her nut." No other children's writer in 1902 would have dared come up with a sentence like that.

Nesbit's other great story *The Railway Children* is the best known of her fiction today after it was so successfully filmed. But for children still wondering what it would really be like if wishes were granted this story could be just the thing.

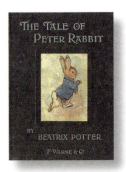

BEATRIX POTTER

The Tale of Peter Rabbit
(1902)

The world's first licensed character, Peter Rabbit is an instantly recognizable figure in his trademark blue jacket. In Beatrix Potter's first book, Peter ventures into the garden where his father was made into pie.

Beatrix Potter (1866–1943) was born in London, England into an artistic upper-middle-class family. An artist from a young age, Potter had her first commercial success with rabbit pictures she sold as Christmas card designs.

Potter's companionable pet rabbit, Peter Piper, used to lie by the fire like a cat. On hearing in 1903 that more than 56,000 copies had so far been printed, Potter commented to her publisher: "The public must be fond of rabbits!"

Potter worked closely on *Peter Rabbit* and subsequent books with her editor, Norman Warne. In July 1905 he proposed to her and Potter said yes to him, but, tragically, he died just one month later.

A young rabbit breaks into a garden, eats some veggies, is chased by the gardener, and makes it home to his mother. In the process, he catches a cold and loses his little blue jacket with its big brass buttons. When Victorian naturalist Beatrix Potter wrote and illustrated this simple fable, she could hardly have predicted that the resulting book would eventually sell 45 million copies and be translated into 36 different languages. Potter's pictures for the story are works of art, lovingly drawn from close observation. Her deep interest in the natural world inspired everything she did as an author, artist, ecologist, and, later, as a farmer and pioneering conservationist.

Born in London in 1866, Potter spent summer holidays in Scotland and Cumbria, England. She stayed on the west bank of Lake Windermere when she was sixteen years old and the location kindled a deep and life-long passion for the Lake District. Her love of art, nature, and animals also started young. Always drawing whatever she saw, Potter wrote in an early journal that she had an "irresistible desire to copy any beautiful object which strikes the eye." She sketched and painted insects, magnified through a microscope, and made hundreds of botanical drawings of fungi, becoming an expert mycologist.

Potter's delicate paintings deftly evoke Peter Rabbit's world, adapting the meticulous dry-brush watercolor technique that she had developed and used to paint scientific specimens. The precision of her pictures makes the story more believable. We are there with Peter inside a damp watering can, trying not to sneeze, or knocking over terracotta flowerpots in his effort to escape from Mr. McGregor's hobnail shoe. The text is lucid, rich in sensory details: French beans and radishes, cucumber frame and gooseberry net, the "scritch, scratch" noise of the hoe, and the soft sand floor of the rabbit hole.

The innocent mischief of Peter Rabbit is peppered with the kind of menacing details and genuine jeopardy that many young readers love. Mrs. Rabbit calmly tells the children not to go into Mr. McGregor's garden because "Your Father had an accident there; he was put in a pie by Mrs. McGregor." Undeterred, Peter Rabbit squeezes under the garden gate and eats so many stolen vegetables he feels sick.

Basing the character on her own childhood pet, a Belgian buck rabbit called Peter Piper, Beatrix Potter first wrote about Peter Rabbit in an 1893 letter to cheer up a friend's five-year-old who was sick in bed. The now-famous "picture letter" to Noel Moore began: "I don't know what to write to you, so I shall tell you a story about four little rabbits whose names were—Flopsy, Mopsy, Cottontail, and Peter. They lived with their mother in a sand bank under the root of a big fir tree." She decorated the letter with sketches that prefigure the iconic illustrations she created for the final book.

Six publishers rejected *The Tale of Peter Rabbit*, partly because they wanted to make a larger, more expensive book. Potter insisted the book should be small so it would be easy for children to hold and to buy: "little rabbits cannot afford to spend 6 shillings on one book," she said. The 250 copies she self-published in 1901 quickly sold out. Trying to help Potter get Peter Rabbit published commercially, family friend Hardwicke Rawnsley rewrote her story in rhyming couplets, though his version ended with a trite moral message about not disobeying one's mother. Luckily the eventual publishers chose Potter's shorter, simpler prose instead. Rawnsley remained a lifelong friend, encouraging Potter's work and sharing her views on the need to preserve the natural beauty of the Lake District. Rawnsley was one of the three founders of the National Trust, a huge British conservation organization that now protects around 620,000 acres of land.

Soon after first publication, Potter produced and patented a stuffed animal based on her story, making Peter the world's oldest licensed character. Potter was the first author to pioneer literary merchandise like this. All kinds of related ceramics, games, and figurines have since been sold in huge numbers. With the royalties from Peter Rabbit, Potter bought Hill Top farmhouse in the Lake District in 1905.

Pictures in her later books show recognizable scenes from inside and outside Hill Top. Peter Rabbit was inspired by a lot of different places, including the landscapes around Derwentwater. The pictures were "composite and scattered in locality," she later explained in a letter, identifying Keswick as the source of the fir tree and saying the vegetable patch and wicket gate belonged to the nearby Lingholm estate, where the walled garden was rebuilt in 2016. The lily pond was painted in Wales while the potting shed and geraniums were in Hertfordshire.

"Now run along, and don't get into mischief." Mrs. Rabbit buttons Peter's iconic blue jacket. Illustration by Beatrix Potter for the first edition.

The First Golden Age

"First he ate some lettuces and some French beans; and then he ate some radishes." Illustration by Beatrix Potter.

The world of Peter Rabbit in later books is recognizably Potter's own Edwardian England, packed with practical details: blackberry picking and scarecrows, bakers selling currant buns, and gardeners weeding rows of onions. But it is simultaneously a fantastical place, where animals speak and wear clothes and drink tea from porcelain cups. Her mixture of delicate natural observation and anthropomorphic inventiveness is one of the things that makes Potter's books so successful.

> "Now my dears," said old Mrs. Rabbit one morning, "you may go into the fields or down the lane, but don't go into Mr. McGregor's garden: your Father had an accident there; he was put in a pie by Mrs. McGregor."

Her first little book was followed by 22 more in the same series as well as other published works. Peter Rabbit himself reappears as a character in several of her subsequent stories. In *The Tale of Benjamin Bunny*, a sequel to Peter Rabbit, he revisits Mr. McGregor's garden with his cousin Benjamin. In T*he Tale of the Flopsy Bunnies*, the original rabbits are grown up and Benjamin is married to Peter's sister Flopsy. The story is about their children, who are kidnapped in *The Tale of Mr. Tod* by a badger called Tommy Brock. Peter and Benjamin rescue them.

In later years, Potter became more involved in farming and conservation. She won awards for her Herdwick sheep and bought up farmland to save it from development. When Potter died in 1943, she left 4,000 acres of Cumbrian countryside and fourteen farms, including her own house, to the National Trust. She wrote in her will: "Hill Top is to be presented to my visitors as if I had just gone out and they had just missed me." The landscape she loved and painted now survives—much as it was in Potter's day—thanks in part to her efforts. She helped save the Lake District for everyone to visit and enjoy.

Between them, Beatrix Potter's books have sold more than 250 million copies worldwide. Peter Rabbit has gone on to inspire countless live-action films, cartoons, ballets, plays, and television shows. In one 2012 animation, Peter is a streetwise, impetuous character with catchphrases like "Let's hop to it!" A 2018 comedy film, featuring a much-expanded adventure, has Peter voiced by James Corden with Margot Robbie as the voice of Flopsy and the film's narrator. The little rabbit has appeared in a lot of different forms, mostly recognizable by his signature blue jacket and playful expression. In the century-and-a-quarter since Peter Rabbit was first published, the book has never been out of print.

SELMA LAGERLÖF

The Wonderful Adventures of Nils
(Nils Holgerssons Underbara Resa genom Sverige) (1906)

The lively perambulations of an elf-sized boy across Sweden disguise a work of calculated moral instruction and self-improvement.

Translated by Velma Swanston Howard (1907).

Selma Lagerlöf (1858–1940) was the first female writer to win the Nobel Prize in 1909. Before she became a full-time writer, she was a teacher in a girls' high school.

The Wonderful Adventures of Nils was originally commissioned in 1902 by the Swedish National Teachers' Association as a geography book for schoolchildren.

The book spawned multiple adaptations including a 1955 Soviet animation, a 1962 Swedish live-action film, and a 1980 Japanese anime.

The Wonderful Adventures of Nils is a remarkable work. Charmed by the extraordinary tale one might easily forget that the story of the spoilt boy Nils, who is transformed into a "thumbietot" by an elf and then must travel the length and breadth of Sweden on the back of a goose before he can return home reformed, is in fact a geographical exploration of Sweden. Within the umbrella of the story, Lagerlöf takes stock of the nation's natural resources, characterizes its inhabitants, draws upon legends and history, and ultimately constructs a *folkhemmet* (people's home), made up of different provinces, social classes and ethnic groups.

The story is a Bildungsroman of sorts, where the protagonist develops and improves through his trials and through his interaction with animals and people. His outer, geographical journey is mirrored in his inner, spiritual awakening, which changes him from the narcissistic and spoilt brat of the opening pages to a mature, considerate and resourceful young man at the end of the adventurous journey.

Interestingly, Lagerlöf never expected *The Wonderful Adventures of Nils* to be a success internationally. The reason it has been is perhaps that the novel's didactic elements are subtle and Lagerlöf's version of nationalism seems essentially unthreatening, even providing an attractive model for some readers in other countries. Moreover, foreign editions, including all English translations, have tended to remove much of the novel's geographical matter, allowing its strong narrative and mesmerizing storytelling voice to stand out.

Both realistic and fantastic elements are combined; it is an elementary school reader, a novel, a children's book, fairy tale, geography book—all rolled into one. As in Rudyard Kipling's Jungle Books—which were an important source of inspiration—it aims to strikes a balance between the realistic and fantastic. The text produces a strong sense of reality: Nils never leaves a realistically portrayed Sweden but enters a magically enhanced version of it. But it can also be read as a fantasy adventure story or, like Pinocchio, as a literary fairy tale—especially so for international readers, as the original photographs were supplanted with more fantastic illustrations.

No one thought any more about struggling. Instead, both the winged and those who had no wings, all wanted to raise themselves eternally, lift themselves above the clouds, seek that which was hidden beyond them, leave the oppressive body that dragged them down to earth and soar away toward the infinite.

The construction of the nation is ultimately bound up with the development of the novel's characters. According to Lagerlöf's friend and collaborator, Valborg Olander, its deepest aim is to make its readers "good human beings and good citizens." And the book works by example. Nils is the everyman-hero for all readers and good citizens to follow.

An illustration by Mary Hamilton Frye of Nils flying on a goose, for the US edition (1913).

LUCY MAUD MONTGOMERY

ANNE OF GREEN GABLES (1908)

The transformational island town of Avonlea enchants its exuberant heroine, who sees that home makes love possible.

Lucy Maud Montgomery (1874–1942) was a Canadian author who produced more than 500 short stories, twenty-one novels, two poetry collections and numerous journals. "I cannot remember a time when I was not writing," she said in one journal.

Anne of Green Gables was first published in 1908, and was followed by 10 sequels featuring Anne, the last of which was published in 2009, 67 years after Montgomery's death.

Since its publication, it has sold more than 50 million copies and has been translated into at least thirty-six languages.

Anne of Green Gables's famed red-headed heroine, whom generations of readers have loved for her loquacious big-heartedness, is slow to make an appearance in the novel that bears her name. Rather than beginning with Anne, this famous Canadian novel begins with an intricate, tripping sentence that focuses on the perspective not of a person, but a place—a *brook*, making its way through the local village. "Mrs. Rachel Lynde lived just where the Avonlea main road dipped down into a little hollow, fringed with alders and ladies' eardrops," we read, "and traversed by a brook that had its source away back in the woods of the old Cuthbert place." The sentence goes on:

> [I]t was reputed to be an intricate, headlong brook in its earlier course through those woods, with dark secrets of pool and cascade; but by the time it reached Lynde's Hollow it was a quiet, well-conducted little stream, for not even a brook could run past Mrs. Rachel Lynde's door without due regard for decency and decorum.

In *Anne of Green Gables* place is a character, but it is also the plot. Lucy Maud Montgomery's beloved novel tells a story of a young orphaned girl, who learns to find a place she could call home—but the setting matters more, and differently, than it does in most other children's fiction. What unites the characters of *Anne of Green Gables* is not any kind of quest, hope, or tribulation—instead, it's simply sharing the place of their distinct Prince Edward Island village, Avonlea.

Many qualities of Avonlea may sound like any late nineteenth-century town with a one-room schoolhouse, village hall, and a church to visit on Sundays. But Avonlea's textures and temperaments render it distinctly Canadian. The villagers of Avonlea have no interest in the American pioneerlike roaming that drives Laura and Pa onward throughout Laura Ingalls Wilder's *Little House* books—but, on the other side, there's none of the British manor-house aristocracy of books such as *A Little Princess* or even *Pride and Prejudice*. Montgomery's *Anne* novels describe a social world

that's democratic but deeply rooted, and profoundly concerned, like the brook is, with "decency and decorum." And Avonlea is not only Canadian, but it is also an island town. The provincial Maritime feel of Prince Edward Island—on the fringes of the world, detached from the sweep of history—allows small events to flourish into meaningfulness. The attentively described seasonal landscape of sea views and verdant gardens takes the place of epic events.

"Anne climbed the ladder amid breathless silence, gained the ridgepole, balanced herself uprightly on that precarious footing..." (Left). Two illustrations from the first edition of *Anne of Green Gables* by M. A. and W. A. J. Claus.

And in this simple world of ice cream socials, spelling bees, and mayflowers, brooks and children are equally fascinating, worthy of our attention. In fact, the novel's opening sentence tells us something about how the story will go—for though she will always keep her "pool and cascade," "headlong" Anne, too, will come to be a "well-conducted little stream" as she courses through the narrative landscape that embraces her.

Children's literature is full of magical destinations, and *Anne of Green Gables* shares some kinship with these stories. Although Anne Shirley pines for romances, not heroic adventures, she begins the novel named after her yearning for drama, and certainly no one around her finds her—with her sparkling imagination, warm heart, and quick temper—anything less than remarkable.

But Green Gables is not a magical kingdom. Prince Edward Island is an island like Neverland, but there are no pirates or crocodiles, and the heroism that happens there revolves not around any terrible antagonist, but rather the more simple, if not less impressive, acts of building a community, and a family, out of people whose hearts, before, had not known how to be opened. The lonely brother and sister, Matthew and Marilla Cuthbert, who adopt Anne, live an orderly life before she arrives. But they are cold, fearful, closed down—they have spent their lives shying away from any personal intimacy—and it is only after Anne arrives that the beauty of their home becomes luminously able to awaken a sense of love within them. They learn that decency can include joyfulness and imagination. And Anne knows from the beginning that home makes love possible.

The deep-heartedness of L. M. Montgomery's story perhaps blooms from her personal connection to it. Like Anne, Montgomery grew up on a small Prince Edward Island farm in the village of Cavendish, which is clearly a model for Anne's Avonlea. And like Anne, Montgomery was adopted—not by strangers, but rather by her grandmother.

So perhaps it's not surprising that Montgomery crafted a novel where the world works differently. Over the course of the novel, Anne grows from a neglected girl to a confident young woman, secure in the love of her adopted family. She realizes that her bitter school rival, Gilbert Blythe, deserves to be her friend; she learns particularly that Marilla, the woman who adopted her, loves her abidingly.

These transformations begin at the novel's opening, when, in the first three chapters, Anne is introduced to Avonlea. But it might be more accurate to say that Anne introduces Avonlea to the adopted family who has always lived there without fully appreciating it. Dazzled with the beauty of her new home, Anne immediately offers up names—the White Way of Delight, the Lake of Shining Waters, the Snow Queen—for paths and ponds and cherry trees that amplify the magical capacity of these seemingly ordinary places. They are not "magical" in the sense that they have an otherworldly power. But when they are fully loved, as Anne loves them, they encourage a full engagement with daily life—an engagement that is sustaining, entertaining, and even ennobling.

Certainly this is the case for Anne, as well as for Matthew and Marilla Cuthbert. While Matthew warms to Anne immediately, Marilla's path forward is different, slower. She remains afraid of her growing love for Anne; she's hesitant to share affection with the child who craves it.

At the novel's ending, Matthew suddenly dies. Montgomery describes mourning him in a way predictably attentive to the emotional experience of place:

> Two days afterward they carried Matthew Cuthbert over his homestead threshold and away from the fields he had tilled and the orchards he had loved and the trees he had planted; and then Avonlea settled back to its usual placidity and even at Green Gables affairs slipped into their old groove and work was done and duties fulfilled with regularity as before, although always with the aching sense of "loss in all familiar things."

> "You mustn't sell Green Gables," said Anne resolutely […] "Nobody could love it as you and I do."

Loss aches, but in that hurt blossoms a kind of hope. Mourning her brother, Marilla opens her heart to Anne for the first time—and their openness to each other is sealed by mutually committing to maintain Green Gables as their home. "You can't sell Green Gables," Anne tells Marilla. "No one will love it like we do."

In the later volumes of the *Anne* series, Green Gables remains a transformative place. In *Anne of Avonlea* for example, two "harum-scarum" twins, Davey and Dora, fall under its pacifying influence. Anne is a part of these transformations, too. But what all eight novels show, and the reason so many readers love them, is an almost alchemical reaction between character and setting that make story possible where it wasn't before. There was a Green Gables, a farmhouse in the small town of Avonlea, before the orphan Anne Shirley arrived there. But it is only after Green Gables shines in Anne's love that it becomes a place where characters' lives and hearts—not only Anne's, but certainly hers—could be transformed. And it's this central lesson, that there can be magic in our home places if we love it into being, that transforms not only Montgomery's characters but also her readers.

Green Gables Heritage Place in Cavendish, on Prince Edward Island, Canada. The building was owned by relatives of Lucy Maud Montgomery and served as the setting for the book.

KENNETH GRAHAME

THE WIND IN THE WILLOWS (1908)

Originally a series of bedtime stories for the author's son, this satirical kaleidoscope pastiches the fads and fashions of the English upper classes.

Kenneth Grahame (1859–1932) spent most of his childhood in England under the care of his maternal grandmother following the death of his mother and his father's descent into alcoholism.

Grahame spent 30 years working at the Bank of England. While there, he would jot down snippets of prose and poetry in a bank ledger, which would later form the basis of his earliest publications.

Though the novel initially received negative reviews from critics, it was loved by the public and sold in such quantities that 100 editions were printed in Britain alone by 1951.

The Wind in the Willows has become part of the mythology of the English countryside, synonymous with "messing about in boats," the wild adventures of the eccentric Mr. Toad, and to many people, it is merely a children's book about little animals. And so it often comes as a surprise to find that the river and boating feature substantially in only two of its twelve chapters, and Mr. Toad in only six; that the book was not originally published as a children's book, and that for about ninety-eight percent of the time it is not about animals at all. Mole, Rat, Badger, Toad, and Otter may have animal names, and some superficial animal characteristics, but they almost always behave like grown men.

The truth is that *The Wind in the Willows* is a kaleidoscope of many books skillfully rolled into one, and readers, old and young, respond to it, and to different parts of it, as and when they can.

The real backbone of the book is the story of Mr. Mole (after all, one of Grahame's original titles for the book was Mr. Mole and his Mates), who very, very rarely behaves like a mole. He makes an engaging central character—naïve, sympathetic, enthusiastic; child readers and adult readers can empathize with him. He is initially vulnerable, and not only is everything interesting and exciting to him, but he moves from being an outsider to being an insider; he grows up.

At the beginning of the book Mr. Mole leaves his spring-cleaning, discovers the River Bank and its bankers, and makes friends with the Water Rat (a gentleman of leisure). He goes on a disastrous camping trip with their neighbor, Mr. Toad; he gets lost in the terrifying Wild Wood in early winter and finds his way to the security of Mr. Badger's house. Later, around Christmas, he goes back to his old home and entertains a local choir of carol singers; he joins his friend the Water Rat in a search for a missing toddler; and finally, he helps to liberate Toad Hall from the invading Wild Wooders.

But the irrepressible spirit of Mr. Toad also runs through the book. A rich insider, he starts as an unsuccessful oarsman, tries horse-drawn

> Believe me, my young friend, there is nothing—absolutely nothing—half so much worth doing as simply messing about in boats.

Ratty takes Mole rowing on the river for the first time, by E. H. Shepard for the 1931 illustrated edition.

caravanning, then (dangerous) motoring; he's sent to jail, escapes, and carouses around the country until he comes home to find Toad Hall occupied.

It is often claimed that the best children's books begin with stories told to an individual child, and it was Toad's story that was the origin of *The Wind in the Willows*. According to Grahame's wife, Elspeth Thomson, Grahame told an endless bedtime story to their son, Alastair (born 1900) "about moles, giraffes, and water rats." These stories are lost, but in the summer of 1907, Grahame wrote a series of fifteen letters to Alastair (they were on vacation separately) containing in 18,000 words the bulk of Toad's subsequently published adventures.

How these beginnings emerged as the complex *The Wind in the Willows* is a fascinating story. Grahame, a rather uptight, conventional Scot, had a successful career in the Bank of England, becoming Secretary in 1898. He led a hearty outdoor life, sailing on the Thames and at Fowey in Cornwall, but also had friends in the bohemian community of writers and artists that

Previous page: Sea Rat tells Water Rat about his adventures, drawn by Paul Bransom for the 1913 edition.

included Oscar Wilde. He published short pieces in the notorious avant-garde magazine, *The Yellow Book*, and made a literary name for himself with two books of short stories about childhood— *the Golden Age* (1895), and *Dream Days* (1898).

John O'Hara Cosgrave, the editor of a popular American magazine, *Everybody's*, was a great fan, and commissioned the English author Constance Smedley to persuade Grahame to write more. She was up against it. As far as writing was concerned, Grahame had said that he was "a spring, not a pump," and that he found writing "a torture" and he had no need of money or notoriety! He had married, somewhat unexpectedly, a rich, lively, and well-connected wife—Elspeth. He was at the peak of his profession, and seems to have been an amiable, unambitious man.

But Constance performed a miracle of persuasion, and Grahame set out to convert the half-book about Mr. Toad into *The Wind in the Willows*. He had a satirical cast of mind, an outsider's view of the upper-class world, a very ready wit, and a remarkable feel for language, but he was not at heart a children's writer. He took the child's story and elaborated it and orchestrated it—and published what was in fact a more or less benign satire on upper-middle-class English society.

More than that—and this explains much of the kaleidoscopic feel of the book—to flesh out Mole's story, and to provide a frame for Toad's, he built each chapter on parody and pastiche of the popular literary fads and fashions of the time.

Thus *The Wind in the Willows* begins with a river story. The Thames was popular as a weekend destination (Grahame was brought up and lived nearby) and was the subject of many best-selling novels. The most famous survivor is Jerome K. Jerome's *Three Men in a Boat* (1889) and there are many resemblances to Grahame's book—especially in the three main characters. Next, in "The Open Road," Grahame drew on the craze for caravanning and caravanning books—the English Caravan Club was founded in 1907. Toad's obsession with cars reflects the many motoring thrillers of the time.

When he was not taking on whole genres, Grahame could not resist a virtuoso cameo: Toad's adventure with the gypsy is a parody of travel writer George Borrow; Toad goes to jail in a flourish of Gilbert and Sullivan–style prose; Mole and Rat in the Wild Wood could be Sherlock Holmes and Dr. Watson.

Grahame called his masterpiece "a book of youth—and so perhaps chiefly for Youth"—but that had nothing to do with the age of the readers. *The Wind in the Willows* is one of the most complex books ever to stumble into childhood—but this is a book that can captivate any reader, on any page, at any stage and at any age; a genuine classic.

FRANCES HODGSON BURNETT

The Secret Garden (1911)

An ill-tempered girl and her malingering male cousin have their lives upturned by a neglected garden with the power to improve both character and health through the power of nature.

Frances Hodgson Burnett (1849–1924) was born in Manchester, England, and emigrated with her mother and siblings to the United States in 1865 after the death of her father.

Like many novels in the Victorian and Edwardian periods, *The Secret Garden* was first published in monthly instalments in *The American Magazine* (1910–11), which was aimed at an adult readership.

While it was well received, the authors' previous novels including *A Little Princess* (1905), far eclipsed *The Secret Garden* in popularity and it only became her most beloved work after her death in 1924.

The garden at the heart of *The Secret Garden* highlights the connection between children and nature, and its power to foster their health and character. After being orphaned when her parents die of cholera in India, nine-year-old Mary Lennox begins the novel as a rude, unlikeable, and sickly girl. She is sent to live with her widower uncle Archibald Craven and his indulged son Colin at Misselthwaite Manor in Yorkshire, England, whereupon all are transformed by the healing qualities of nature. Colin's mother, Lilias, died when a branch from a tree in her treasured garden struck her, and her grieving husband locked up the walled garden and buried the key. The mysterious garden has been abandoned for ten years when a friendly robin helps Mary discover the key hidden in the soil, and she notices signs of life among the dormant bushes and flower bulbs.

Mary learns much about reviving the garden from a twelve-year-old boy named Dickon, who is the brother of kindly servant Martha Sowerby. Dickon spends much of his time on the moors and is the picture of health. As Mary gains weight and her complexion improves with the time she spends outdoors, she discovers her cousin Colin living in a hidden bedroom in the house; he believes himself to be a sickly "cripple" who must remain confined to bed. Mary's stories of her time in the garden with Dickon soon lead to Colin making his first trip outdoors in years. When he visits his mother's garden, he rises from his wheelchair to stand, proving that he is able to walk, after all. His repeated days in the garden with the other children soon improve his health and happiness to the point where he, too, can run and play with Mary and Dickon.

The radical shift toward urban life in the nineteenth century meant that childhood experiences within the natural world changed dramatically, and connections with plants and animals were severed. Belief in the need to recapture the restorative power of nature for children was visible in the introduction of kindergartens (or children's gardens) in Britain, and in the almost supernatural power of the secret garden. As Colin and Mary's health and tempers begin to improve with time spent among the masses

It was the sweetest, most mysterious-looking place any one could imagine. The high walls which shut it in were covered with the leafless stems of climbing roses which were so thick that they were matted together.

"If you look the right way, you can see that the whole world is a garden." Mary as illustrated by Charles Robinson for the original 1911 British edition.

Previous page: "Mary, Colin, and Dickon in the secret garden," illustration by Charles Robinson.

of blooming flowers, they debate whether the garden's "Magic" is real or whether it requires them to pretend. Mary is emphatic that it is real and pure: "It's Magic . . . but not black. It's as white as snow."

While *The Secret Garden* is not a fantasy novel, there is something inexplicable about the positive influence of Lilias from beyond the grave via the garden. Martha's mother, Susan, is convinced that Lilias still inhabits the garden. Indeed, it is a vision of his late wife calling to him in a dream from the garden with a voice "like a sound from a golden flute" that compels Archibald Craven to return from Europe and reconnect with his son, whom he has long neglected due to his grief.

Through the maternal love manifested through the garden to which she had once lovingly tended—"a wilderness of autumn gold and purple and violet blue and flaming scarlet"—the characters of Archibald, Colin, and Mary, and the relationships between them, are able to flourish.

J. M. BARRIE

Peter and Wendy (1911)

A novel written for a dual audience of adult and child readers about the thrilling adventures enabled by children's imaginations and the impossibility of remaining young forever.

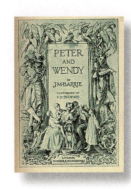

Among the most famous of all fantasy worlds in children's literature is Neverland, an island that represents the fleeting pleasures of childhood. While Peter Pan first appeared in James Matthew Barrie's novel *The Little White Bird* (1902), Neverland first featured in the stage play *Peter Pan, or The Boy Who Wouldn't Grow Up*, performed in London's West End in December 1904 and as warmly embraced by adult audiences as by children.

Peter Pan's entry into children's books began when the chapters in which he appeared in *The Little White Bird* were published separately as *Peter Pan in Kensington Gardens* in 1905. It is in *Peter and Wendy* (1911), which evolved from the play, that Barrie fully describes this imaginary world. In this novel, Peter Pan visits Wendy Darling in her London home at night and entices her to travel to Neverland with him to be a mother to the Lost Boys. Wendy's younger brothers, John and Michael, join them on this journey.

Peter Pan and Neverland are almost universally recognized across generations today. Neverland is an ideal scene for childhood adventures, a natural setting with no signs of the modern world: Peter and the Lost Boys live in a home under the ground, which they reach via hollowed-out trees. In locations such as the Neverwood and the Mermaid's Lagoon, the children encounter fairies (notably Tinker Bell), mermaids, pirates, wild animals, and a Native American tribe.

Neverlands are "always more or less an island," according to Barrie's novel. Yet they vary and change because they are the product of each child's imagination. Each child's Neverland varies depending on their age and individual fantasies of nature and play:

> John's, for instance, had a lagoon with flamingos flying over it at which John was shooting, while Michael, who was very small, had a flamingo with lagoons flying over it. John lives in a boat turned upside down on the sands, Michael in a wigwam, Wendy in a house of leaves deftly sewn together. John had no friends, Michael had friends at night, Wendy had a pet wolf forsaken by its parents.

J. M. Barrie (1869–1937) never had children of his own, but he developed a friendship with the five boys in the Llewelyn Davies family, George, John ("Jack"), Peter, Michael, and Nicholas, whom he cared for after their parents died.

He invented the character of Peter Pan when telling stories to George and Jack about their brother, Peter.

Barrie gave the rights to Peter Pan to the Great Ormond Street Hospital in 1929 to provide ongoing financial support to sick children, an arrangement that continues to this day via a special amendment to the British Copyright Designs and Patents Act.

Previous page: Poster advertising the first production of J. M. Barrie's *Peter Pan* at the Duke of York's Theatre, December 27, 1904. Color lithograph by Charles Buchel.

The Darling children's imaginations draw on elements of Victorian and Edwardian children's literature, such as popular castaway stories inspired by *Robinson Crusoe* (1719), including R. M. Ballantyne's *The Coral Island* (1857), and boys' adventure fiction. However, while her brothers are immersed in adventures with pirates and Native Americans in Neverland, Wendy rehearses for her future role as a wife and mother. She utilizes her needlework skills to sew a shelter and assumes the care of a wolf so that she may play at mothering (shades of *The Jungle Book*). Indeed, the British term "Wendy House" for a children's playhouse originated from Wendy's home in *Peter and Wendy* in which she cares for the Lost Boys by darning their clothing and telling them stories.

Potentially sharing a connection with the Australian term "Never Never," used to refer to a remote location, Barrie's Neverland is distant from the real world. Peter Pan's iconic direction to the Darling children to fly "Second to the right, and straight on till morning" locates the island nonsensically in relation to space and time. The children's long journey to reach the island symbolizes the way in which adults cannot access the magic of childhood play and imagination. Barrie directly addresses adult readers' feelings of nostalgia:

> On these magic shores children at play are for ever beaching their coracles. We too have been there; we can still hear the sound of the surf, though we shall land no more.

This wistfulness for childhood is especially evident in the lives of some the most influential authors of children's fantasy literature in the late nineteenth and early twentieth centuries. Barrie, Carroll, and fairy tale author Hans Christian Andersen have all been understood as finding solace for their loneliness, awkwardness, and shyness in a nostalgic retreat into childhood. Both men without families of their own, Barrie and Lewis Carroll notably developed close friendships with other people's children and *Peter Pan* and *Alice's Adventures in Wonderland* (1865) had their origins in stories told aloud to entertain their young companions. In popular psychology today, adults who wish to remain childlike are described as exhibiting "Peter Pan syndrome." While it is not a clinically diagnosable condition, the term is used to refer to people who struggle to maintain adult responsibilities.

Of course, all children—except Peter—must grow up. A place where childhood adventure and play can flourish away from modern life and adult logic and rules, Neverland cannot be inhabited forever. In *Peter and Wendy*, the Darling children return to London with the Lost Boys to resume the regular structures of time and formal schooling. The Lost Boys feel duped once they realize what schools entails and "saw what goats they had been not to remain on the island."

Only Peter successfully resists a permanent departure from Neverland, a place that keeps him from ever maturing. In contrast, after she has returned to London, Wendy ages at a normal rate, gradually outgrows her dress

"Peter flies into the nursery," by Francis D. Bedford, for the 1911 edition.

woven from leaves and berries in Neverland, and her daughter, Jane, then her granddaughter, Margaret, take her place by flying to Neverland with Peter when he visits annually. The transfer of these adventures between generations represents the natural life cycle as the child becomes an adult and imagination and play are replaced with duty and responsibility.

Peter Pan's endless childhood is unnatural and tragic. For instance, Peter retains his baby teeth as an older boy, which creates a disconcerting experience when "he gnashed his little pearls" at Mrs. Darling. Like all children, Peter is also preoccupied with himself. As time passes, he soon forgets his encounters with Wendy, only thinking of his immediate desires, such as the need for a girl to clean his home. Though *Peter and Wendy* celebrates the delight of belief in mythical creatures and fantasies of dangerous battles in the wilderness, a perpetual childhood in Neverland is an unpleasant fate, with no possibility of change, and no connection with family. While all children have a selfish side and are "innocent and gay and heartless," their journeys to Neverland with Peter Pan must naturally stop with adulthood.

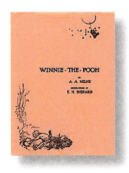

A. A. MILNE

WINNIE-THE-POOH (1926)

Our first introduction to Winnie-the-Pooh and his friends, perpetual residents of the Hundred Acre Wood, in a set of hugely charming stories that has become one of the best-loved children's books of all time.

Alan Alexander Milne (1882–1956) had a moderately successful career as a humorist and playwright before the phenomenal popularity of *Winnie-the-Pooh* (1926), which sold 35,000 copies in the UK and over 150,000 in the US in the first year.

The toy Winnie-the-Pooh now lives in the New York Public Library.

Milne borrowed his name from "Winnie," an American black bear cub at London Zoo, and a swan called "Pooh," whom Milne met on vacation.

Is *Winnie-the-Pooh* a classic? There are plenty of indicators to suggest that it is, which have more to do with its afterlife, and its adaptations and exploitations than the considerable merits of the book itself. Think of, say, the proliferation of memes and inspirational quotes online attributed—via Pooh—to Alan Alexander Milne (most of them never written by A. A. Milne in reality); or the Disney incarnations with all their associated commodities; or the ways in which Milne's words and characters have filtered into our conversational language.

Winnie-the-Pooh and its sequel, *The House at Pooh Corner*, are collections of linked stories featuring the same little group of characters living around the lovely Hundred Acre Wood, a place where many of us might have spent much of our earliest years. Pooh, Piglet, Rabbit, Kanga and Roo, Eeyore, and Wol Owl are—for anyone who doesn't know them—anthropomorphized stuffed animals, each with a couple of consistent personality traits to define them. Pooh is a bear who likes honey, a lot, and if ever you leave him in the presence of a large pot of honey, you can assume that large pot of honey is done for. Self-sacrifice means not eating the honey; risks are worth incurring to secure more honey; punishment and guilt come from eating the honey that was not to be eaten, etc.—that's the basis for much of his particular moral universe.

The animals live independently, each in their own home, but in all other respects they behave as children. There is one actual human child in the books, Christopher Robin, named for the author's son, who acts as their useful, responsible adult. They go off on adventures around the—sometimes perilous-seeming but fundamentally very safe—forest; they do benign things that are endearingly foolish but well-intentioned, clumsy but never actually mean; and at chapter's end, they always make it back, misunderstandings are always resolved. They might not have found the woozle they were hunting or trapped a heffalump (oh, bother), but they're home and they're safe and the rain has stopped and everyone is still good friends. Simple enough.

But oh, that narrative voice. Its confident warmth and its humor. And alongside that, you have the gorgeous E. H. Shepard illustrations, originally

> You can't stay in your corner of the Forest waiting for others to come to you. You have to go to them sometimes.

Pooh, Piglet, and Christopher Robin standing on what was originally called Posingford Bridge. The bridge, which spans a tributary of the River Medway was replaced in 2005 but kept its original form so fans of the books can continue to play "Pooh Sticks." Illustrated by E. H. Shepard for the first edition.

just in black and white, that never do too much, yet are how we remember what we remember. Though the toys of the real Christopher Milne inspired the stories, Shepard based the illustrated Pooh on a toy bear of his own son's; and just as Milne based his characters' world on his own home at Ashdown Forest, East Sussex, Shepard used views of the same location, with its familiar heather and pines, when creating the books' visual world. The real forest and the book forest, Christopher Milne would write, "are identical." Importantly, the book opens with a memorable map. I'd bet a large proportion of readers today who love the promise of a good map at the start of their books learned that love from Shepard's introduction to the 100 Aker Wood (see overleaf).

There's all that skill in the voice and the illustrations . . . and now, a part of the reading pleasure is of course nostalgia, too, for the enchanted place that was one's own childhood, or the childhood one might have liked to have. The second book concludes with Christopher Robin leaving, going off to school —it's one of the most guaranteed tear-jerker endings I know. But it is also a celebration of enduring childhood memories, that feeling we have that back there, somewhere in the Hundred Acre Wood, "a little boy and his Bear will always be playing."

Winnie-the-Pooh is not to everyone's taste. It is sometimes considered sentimental, whimsical, twee. (Tiddly-pom.) Reviewing it in her "Constant Reader" book column in the *New Yorker*, Dorothy Parker famously wrote "Tonstant Weader Fwowed Up." But however admittedly funny the review, the criticisms are not reading the books quite right, I think, nor tuning in to their young audiences. In any case, as we approach the book's 100th birthday (HIPY PAPY BTHUTHDTH THUTHDA BTHUTHDY!), it endures, holding its rightful place more or less invincibly on classics lists, and contemporary bookshelves, in readers' memories and affections.

100 Aker Wood map illustration by E.H. Shepard. His illustrations were so integral to the series' success that A. A. Milne arranged for Shepard to receive a share of the royalties.

ERICH KÄSTNER

EMIL AND THE DETECTIVES
(EMIL UND DIE DETEKTIVE) (1929)

Vividly bringing to life the sights and sounds of Weimar Berlin, this is the exuberant tale of the schoolboy Emil Tischbein and the gang of child "detectives" with whom he teams up to catch a thief.

Translated by Eileen Hall (1959).

Erich Kästner (1899–1974) was born in Dresden and worked as a journalist and critic in Leipzig and Berlin.

Other works include *Das doppelte Lottchen* (*The Parent Trap*, 1949), and the adult novel *Fabian* (1931). After 1933, despite having his work banned by the Nazis, Kästner remained in Berlin, publishing a sequel to *Emil and the Detectives, Emil und die drei Zwillinge* (*Emil and the Three Twins*) outside Germany in 1935.

There have been at least six film adaptations of *Emil and the Detectives*, the first of which, in 1931, features a screenplay co-written by Billy Wilder and (uncredited) Emeric Pressburger.

Emil and the Detectives is one of the most charming and original children's novels of the interwar period. An immediate bestseller when it was published in Germany's Weimar Republic, it is the prototype of adventure stories featuring "meddling," crime-solving children, and a great novel about the transformative impact of the modern city. In a fast-paced narrative covering just over one day, it tells the story of Emil Tischbein, a schoolboy from a provincial town who falls victim of an opportunistic thief when he falls asleep on the train to Berlin, losing the cash he had been entrusted with by his mother.

Throughout, the novel demonstrates the value of trusting one's instincts and of overcoming setbacks through action. Thus, when Emil spots the man he suspects to be the thief among the crowds at Berlin's Zoo station, he immediately gives chase, trailing him through the unfamiliar metropolis. A turning point comes when Emil, just when he is beginning to feel isolated and uncertain, encounters Gustav, a local boy who is excited at the prospect of catching a thief. Gustav summons a gang of willing classmates and together they devise a plan, as the outsider Emil finds his feet in this alien world through the power of friendship. In a gentle pastiche of German bureaucracy, the self-styled "detectives" embrace a rational, disciplined approach, surveilling the suspect and staking out his hotel. At the novel's climax the man, surrounded by intimidating hordes of children, attempts to deposit the stolen money at a bank, only to be exposed as a thief when Emil provides physical evidence that the bank notes were his. In the story's satisfyingly happy ending the thief turns out to be a wanted bank robber, earning Emil a 1,000 Mark reward, and allowing this notably selfless son to treat his beloved mother from the money he has earned.

Unlike many successful children's books, the success of *Emil and the Detectives* derives not from fantastical or exotic settings or complicated plot devices, but rather from a sense that adventure is possible in real places and everyday scenarios. Kästner, drawing on his talents as a journalist and satirical poet, brings observational precision, warmth, and wit to the

> They say you should always assume the best about people until they've proven themselves to be otherwise.

Gustav (left) introduces Emil (right) to the gang of children who help to solve Emil's case. Illustration by Walter Trier, a longtime collaborator with Kästner.

depiction of a teeming metropolis that bewilders and entrances the young protagonist in equal measure. He vividly evokes its sights and sounds as Emil bonds with his new friends and navigates the city's topography—you can even plot his movements on a map of the city. Writing in an authentic register, replete with colloquialisms, Kästner evokes a magical, parallel world inhabited by prepubescent, streetwise children, which is memorably enhanced by Walter Trier's much loved illustrations.

Emil and the Detectives has been widely translated and adapted into film versions, radio plays, and stage productions. It is, in a way, a product of its time, playfully riffing on the detective genre that was hugely popular in the 1920s, and also bearing comparison with other cultural responses to Berlin from the era. We might mention Alfred Döblin's polyphonic novel *Berlin Alexanderplatz* (1929), the innovative film *People on Sunday* (1930), which depicts Berlin's youth during summer, or Fritz Lang's crime drama *M* (1931), which also sees a criminal hunted by unlikely, amateur "detectives" —the city's street beggars. Yet *Emil and the Detectives* also manages to transcend time and place.

Almost a century on, its lasting influence is discernible in many later texts, films, and television shows, from Enid Blyton's *Famous Five* to the Harry Potter novels and *Stranger Things*. This children's classic is as relatable to readers in the 2020s as it was in the 1920s.

2 NEW HORIZONS

1930 TO 1959

Conjuring fantasy lands and reimagining those close to home, radical narratives proved popular in a rapidly changing world.

Still from the 2015 film adaptation of *The Little Prince*, directed by Mark Osborne.

ANDRÉ MAUROIS

Fattypuffs and Thinifers
(Patapoufs et Filifers) (1930)

An adventure story with a satirical twist; two young brother—surface-dwellers—fall into a surreal new world at the centre of the earth.

Translated by Rosemary Benét (1940); Norman Denny (1968).

André Maurois was born Émile Wilhelm Herzog (1885–1967) and changed his pen name after the First World War. He legally adopted the name in 1947.

A respected biographer and novelist, Maurois was elected to the Académie Francaise in 1938.

Although upon first publication *Fattypuffs and Thinifers* (1930) featured illustrations by French artist Jean Bruller, the most iconic representation of Maurois' characters arguably came in 1941, when Fritz Wegner's caricatured artwork accompanied the illustrated English translation.

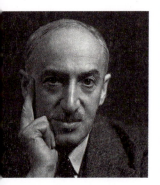

A couple of made-up words can stick and bestow cult status. In the original French edition from 1930, the title was *Patapoufs et Filifers*. Now, patapoufs is established in the French lexicon and dictionaries. The English translation is only slightly less onomatopoeic.

On a Sunday morning walk in the forest with their father, Terry Double "who never thought of the consequences" and Edmund Double, fall down the side of the pillars of the Two Rocks and ride the escalator down to a fantastical harbour. They are then taken separately to two rival countries—Fattyland and Thiniport—inhabited by equally rival tribes. Edmund, being slightly chubbier, is despatched on the ferry to Fattyland where he marvels that: "The chocolate eclairs were almost as fat as motor tyres, and the cream buns were as big as bath sponges." Terry, meanwhile, is consigned to Thiniport.

The Thinifers are tall and skinny. They drink only water and eat spaghetti—because it is thin. They live in tall thin houses and stand in thin trains with no seats. They are obsessive time keepers, ambitiously neurotic, hardworking and often quarrelsome. The Fattypuffs live on the other side of the lake. They are easygoing, kind-hearted people who enjoy lobster and egg sandwiches on the hour and a nap afterward.

The Fattypuffs and Thinifers have grown to despise each other's ways of life. Edmund loves the Fattypuffs. "Nearly all day long they laughed and played and made jokes and most of their conversations were about food." The Thinifers, Edmund is told, "are horrible to look at, being excessively thin, bony as skeletons and yellow as lemons." Terry, on the other side, thinks that the Thinifers are remarkable people who work hard and are wonderfully good at arithmetic. "He liked this exactness on the part of the Thinifers. At least you always knew where you were."

This symbolism of Franco-German antagonism was a relationship André Maurois knew well; the son of a Jewish textile manufacturer, his family fled Alsace during the first Franco-Prussian conflict of 1870. He then served in World War 1 as a French liaison officer-cum-translator to the English. His

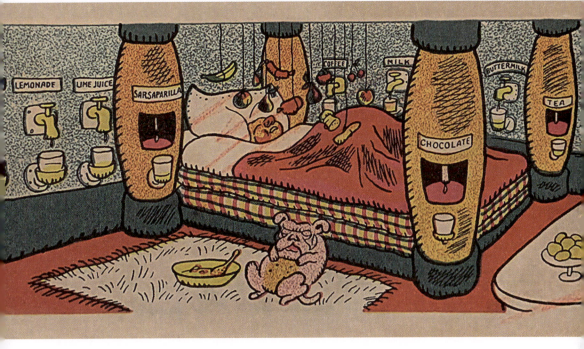

An illustration of a "Fattypuff Bedroom" by French illustrator Jean Bruller for the first edition.

conciliatory vision did not last the Vichy government of the Second World War and he decamped to America where he lectured at Princeton University and helped organize anti-Nazi propaganda.

There is a lot of playfulness in the book, built around childish interests of supper, sibling rivalries and grown-ups making fools of themselves. And there are indeed a few side jokes for the grown-ups like the musician *Tumski-Korsapuff*, composer of the of the Hymn to Plumpness.

But Maurois' storytelling is also skilfully satirical. He was an early science fiction pioneer, drawing on the styles of Lewis Carroll and Jonathan Swift, and, in turn, surely influencing Roald Dahl. With its episodic chapters alternately focusing on each country (and boy), both sides are portrayed equally throughout. By removing the "us" and "them" Maurois makes it impossible to "support" one side in the conflict. The diplomatic conference, one of the funniest scenes in the book, similarly introduces nuanced political issues. He also plays games with scale, delighting the reader in the numerous details of these imaginary countries and their inhabitants that are defined by their size.

Like all great children's stories, *Fattypuffs and Thinifers* introduces a slice of dark realism as war intervenes; and, ironically, Maurois's story from 1930 was a prescient warning of the forthcoming second world war.

Yet, the book also has an enduring message of compassion, reconciliation and hope, right to the end. And now, across almost a century, Maurois's humor appears even sharper, more painful, while the moral seems more relevant, not less.

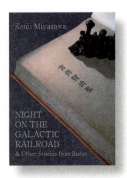

KENJI MIYAZAWA

Night on the Galactic Railroad
(Ginga Tetsudō no Yoru) (1934)

A lonely schoolboy boards an enchanted train and is whisked off through the night's sky on a surreal interstellar voyage to the Milky Way.

Translated by J. Sigrist & D. M. Stroud (1971).

Kenji Miyazawa (1896–1933) was a Japanese teacher and scientist as well as a prolific author and poet.

Night on the Galactic Railroad was written around 1927 but remained unpublished until 1934, a year after Miyazawa's death. Since its publication, the story has been adapted for stage and was turned into an animated movie in 1985.

Miyazawa was fascinated both by Buddhist and Christian mysticism and influences of these two belief systems are scattered throughout his works.

Of all the places we visit in life, it is the unknown destination to which we travel after death that has been the focus of so many of history's most renowned poets, artists, and writers. This is equally true of Kenji Miyazawa, one of Japan's most beloved poets and children's authors, who spent much of his short time on earth pondering what he and his loved ones would encounter in the afterlife. *Night on the Galactic Railroad* is an example of just such a musing, in which readers follow Miyazawa's reluctant protagonist, Giovanni —a poverty-stricken schoolboy—on a mystical train ride through the star-filled galaxy.

Miyazawa was an accomplished scientist and teacher. He grew up in a Buddhist household in the small city of Hanamaki in northern Japan, where, alongside his writing, he threw himself into an exploration of Eastern and Western scriptures, mysticism, and esotericism. The teachings of these seemingly divergent belief systems are brought together in the fantasy world Miyazawa builds—a world in which the stars seem to come alive and where the souls of the dead depart from the Earth on a train bound for the heavens. The world Miyazawa describes invites readers to ponder the mysteries of the cosmos while simultaneously reflecting on their own place within it. A bit too much for a child to contemplate? Perhaps so. Yet, in *Night on the Galactic Railroad* it is not so much philosophical complexity that readers encounter, but depictions of love, beauty, companionship, joy, and sorrow; aspects of the physical world that are familiar to readers of all ages. But any semblance of the "real" is soon taken away, as Miyazawa paints a picture of an interstellar journey through the night sky.

Miyazawa's story unfolds in a fictionalized version of his hometown of Hanamaki. The main characters in the town are given European names, making the imagined geography of the story feel more like that of a Western fairy tale. He begins within the familiar setting of a school, where a nervous Giovanni reluctantly raises his hand to answer his teacher's question about whether the Milky Way is, in fact, a river of spilled milk. Giovanni finds himself unable to answer the question, and so Miyazawa takes his readers

Previous page: Front cover of the 2015 edition of *Night on the Galactic Railroad*, illustrated by Toshiya Kobayashi.

> No one knows what true happiness is, least of all me. But no matter how hard it is, if you keep to the path you deem to be true, you can overcome any mountain. With each step in that direction, people come closer to happiness.

on an mesmerizing journey to find out. When class ends, the children head down to the river to celebrate the Milky Way Festival, where, among the various festivities, hollowed-out gourds are lit with candles and placed in the water as floating lanterns—mirroring traditional festivities that took place in the town where Miyazawa grew up. But Miyazawa doesn't indulge in a nostalgic retelling of seasonal celebrations; instead he describes how a bullied Giovanni makes his way to the festival, only to flee after being teased by his classmates. Running to the top of a nearby hill, Giovanni sits and stares up at the stars—his entry point to an extraordinary world. Realizing that the very spot where he was resting has mysteriously become a train platform, the young boy rubs his eyes in astonishment as he hears calls for "Milky Way Station." An enchanted train glides toward the boy, the lights of its carriages illuminating the sky like "a billion fireflies." Giovanni opens his eyes to find himself aboard an old railroad car with his school friend, Campanella. This train, Miyazawa writes, does not run on fuel, but races toward the stars simply because it is willed to do so.

Together, the two boys ride the train through the night sky as it heads toward its final destination—that great cosmic river of spilled milk, the Milky Way. Miyazawa imagines this extraordinary world through constellations of stars, ancient myths, and all manner of unusual folklore; his descriptions of the various passengers and places the two boys encounter on their galactic journey are filled with a mixture of Buddhist and Christian symbolism. As the children watch through the train window, they see magical sights of phosphorescent signals in all the colors of the rainbow, meadows of silver reeds, and bejeweled flowers—all of which are just out of Giovanni's reach as he grabs at them from the window. There are further signs that this train is unlike any other: The number of passengers on board magically appears to increase and decrease without explanation as the train passes its various stops, which include Swan Station where the streets are lit with the blue light of the Milky Way, described by Miyazawa as a celestial river filled with crystals, topaz, and shimmering jade.

At the next constellation, the Leo Observatory, readers are introduced to the train's conductor, who informs Giovanni that his ticket seems to have been brought from the Third Dimension. A nearby passenger—a man who catches "snowy herons"—describes how this ticket allows its holder to travel freely along the Fourth Dimension Milky Way Railroad. Other passengers, such as a pair of children who board the galactic train after the ship they'd

Giovanni (right) and Campanella (left) aboard the train in the 1985 anime movie adaptation of *Night on the Galactic Railroad*. In this adaptation of Miyazawa's story, the protagonists are depicted as anthropomorphic cats.

been sailing on hits an iceberg and sinks, suggest that something darker underpins Miyazawa's tale.

The magic and wonder of this galactic world are further revealed through a series of spectacular stations based on well-known constellations. A dense forest in the formation of a harp player, filled with peacocks, is named as the place where the musicians of the past end up to once again play together. In addition, a red-flamed scorpion glimpsed from the carriage window is said to have been placed in the heavens to bring light to the darkness of night, providing a unique reimagining of a familiar sign from the Greek zodiac. When Campanella, the shipwrecked children, and the other passengers end their journey at the Southern Cross, they depart the train to enter heaven, leaving a broken-hearted Giovanni on the bank of the Milky Way River.

Here, Miyazawa bursts the bubble of this enchanted land, bringing both Giovanni and readers back to the meadow where the fantastic journey began. Readers learn that, while trying to sail a hollowed-out gourd, Campanella had fallen into the river and drowned, thus becoming aware that Giovanni's galactic train ride saw him accompany his friend on the journey to the afterlife. Miyazawa brings his readers back to Earth with a bump, but like all the best children's stories the fantastical world they've traveled through is never fully explained, and is neither fully real nor entirely fictional. *Night on the Galactic Railroad* imagines a world beyond our own, but it is, perhaps, one Miyazawa believes we are all destined to visit.

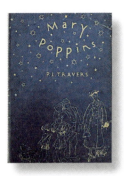

P. L. TRAVERS

Mary Poppins (1934)

A magical nanny who blows into the lives of the Banks family on the East Wind—with a promise to stay and care for the children, but only until the wind changes.

Pamela Lyndon Travers (1899–1996) began her career as a dancer and Shakespearean performer in Sydney in the early 1920s. She moved to London in 1924 to pursue her writing career. Mary Poppins first appeared in *The Christchurch Sun* in 1926, before taking book form in 1934.

In total there were eight books in the Mary Poppins series. The final one, *Mary Poppins and the House Next Door*, was published in 1988.

P. L. Travers fought hard against the changes to her story that she saw in the Disney film—ultimately, she lost. She was so unhappy with the way she and her novel were treated that she ruled out any further adaptations.

Mary Poppins arrives at 17 Cherry-Tree Lane in a gust of wind. Instantly hired to take care of the Banks family's four children—Jane, Michael, and infant twins Barbara and John—it is clear from the moment she slides up the bannister to the nursery, that this is a nanny unlike any other.

Written by the Australian English writer Pamela Travers, who published as P. L. Travers, the character of Mary Poppins was first introduced to the world via a newspaper short, from there, it seems Travers was propelled forward by the muse. "The book was entirely spontaneous and not invented, not thought out," Travers said in an interview. "I cannot summon up inspiration; I myself am summoned."

Who Travers was summoned to create was a nanny brimming over with magic. Mary Poppins can talk to animals and the elements; she can jump into pictures drawn with sidewalk chalk; she can whisk the children around the world with nothing more than the spin of a compass; she can hang the stars. She can also do the ordinary, exceptionally well: unbutton pesky buttons, tuck children in for the night, tidy the nursery. And if you ask her about the things she does that seem magical, she'll shoo away your curiosity with an admonishment about manners.

Much like the novel's main character, *Mary Poppins* balances itself between the real world and the imaginary; it's a balancing that many of us likely remember from our own childhoods. One moment the Banks children are strolling through London, and the next they are speaking with polar bears on the North Pole. One moment they're putting on their hats and gloves for a day out, and the next they're shopping with a star to buy gifts for the sister stars in her constellation. As readers, we predominantly experience these adventures through the eyes of Jane and Michael, who wonder at the magic with a mix of joy and disbelief. "Jane and Michael gazed at each other. Was it a dream from which they would wake?" Was it real? What is real? Does it even matter?

Julie Andrews as Mary Poppins flying over London in the 1964 movie adaptation.

Alongside the undeniably magical characters peppered throughout, are the types of everyday people who seem magical to children: the woman feeding pigeons on the church steps, for example. Magic, the book reminds us, can be found everywhere as long as we're willing to look. Indeed, all of us, the ordinary and the extraordinary, are cut from the same celestial cloth. A king cobra says at one point:

> We are all made of the same stuff, remember, we of the Jungle, you of the City. The same substance composes us—the tree overhead, the stone beneath us, the bird, the beast, the star—we are all one, all moving to the same end.

While we may be composed of the same substance, the book purports that there is a magical ability humans are born with that we lose over time. That ability enables us to speak with animals and elements; to view the world with magic. But people lose that quality as they grow; all people, that is, except for Mary Poppins. The babies Barbara and John

New Horizons 95

may not be understood by their parents, but for much of the book they speak a language that birds and wind and stars understand and, of course, their magical nanny. "There never was a human being that remembered after the age of one—at the very latest—except, of course, Her," a starling tells Barbara and John. Mary Poppins, it seems, is the only human to keep that magic.

Through all the fantasy of the book, there is a very real anxiety that plays on the dependence children have about the grown-ups who take care of them. At one point Michael cries out to Mary Poppins, "you'll never leave us, will you?" It really is the question that every child has when their grown-ups tuck them in at night, or leave for work in the morning—you'll come back and take care of me, won't you? "I'll stay till the wind changes," Mary Poppins replies. And so she does.

Through its popularity the mythology of Mary Poppins has focused on the abilities of a magical nanny; but the book really does strive for its readers to re-focus on the magic of the whole wide world.

Mary Poppins sighed with pleasure, however, when she saw three of herself, each wearing a blue coat with silver buttons and a blue hat to match. She thought it was such a lovely sight that she wished there had been a dozen of her or even thirty. The more Mary Poppins the better.

NOEL STREATFEILD

Ballet Shoes (1936)

An innovative and empowering tale of three girls training for the stage in 1930s London.

Ballet Shoes was a phenomenon from the minute it arrived in British bookstores in 1936. For the first edition, at least one London bookstore had to ration customers to a single copy each. It was immediately reprinted and has never since been out of print. Given that the title seems to be directed at a very specific market segment—ballet-crazy girls—the book's immediate international success is surprising. The author herself was astonished; at the time, Noel Streatfeild had recently retired as a moderately successful actor in a touring Shakespeare company, an experience on which she drew substantially for *Ballet Shoes*.

She was starting to have some success as a novelist when asked by J. M. Dent's children's editor to write a book about the theater for children. She rapidly recycled material from her first novel, *The Whicharts* (1931), which follows the lives of three illegitimate daughters of a brigadier who are raised by one of his mistresses and find careers on the stage. *Ballet Shoes* has essentially the same plot, but omits the mistresses, bad language, and illegitimate children.

The story introduces sixteen-year-old Sylvia, who had been adopted by her paleontologist great uncle Matthew (Gum) as a small child. In different incidents, Gum rescues three more baby girls, who later call themselves the Fossils in honor of Gum's profession. Gum then embarks on a long expedition. Sylvia and her old nurse, Nana, are left with three infants and just enough funds to last for five years. With the money running out and no sign of Gum, Sylvia decides to take in boarders. One of these, a dancing teacher, suggests the girls could be trained to earn their living on the stage. And here the story really begins. They enter Madame Fidolia's Children's Academy of Dancing and Stage Training; Pauline, the oldest, becomes a successful actor, Posy, the youngest, is set to become a *prima ballerina*, and Petrova, the middle girl, learns to fly airplanes.

Ballet Shoes was the right book at the right time. In the 1930s, tours by celebrity dancers such as Anna Pavlova and Sergei Diaghilev's *Ballet Russes* created a ballet-fever in the United Kingdom and the United States. Girls

Noel Streatfeild (1895–1986) worked as an actor, a novelist, and a committed distributor of aid to bombed areas of London during World War II.

The book is credited with introducing the "career" story to the United Kingdom. It has encouraged generations of readers to recognize children as competent and capable of dedication to a chosen career.

Ballet Shoes was adapted into a film starring Emma Watson in 2007 and a stage production at Britain's National Theatre in 2024.

New Horizons

Illustration by Ruth Gervis, the author's sister, for the first edition of the book.

flocked to ballet classes and in 1931 the company that became the Royal Ballet was established. Dent splashed out on a publicity campaign: a silver cover, a window display featuring the ballet shoes of a famous ballerina, and photographs of young dancers. The child posing as Posy Fossil in the photos was Moira Shearer, star of Powell and Pressburger's *The Red Shoes* (1948).

While a book very much of its time, *Ballet Shoes* remains relevant today. It is an innovative and empowering children's story about female creativity and ambition; an original take on the school story, and a highly unusual (since only Sylvia and Gum are related by blood) family story. Much of its power comes from the way *Ballet Shoes* draws on Streatfeild's own experience of growing up as a creative and unconventional girl in a wealthy and conservative vicar's household along with her bohemian life among actors when she left home.

Streatfeild's portrayal of competent children working alongside adults to solve problems and keep their family afloat in the lean 1930s gives it layers beyond what subsequently became an entire subgenre of the "ballet book."

J. R. R. TOLKIEN

THE HOBBIT (1937)

The unheroic hero who became the standard-bearer for British fantasy writing and introduced Tolkien's Middle Earth to the reading public.

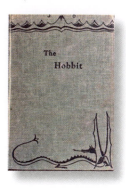

One summer's day in 1930, John Ronald Reuel Tolkien, Professor of Philology at the University of Oxford, was at home, grading exam papers in his study when he came across a blank page. Taking a break from his work, he idly wrote in it: "In a hole in the ground there lived a hobbit."

Tolkien could not have known it, but he had just produced one of the most famous opening lines in English literature. *The Hobbit* is now a recognized classic of children's literature. The story's setting is a fantasy world inhabited by creatures familiar to us from legend and fairy tale, but also by some of Tolkien's own invention. Bilbo Baggins, the book's reluctant hero, is a hobbit, a creature half the size of a human, with hairy feet and leathery soles that render shoes unnecessary. Like most of his kind, Bilbo is an intensely domestic being whose life centers on his hobbit hole and the dependable routines and comforts it offers. He is thus deeply discomfited by the arrival at his home of the wizard Gandalf, and later the dwarf Thorin Oakenshield and a dozen of his companions, who are intent on recruiting Bilbo for their forthcoming adventure, involving a journey through the goblin-infested Misty Mountains and the treacherous forest of Mirkwood to the Lonely Mountain, where the dragon Smaug guards the treasure that Thorin claims as his own.

Though appalled by the prospect of danger, Bilbo is able to draw on an unsuspected talent for adventure, and surprises everyone (including himself) with his quick thinking and level-headedness, proving to be a vital member of the party. His encounters with trolls, goblins, giant spiders, elves, and humans make for an unforgettable story, in which fantastic and sometimes terrifying events are set against Bilbo's unheroic desire to return to the comfort of his hobbit hole. Among the characters he encounters are the "skin-changer" Beorn, at times a fierce bear and at others an equally intimidating bear of a man; the warrior, Bard, who appears to have stepped out of the pages of Beowulf; the suave and corrupt dragon Smaug himself; and the subterranean, cave-dwelling creature known as Gollum, with whom Bilbo trades riddles in an attempt save his own life, and from whom he obtains a ring of invisibility. The world of *The Hobbit* was influenced by Tolkien's immersion in the Old

J. R. R. Tolkien (1892–1973) was an Oxford professor of philology who brought his deep knowledge of language and literature to bear on his writing.

The Hobbit is a classic example of a story that takes its hero (and its readers) out of their domestic, everyday life, puts them through innumerable dangers and excitements, and finally returns them to the place they started

The landscapes of *The Hobbit* are invented, but in many places, the world we know bleeds through to the surface of the story.

The Road goes ever on and on, down from the door where it began.
Now far ahead the Road has gone, and I must follow, if I can.

Norse and Old and Middle English literatures that were his stock in trade as a scholar, as well as his childhood love of nineteenth-century writers such as George MacDonald and William Morris. However, a more immediate context for the story was Tolkien's own unpublished writings. *The Hobbit* was his first published novel, but the world it was set in was created much earlier. Tolkien had begun developing Middle-earth (as it was later called) more than twenty years before Bilbo's story was published. Starting in 1914, with the poem, "The Voyage of Éarendel, the Evening Star," he had built a large corpus of unpublished stories and poems centered on Middle-earth's early history, delineating an extensive fantasy world with its own mythology, chronology, geography, languages (which Tolkien, as a philologist, described in detail), races, and cultures. Much of this material, referred to by Tolkien scholars as the legendarium, would not see publication until after Tolkien's death, but it provides the context and setting for both *The Hobbit* and his later novel, *The Lord of the Rings* (1954–55). Indeed, Middle-earth might reasonably be called Tolkien's real life's work, at least as much as the stories he set there.

As one might expect of a project pursued over a lifetime, Middle-earth changed as Tolkien developed and refined it. While Middle-earth has at times been regarded as the very model of a self-contained fantasy world, Tolkien sometimes suggested a connection between its geography and that of Europe, even hinting that Middle-earth is Europe, during an imaginary prehistory. The Shire, heartland of the Hobbits, is set at about the latitude of southern England, and Bilbo's habits and worldview are very redolent of the English bourgeoisie; indeed, the book's humor partly derives from the contrast between Bilbo's outlook and the landscape of monsters and heroes in which he finds himself, while his possession of such modern items as an umbrella and a mantel clock set him apart from the dwarves, elves, and wizards.

This mismatch is not accidental. Although Middle-earth had existed long before Tolkien wrote *The Hobbit*, hobbits themselves were a new creation, and to some extent Tolkien had to retrofit them. He made various adjustments in terms of language and style. This is seen most clearly by contrasting *The Hobbit* with *The Lord of the Rings*. In *The Hobbit*, orcs are goblins, the dark lord Sauron is named (albeit in passing) only as the Necromancer, and the settlement of *Esgaroth* (an Elvish word), where Bard's people reside, is generally referred to simply as "Lake-town."

The writing of *The Lord of the Rings* necessitated yet another kind of retrofitting, with certain features of *The Hobbit* being altered in later editions to fit Tolkien's plan for the later, larger work. Bilbo's riddle contest with Gollum is the most important example. In the first edition of *The Hobbit* the

"The Lonely Mountain," illustrated by J. R. R. Tolkien himself.

prize is Gollum's ring, and when Gollum loses he is willing to give it to Bilbo. By the 1951 edition, Tolkien had reconceived the ring, not just as a means of conferring invisibility but as the One Ring, the source of Sauron's power, which casts its baleful influence over all who possess it. For the Gollum of *The Lord of the Rings* to have willingly parted with his "precious" would have been inconceivable. So, Tolkien changed the text of *The Hobbit* to make clear that Gollum had no such intention. The 1937 version remains only as a lie told by Bilbo to his companions to account for his possession of the ring.

The Hobbit stands as a milestone in children's literature. Its initial popularity was boosted by atlases, encyclopedias, and handbooks, as well as inspiring novelists, musicians, game designers, and others to imitate or pay homage to Tolkien's achievement. In the early 2000s, a new generation was enthralled by Peter Jackson's film adaptations of the three volumes of *The Lord of the Rings*, and later of *The Hobbit* itself.

It is a long way from that fateful meeting in the study in Oxford, between a blank sheet of exam paper and the mind of J. R. R. Tolkien—as far, perhaps, as the Lonely Mountain was from Bilbo's hobbit hole.

T. H. WHITE

THE SWORD IN THE STONE
(1938)

A joyous muddle of time, space, and imagination, come together to reveal the story of King Arthur's childhood in Britain.

T. H. White (1906–1964) was naturally reclusive, isolating himself for long periods of time in the English countryside hunting, fishing, and engaging in falconry.

White had written his thesis on Malory's *Le Morte d'Arthur* while at the University of Cambridge. He revisited Malory's work in 1937 and it inspired him to write this "preface."

Revised in 1958 to better fit the overall context of *The Once and Future King*, later extending Arthur's story into four novels.

Raised by Sir Uther in a remote castle outside the great Forest Sauvage, Arthur—or "Wart"—is a child of uncertain origins and an inauspicious future. Despite playing second fiddle to Uther's son, Kay, Wart's childhood is nothing less than bucolic. His friendship with the brash, but sensitive, Kay, a small village full of quirky retainers, and the pure joy of living in such close proximity to nature all sustain and delight Wart. His world is small, but perfectly formed. It is full from day to night, stuffed with activities and work and play. It is the ultimate summer kingdom: unchanging and delightful. The passage of time is marked by quirky annual rituals, the outside world is far, far away, and the walls of the castle will always stand indomitable.

With the coming of Merlyn, Wart's understanding of his world begins to deepen. Merlyn is born out of time and has lived his life backward. His goal, known to the reader, if not to Wart, is to prepare the boy for rule. Constructed as a "preface to Malory" and *Le Morte d'Arthur*, the result is a magical, whimsical story of Arthur's coming of age—quietly underpinned by the bittersweet tragedy of his ultimate fate.

Merlyn doesn't try to expand Wart's horizons as much as stretch them, showing him the hidden worlds that lie adjacent or beneath his own—sometimes literally. Over the course of *The Sword and the Stone*, Wart is transformed into a series of animals— a fish, an owl, and a badger. Merlyn's lessons are sneaky but effective, and Wart learns about power, honor, legacy, and (ironically) humanity. All vital for his eventual role as an absolute monarch, as he "learn[s] why the world wags and what wags it."

Wart is also repeatedly sent off into the forest itself. The Forest Sauvage acts as a barrier between Uther's rural realm and the rest of Britain. It is simultaneously full of horrors—giants, dragons, witches, cannibals—and heroes—even the legendary Robin Hood (referred to as Robin Wood in the novel). It is a cauldron that is constantly producing adventures, a land of possibility that is just dangerous enough to serve as part of Wart's challenging curriculum.

Merlin Presenting the Future King Arthur, painted by Emil Johann Lauffer (1837–1909).

White neatly elides the nasty, brutish, and short reality of the Dark Ages in favor of a deliberately rose-tinted, ahistoric view. There are asides about the happiness of the peasantry, the cleanliness of the air, and the tastiness of the food. Every summer was luxurious, and in every winter ("confined by statute to two months") the snow "lay evenly, three feet thick, but never turned to slush." In Arthurian Britain, even the weather "behave[s] itself." White's depiction or view of the past, such as it is, is further obfuscated by deliberate anachronism. Merlyn is, for all practical purposes, a time traveler, and his odd remarks about the future can be forgiven. But all the characters are prone to ahistorical allusion and unreasonable references. Sir Grummore's obsession with Bolsheviks is particularly amusing.

White's vision of the Arthurian world goes beyond nostalgia and becomes the stuff of myth itself. It is a compression of all of British history, cherry-picking the best of all times, and of none. It is village life, it is the Blitz spirit, it is the glory days of a yore that wasn't. It is a vision of a British history that never was, but is simultaneously deeply engrained in the land's collective subconscious. King Arthur is the closest Britain has to a national myth: not only an origin story for a united Britain, but also an aspiration for what Britain could be (in this case: pastoral, feudal, bumblingly chivalric, and an understated force for good). White's imaginary world is the only fitting setting for a King that, rather than being once and future, never was and never will be. A figure, and a land, that is both impossible and inspirational.

HERGÉ

The Adventures of Tintin: The Secret of the Unicorn
(Le Secret de la Licorne) (1942)

A classic adventure following Tintin and his friend Captain Haddock on a quest to discover the Unicorn, a shipwreck filled with pirate treasure…

Translated by Leslie Lonsdale-Cooper & Michael Turner (1959).

The Tintin stories were the creation of Belgian artist-writer George Remi, who took Hergé as his pen-name—made up of his initials reversed: R-G.

Since their first publication, Hergé's *The Adventures of Tintin* have been translated into more than seventy languages and have sold more than 200 million copies worldwide.

Tintin stories have been adapted for the big and small screens, including a Spielberg movie substantially based on this specific volume; and there is a very healthy merchandise industry in Tintin's native Belgium and beyond.

Though Tintin's stories first appeared serialized in the children's supplement to a newspaper, it was *Tintin in the Land of the Soviets* that gave the Francophone world its comic-book-form introduction to the intrepid young reporter, in 1930. The hero of this volume would go on to accompany us over many decades, through two dozen volumes of adventures set all over the world (and a couple of times on the Moon), always with his trusty white fox terrier Snowy (Milou) at his side. The series would establish itself as one of the landmarks in the Franco-Belgian *bande-dessinée* —graphic novel— tradition, and one of the few that eventually managed to break successfully into the sphere of Anglophone readers.

The popularity of the volumes endures, despite some discomfort about the politics and, especially, about the sometimes stereotyped and patronizing depictions of non-white characters, which has complicated our attitudes as readers today. The most problematic of the stories, *Tintin in the Congo*, has long faced accusations of racism, and it is now discreetly missing from many series lists.

The Secret of the Unicorn, the eleventh in the Tintin series, was published as a volume in 1943 (having likewise first been serialized), though— typically—it took another sixteen years to make it into English.

Having mentioned that Tintin is notionally a reporter, it's worth pointing out that in this book—indeed in many of those to come—there is no reporting work to be seen. He is most often found dashing off on one of his adventures, perhaps trying to solve a mystery, and *The Secret of the Unicorn* is one of the prime examples. "I've a hunch that we're off on one of our adventures again," remarks Snowy—who is occasionally able to speak—and he's right.

And this one is a particularly well-told story: expertly paced, narratively sophisticated, including a lot of action and some very cleverly integrated flashbacks. It begins with a mysterious old model warship, the *Unicorn*, which Tintin buys in a Brussels flea market, and then goes mysteriously missing (Great snakes!), and ends with our hero setting off on a hunt for sunken pirate treasure. Along the way, there is intrigue, there is plenty of peril

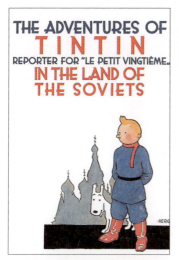
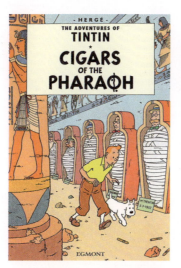
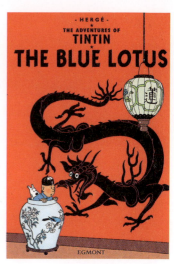
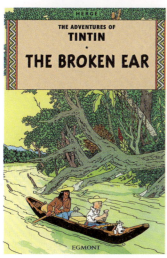
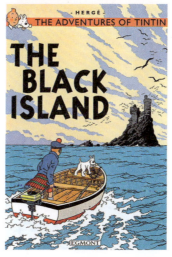

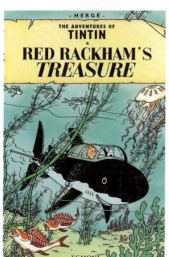
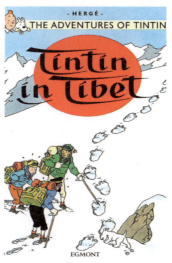
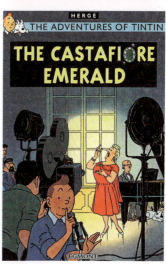

Tintin (voiced by Jamie Bell) and Captain Haddock (Andy Serkis) in the 2011 animated movie *The Adventures of Tintin*, directed by Steven Spielberg.

Previous page: Covers from Hergé's The Adventures of Tintin series beginning with Tintin in the Land of the Soviets published in black and white in 1929-30. All subsequent Adventures were drawn in color or reprinted in a second colorized version from 1942 onwards.

(Tintin himself always survives, but people do actually get shot dead in this one, and there are various other high-stakes moments), there are chases and a code to crack. (Also in this book: a kleptomaniac, a pair of evil antique-dealer brothers, a big dog, and a butler called Nestor.)

The main supporting player in this story—and in all the stories from *The Crab with the Golden Claws* (vol.9) until the end of the series—is Tintin's friend Captain Haddock, a retired sea captain who likes a drink (many drinks) and is characterized in part by his enthusiastic loyalty to his friend, and in part by his temper and the high-voltage language with which he expresses it. Get on the wrong side of him, you will undoubtedly hear an explosive "Billions of bilious blue blistering barnacles!" and you might well find yourself called a *bashi-bazouk*, or worse.

Tintin himself is permanently young; he is straight-forwardly daring, untemperamental, and unlike his friends, not very funny. But there is further support, and comedy, from a pair of bowler-hatted detectives who are almost identical but not quite, and who are, surprisingly, not related. One of them is called Thompson ("yes, with a P, as in Philadelphia"), the other Thomson ("no, without a P, as in Venezuela"). They are not hugely clever, and spend a lot of time arresting the wrong person or trying to extract themselves from their bowlers, which seem to have gotten jammed on their heads when something heavy fell on them.

The globe-trotting series takes Tintin and co. to all sorts of exciting locations—introducing young readers to countless places, real (the Amazon,

> Avast you dogs! Sea-gherkins! Baboons!
>
> Bucaneers! Filibusters! Bagpipers! Gallows-fodder!
>
> We've won! That's got them on the run!
>
> Yo-ho-ho and a bottle of rum!

the Sahara, the Himalayas, the Moon . . .) and invented; on their adventures, our friends are exposed to all sorts of dangers, ranging from bombs and guns to political coups and kidnappings.

The Secret of the Unicorn is notable, among other reasons, for being the volume where we pay our first visit to Marlinspike Hall (*le château de Moulinsart* in the original), which is originally home to the book's villains, but that will turn out to be Captain Haddock's ancestral estate and that will play a major role in subsequent adventures; as the story continues, *Red Rackham's Treasure* introduces us to Professor Cuthbert Calculus—a brilliant inventor, and comically hard of hearing (to Captain Haddock's infinite cursing frustration)—who will become a part of the core cast from here on.

Over his career, Hergé he would develop the distinctive *ligne claire* style that would come to characterize his work—clear lines, the pictures usually unhatched, with strong flat color; even where the backgrounds are detailed, the characterization is usually relatively simple; even Tintin himself hardly changes: a round face, dot eyes and a quiff, and that's all you need to recognize him. Hergé's *ligne claire* became so widely copied that it's easy to look at the books today and miss the originality of his style, groundbreaking in its day.

ENID BLYTON

THE MAGIC FARAWAY TREE
(1943)

From the liberating Land of Do-As-You-Please to the terrifying Land of Tempers, the Faraway Tree was inspired by Norse mythology and filled with British delicacies like jelly and boiled sweets.

Enid Blyton, Britain's most prolific children's writer, never did anything better than this story, a particular and enduring favorite with younger readers. The idea of a tree reaching up to other magical lands, also familiar in folklore, gave her the chance to write her own version perfectly tailored to children's favorite fantasies. Brother and sisters Jo, Bessie, and Fanny already lead a charmed life in a cottage deep in the countryside, with their mother providing generous lunches before allowing her children to play outside for the rest of the day unsupervised. Their father is almost invisible. Joined by cousin Dick, what follows is a series of hectic, fun-filled adventures in the nearby Enchanted Wood. This magical place, with its friendly talking birds and animals, is dominated by the Faraway Tree. Inhabited by "all sorts of queer folk" living on different levels, it also provides access to a succession of magical lands coming and going at the very top.

And what lands! One offers unlimited treats, which would have meant so much to first readers in 1943 at a time when such goodies were strictly rationed. Another provides a choice of as many presents as you liked and a third allows unlimited fairground rides, either free or else paid for by Moon-face, an obliging middle-aged tree inhabitant and new friend to the children. Other residents include the Saucepan Man and Silky, a fairy. But Blyton knew that descriptions of endless pleasure eventually gets boring, so she also builds in regular mini-dangers that briefly threaten. Is the slippery-slip on which the children slide down from the tree on cushions at the end of each perfect day now blocked? Will Dick, who is the only mildly naughty child, get into another scrape, such as accidentally growing into a giant and then almost disappearing when he goes into reverse? Will Jo, suddenly up-ended in Topsy–Turvy land, ever be able to stand up straight again?

Many other writers have re-created small children's most satisfying daydreams in their stories, but none on the same scale as Blyton. Short, snappy chapters written in easy English race from one imaginative excess to another with never a dull moment. Six ice-creams for one greedy child

---

Enid Blyton(1897–1968) had a long career and published more than 700 books for children including the Famous Five and Secret Seven series.

The first book in the Faraway Tree series, *The Enchanted Wood*, was published by Newes in 1939, followed in 1943 by *The Magic Faraway Tree* and *The Folk of the Faraway Tree* in 1946

Hugely popular around the world, Blyton's works have sold more than 500 million copies and have been translated into more than 40 languages.

It was so lovely when a really nice Land was at the top of the Faraway Tree. They had been to the Land of Birthdays before, and the Land of Take-What-You-Want. The Land of Goodies had been nice, and the Land of Do-As-You-Please. The Land of Presents sounded just as exciting!

are followed by treacle tarts, chocolate blancmange, and finally a store made out of marzipan and gingerbread. This building is surrounded by trees that grow British delicacies: current buns, biscuits, jelly, and magical boiled sweets. Instant danger is quickly avoided with the help of flying beds and tables or steam trains the children have no problem driving. Spells conveniently at hand allow for elephant rides or trips to the warm sea. Action is incessant; the only equivalents would be those imaginary games children make up for themselves, whether playing with others or else on their own.

And there is also regular input from the author herself, encouraging young readers to continue to believe at least for the moment that all this is actually happening. "And there they were," she concludes one chapter, "in a new and strange land again, out of breath and most astonished. How they stared around in surprise!" Another time she writes "What exciting times they do have, to be sure!"

Contemporary editions of this story have made a few alterations in tune with changing modern susceptibilities, but Blyton's fertile imagination, always more appreciated by children than by their parents and teachers, still comes over as strong as ever. Some adults have claimed that this was the book that first turned them into readers. It is not hard to see why.

As a child, Enid Blyton was fascinated with Norse mythology, and the Magic Faraway Tree itself was inspired by Yggdrasil, an enormous ash tree that connects the nine worlds in the Norse mythological tradition.

ANTOINE DE SAINT-EXUPÉRY

The Little Prince
(Le Petit Prince) (1943)

The Little Prince from a faraway asteroid brings moral magic and religious insights.

Translated by Katherine Woods (1943).

Antoine de Saint-Exupéry (1900–1944) led a life as diverse as his writing: failing his exams for the French naval academy, training as an architect and aviator, circling his plane in the skies of Algiers while finishing a novel.

Le Petit Prince is the second most widely translated book (after *Pinocchio*, 1883).

The B612 Foundation, an NGO conducting research to defend Earth against asteroid collision, is named after the tiny home "planet" of Saint-Exupéry's Little Prince. A real asteroid has been named B612 to honor *The Little Prince*.

The Little Prince—published first in French as *Le Petit Prince*—is a bittersweet palimpsest that has entranced generations, deploying multiple layers of meaning to acknowledge gently the hard truths of life, leaving adults sad but hopeful, yearning for the child from the stars and his laughter. It is the best-known work of the French writer, poet, and aviator Antoine de Saint-Exupéry and remains one of the most-translated books ever, a modern classic suggesting that the simplest things in life are the most important.

In writing *The Little Prince*, Saint-Exupéry drew on his own experiences as a pilot, he had qualified as one in 1922, including a period serving in North Africa. In 1944 during World War II he attempted a reconnaissance mission over France and never returned. In 2004 the wreckage of his plane was recovered, although the exact cause of the crash remains unknown.

The story begins with one of Saint-Exupéry's watercolors, an image copied from a "true" jungle book the narrator read at age six. A boa constrictor coils around a "wild beast" whose eyes bulge as the snake's mouth gapes to consume him (opposite). As a child, the narrator explains, he attempted to recreate the image; resulting in something "grown-ups" took for a hat, but which the six-year-old clearly saw as a snake digesting an elephant. In this simple depiction of mortality Saint-Exupéry demonstrates the clash of potential meaning—which children see directly—and mundane interpretation, which blinds adults to seeing the potential. Within the narrative, however, this clash is productive: *The Little Prince* chides grown-ups, but enriches them, too.

The narrator, now an adult, has grown up to become a pilot who has crashed in a barren desert with no signs of civilization. While he struggles to fix his plane, a young boy with golden hair and a scarf appears as if from nowhere. Over the next eight days the Little Prince tells the narrator vivid tales of his home on a faraway asteroid, his adventures on other planets and how he fell to Earth. These tales are parabolic and present culturally symbolic themes. The Little Prince tells the narrator, for example, of a man on a tiny planet who forgot to tend to his bushes. Three of the seeds should have been

—Tu es une drôle de bête, lui dit-il enfin, mince comme un doigt...

An illustration by Antoine de Saint-Exupéry of the Little Prince standing on Asteroid B-612.

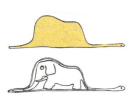

The "grown-ups" mistook the first drawing for a hat, whereas a six-year-old clearly understands it is a snake digesting an elephant.

Previous page: An illustration by Antoine de Saint-Exupéry that appeared in *The Little Prince*'s first edition (1943).

plucked when they began to sprout, because they were "bad." Instead, they grew to be powerful baobabs that he could not cut down, trees that sucked the life out of his planet and shattered it. "Children," the narrator writes, recounting this story, "Watch out for baobabs!" (We must learn for ourselves, of course, what are the baobabs in our own lives.)

This boy who fell to Earth is not an avatar of Jesus. His views, story, and effect are, however, consonant with the Christian thread in Western culture: "Unless you change and become like little children, you will never enter the kingdom of heaven" (Matthew 18:3). Furthermore, as Jesus told his doubting disciple Thomas, "Because you have seen me, you have believed; blessed are those who have not seen and yet have believed" (John 20:29), the Little Prince tells the pilot: "The important thing is what can't be seen." The Little Prince does not die for his friend, however. He dies to get back to his rose, which he loves because he has tended her. Still, his home asteroid, B-612, bears the number 4 (symbolic in the Bible of Earthly completeness) multiplied by 153 (the number of miraculous fish—or souls—that Peter nets in obeying the risen Jesus [John 21:11]).

The last image of the book shows a desert landscape with only a star. The narrator asks us to let him know if we ever see this landscape, and under that star, a child. "Don't let me go on being so sad: Send word immediately that he's come back."

ASTRID LINDGREN

Pippi Longstocking
(Pippi Långstrump) (1945)

The outragious Pippilotta Delicatessa Windowshade Mackrelmint Efraimsdaughter Longstocking brings laughter into a dark world.

In 1941, Astrid Lindgren's daughter Karin suffered from pneumonia and asked her mother to tell her a story, and Lindgren invented the character of Pippi Longstocking to entertain her sick child. Pippi took shape over the next four years, in stories orally related to Karin and her cousins, who could not get enough of this wild and wonderful girl. Only in April 1944, when Astrid Lindgren was bedridden herself after she sprained her ankle, did she write down the stories and send them to a publisher, Bonniers, who promptly refused to publish the manuscript because Pippi was just too unruly. Lindgren entered the manuscript into a children's book competition with Rabén and Sjögren and won, which eventually led to the stories being published in 1945. However, Lindgren had to alter and tame the original manuscript ever so slightly because her editor, Elsa Olenius, deemed it somewhat inappropriate and uncouth that there would be horse dung in the circus, or that the contents of a chamber pot would be used to put out a fire.

Pippi's adventures became an instant success, and before the end of the 1940s, the book had sold more than 300,000 copies in Sweden alone. What is it, though, that makes Pippi so successful?

Imagine a small town in Sweden where everything runs its proper course, where people are polite to each other, where children are well-behaved and play nicely within the confines of their yards. Then, one day, a nine-year-old girl moves into the house at the end of town, with her monkey, Mr. Nelson, and her horse, but otherwise all alone. She is red-haired and freckled, with stiff pigtails standing up from her head, wearing one long brown stocking, the other one black, and with shoes twice the size of her feet. Pippi is rich, owning a suitcase full of gold coins, and so strong that she can lift her horse single-handedly. Most outrageously, though, Pippi does whatever she wants because "there was no one to tell her to go to bed just when she was having the most fun."

Pippi befriends the children next door, Tommy and Annika, and together they experience many hilarious adventures made so by their situational comedy. With her clownish appearance and unconventional behavior,

Translated by Florence Lamborn (1950); Edna Hurup (1954).

Pippi Longstocking was a quick success, selling 300,000 copies by the end of the 1940s. The series has been translated into 76 languages.

After Astrid Lindgren's death in 2002, the Swedish government created the Astrid Lindgren Memorial Award in her memory. It is the world's largest monetary prize for children's literature.

As well as writing, Lindgren was a committed humanist who fought for equality, ecology, the rights of children, and animal welfare.

Tommy (Pär Sundberg), Pippi (Inger Nilsson), and Annika (Maria Persson) in the 1969 TV adaptation. The series covers the original *Pippi Longstocking* book as well as the sequels *Pippi Longstocking Goes on Board* (1946), and *Pippi in the South Seas* (1948).

Pippi mocks the narrow-minded norms of bourgeois society and refuses to be reined in by the authorities. However, Pippi is not just a fibs-telling brat. She is a warm, generous, kind-hearted friend with a strong sense of justice, always on the side of the weak.

When, for example, the children come upon a group of bullies who attack one boy much younger than them, Pippi uses her superpowers to simply lift up the older boys into a tree: "You are cowards! Five of you go after one boy. That's cowardly. And then you begin to push a little defenseless girl around. Oh, how disgraceful! Nasty!" Here, Pippi is not just superior because of her strength, but also because of her innate sense of fairness.

Conceived during one of the darkest times in Europe—World War II—Pippi resembles an antidote to violence, cruelty, and the corrupting effects of power. It would be fair to assume that Astrid Lindgren created Pippi out of her wish to escape the anguish of the war years, and to create a character who could inspire both hope and happiness. It certainly contributed to Pippi's success that, when the first volume was published in 1945, Swedish families wanted to forget about the war, and laughter was one way of doing so. However, Pippi's power is more universal than that. As an independent, emancipated girl who is fiercely antiauthoritarian, she is the perfect outlet for the compensatory fantasies of her young readers: in a similar way in which Tommy and Annika are empowered by Pippi, so are the children reading about her.

TOVE JANSSON

The Moomins and the Great Flood (SMÅTROLLEN OCH DEN STORA ÖVERSVÄMNINGEN) (1945)

Fantastic, familiar, frightening, Jansson's much-loved tales of Moomin trolls taught generations of children kindness and good manners.

Tove Jansson is a Scandinavian institution, and her strange, gentle, unfailingly polite little creatures have delighted millions around the world. Jansson originally came up with the Moomins, or something very like them, in her childhood, and continued developing them when she became a professional artist and illustrator. They first appear in her adult work in political cartoons she drew for the satirical magazine *Garm*.

The first of the Moomin books published, *The Moomins and the Great Flood* (really a short story of about sixty pages), is not "officially" part of the Moomin series. It can, however, be seen as proof of concept for the ensuing series (and the enormous franchise that they later became). The world described in the book is one in flux. The Moomins travel from forest to swamp to cliffside cave to beach, before finally being swept away by the titular flood. (They even spend the night in a candy meadow with rivers of chocolate and jam, perhaps inspiring Roald Dahl's *Charlie and the Chocolate Factory*). The book ends with the family reuniting, and with Moominpapa announcing he has found the perfect valley for them to build a house to live in, which serves as the setting for all future Moomin books.

And yet the world of this book is much more civilized than we might expect. When the Moomins part from friends, Moominmama promises: "We'll send you both a letter and tell you what happened." Even in the midst of this wilderness, it seems, one can still rely on the mail. And after the flood, the various displaced creatures sit together around campfires, sharing their surviving utensils and making each other warm drinks, as good neighbors should. Manners, and neighborly behavior, are central to these books and their world, which for all its fantastic qualities, is rooted in the Finnish landscape and Swedish culture in which Tove Jansson grew up. The Moomins are earthy, eager for both diversion and comfort, and keen to have everything in its right place. The world they construct for themselves reflects these preoccupations: The Moomins' house is cozy and full of all the odds and ends that one needs to feel fully at ease. Moominmama, meanwhile, never sets out on an excursion without a full meal, complete with cutlery and a butter dish, and a purse full of whatever she and her children might need to be well and happy.

Translated by David McDuff (2005).

Though *The Moomins and the Great Flood* was the first book starring the Moomins, it was the last to be translated into English, having to wait a full 60 years after its initial publication.

In addition to the Moomin novels, Jansson (1914–2001) wrote a regular comic strip featuring the Moomins. The strip was eventually taken over by her brother, Lars.

Jansson also wrote novels and short stories for adults. Several of these include characters who write children's books or cartoons.

At last they came to a small valley, that was more beautiful than any they had seen that day. And there, in the midst of the meadow, stood a house that almost looked like a tall stove, very elegant and painted blue.

Moomintroll and Snorkmaiden, illustrated by Tove Jansson.

Opposite: Original illustration by Tove Jansson for *The Moomins and the Great Flood*.

The change of the seasons determines the shape and nature of the Moomin world. A later novel, *Finn Family Moomintroll* (1948, English translation 1950) takes place over a long summer, and features such quintessentially Scandinavian summer excursions as a boat trip to the islands and a night under the stars. In *Moominland Midwinter* (1957), Moomintroll wakes up unexpectedly during his hibernation, and finds the world altered and frighteningly foreign. Too-Ticky, whom he finds living in the family's beach house (thus transforming it, too, into something unfamiliar), explains:

> There are such a lot of things that have no place in summer and autumn and spring. Everything that's a little shy and a little odd. Some kinds of night animals and people that don't fit in with others and that nobody really believes in. They keep out of the way all the year. And then when everything's quiet and white and the nights are long and most people are asleep—then they appear.

The world of the Moomins is simultaneously fantastic and familiar, cozy and frightening, eternal and ever-changing—a tension that explains why this series of books has resonated so powerfully with generations of children who are just starting to discover their own world.

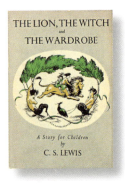

C. S. LEWIS

THE LION, THE WITCH, AND THE WARDROBE
(1950)

"Always winter and never Christmas; think of that!" C. S. Lewis's enchanted realm beyond the wardrobe.

C.S Lewis (1898–1963) wrote The Chronicles of Narnia over two years while nursing a dying (and querulous) old woman, coped with a binge-drinking brother, and continued his work as an Oxford University lecturer specializing in medieval and Renaissance literature.

The books were originally published by Geoffrey Bles and The Bodley Head, the latter publishing the final two books of the series.

The Lion, The Witch, and The Wardrobe has reached both the big and small screens since its publication, including three separate television series and a blockbuster Disney film adaptation in 2005, which grossed $745 million at the box office.

Born to a middle-class, Anglo-Irish family in Belfast, Clive Staples Lewis (known to his friends and family as Jack), described himself as "a product of long corridors, empty sunlit rooms, upstairs indoor silences, attics explored in solitude, distant noises of gurgling cisterns and pipes, and the noise of wind under the tiles. Also, of endless books." His mother died when he was nine and, although he remained close to his older brother Warren for the rest of his life, his relationship with his father was difficult.

As a youth, Lewis discovered Norse mythology, which impressed him as ineffably severe, melancholy, and beautiful. This infatuation with what he called "Northerness" provided common ground in his early acquaintance with J. R. R. Tolkien as fledgling dons at Oxford in the 1920s.

The medieval literature Lewis loved and that underpinned his own work was essentially a fusion of pagan, folkloric, and Christian elements. It's a deliberately patchwork aesthetic that seeks to collect and harmonize rather than to unify and homogenize, on the principle that all the things of this world testify to the infinitely varied goodness of God. So, likewise, the talking animals, Northern European dwarves, classical fauns, and Arthurian knights of Narnia all happily coexist under the banner of the lion god, Aslan. The underlying thinking is platonic—or, rather, neoplatonic: All these seemingly incompatible elements are not lies that contradict the truth and each other, but rather the many shadows that human beings have invented to conjure the one great reality we can never encounter directly in this life.

The closest model for Narnia is the Faerie Land of Edmund Spenser, the sixteenth-century English poet whose work was Lewis's academic speciality. Like Faerie Land, and the Celtic notion of the underground kingdom of the Tuatha Dé Danann (which Lewis heard about as a boy from his Irish nurse), Narnia is a separate world that nevertheless intersects with our world at certain places and times, permitting the traffic of people between the two. The four Pevensie children enter Narnia through an enchanted wardrobe in *The Lion, the Witch, and the Wardrobe*, to find the land suffering under the tyrannous reign of the White Witch, who has cursed it to be "always winter and never Christmas." The siblings are enlisted by Aslan to defeat the witch, but first the lion god must sacrifice his own life to pay for the treachery of Edmund, then be triumphantly resurrected.

In each of the other six Chronicles (with the exception of *A Horse and His Boy*), children from our world are brought over to save Narnia or Narnians. Yet, notably, surprisingly little of the action takes place in Narnia itself and, when it does, it is a Narnia gone wrong: frozen by the White Witch; its magical nature suppressed by the Telmarines in *Prince Caspian*; or sliding into corruption in the final Chronicle, *The Last Battle*. The quintessential Narnia—best captured in the fireside tales of Mr. Tumnus in *The Lion, the Witch, and the Wardrobe*—is almost always seen from a distance, either in space or time, or else savored in brief snatches before the children are back to this world. This ideal Narnia is a never-ending round of pastoral revelry:

> he told about the midnight dances and how the Nymphs who lived in the wells and the Dryads who lived in the trees came out to dance with the fauns; about long hunting parties after the milk white stag who could give you wishes if you caught him; about feasting and treasure seeking with the wild red Dwarves in deep mines and caverns far beneath the forest floor: and then about summer when the woods were green and old Silenus on his fat donkey would come to visit them, and sometimes Bacchus himself, and then the streams would run with wine instead of water and the whole forest would give itself up to jollification for weeks on end.

So powerful is the Arcadian resonance in these books, that most readers —including the series' most famous illustrator, Pauline Baynes—persist in seeing Narnia as a landscape of rolling hills and meadows with the occasional picturesque stand of trees. Lewis, however, described it as largely forested. Its population consists of talking beasts, larger and visibly more intelligent than ordinary "dumb" beasts and treated by all good Narnians as free, sentient beings. Other Narnians include fauns, satyrs, dwarves (who come in "red" and "black" varieties), dryads and naiads (tree and water spirits), centaurs and assorted mythical creatures, ranging from minotaurs to werewolves. The magical population concurs that while Narnia is "not men's country," it nevertheless ought to be ruled by a small elite of human beings in obedience to a decree made by Aslan at the dawn of the world (*The Magician's Nephew*, 1951).

Narnia is bordered on the west and north by rugged and sparsely inhabited mountains, and its marshy northern borders are occasionally harried by hostile, man-eating giants. To the south lies Archenland,

Above: Mr. Tumnus is the first creature Lucy Pevensie meets in Narnia, when she comes across the faun carrying his umbrella and packages through a snowy wood in an early passage of *The Lion, the Witch and the Wardrobe* (1950).

The four Pevensie children (Susan, Peter, Lucy, and Edmund) discover the snow-covered land of Narnia in the 2005 movie adaptation directed by Andrew Adamson and co-produced by Walden Media and Walt Disney Pictures.

a friendly nation populated by a feudal human society. A harsh desert separates Archenland from the vaguely Turkic empire of Calormen, whose dark-skinned and be-turbaned rulers frequently entertain imperial designs on the "Northern barbarians."

To the east of Narnia lies the Great Eastern Ocean, speckled with the allegorical islands visited in *The Voyage of the Dawn Treader*—the most medieval of the Chronicles and many readers' favorite. Because Narnia's world is flat, the furthest reaches of the Great Eastern Ocean abut on a wall of flowing water, beyond which is Aslan's country, home to the souls of the virtuous dead. Far beneath the surface of Narnia lies the land of Bism, whose gnome inhabitants live happily on the banks of a river of fire and pick diamonds like fruit to squeeze for their juice.

Opposite: A map of Narnia, illustrated by Pauline Baynes for a 1972 Puffin Books poster.

> She did not shut it properly because she knew that it is very silly to shut oneself into a wardrobe, even if it is not a magic one.

The marginal detail work on Narnia is cursory; it's like an old-fashioned movie set, the facades just convincing enough to serve as a setting for the narrative. Even Narnia itself is scantily shaded-in. Narnia has no major cities—just two castles and a briefly mentioned market town, Chippingford. Despite the absence of any industry or agriculture, the inhabitants have somehow obtained such commodities as a sewing machine, orange marmalade, tea, and a seemingly endless supply of sausages and bacon.

Does this incongruity matter? Not to millions of young readers, that's for sure. Children, as a general rule, don't even detect the religious symbolism that many adults find so glaring in the Chronicles. We seldom notice the flaws in the object of our desire, and that is what Narnia is—a shimmering, delicious mirage, just out of reach. Within its elusive borders is collected every wonder that ever delighted Lewis in the thousands of books he read, every adventure he longed for, every brave prince and doughty badger, every enchanted pool and misted mountain, every mermaid and leafy-haired dryad, every spired castle and green hill. It would be a motley collection if it were not unified by the intensity of his desire, which, because it is effectively a child's yearning, mysteriously preserved in the mind of a formidably well-read, middle-aged man, communicates most immediately to child readers.

That doesn't, however, make it merely childish. The desire to bring all of life's joys together in celebration is an impulse that, even those who can't subscribe to Lewis's faith, can nevertheless still understand and share. In the case of Narnia, it isn't the elaboration of the backdrop that casts the spell, that makes the place seem real in spite of its many absurdities, but the inexhaustible delight of the dancers who inhabit it, as well as the man who made it.

E. B. WHITE

CHARLOTTE'S WEB (1952)

A love song to the farm from a virtuoso master of grammar starring a spider and a pig.

After graduating from Cornell University, Elwyn Brooks White (1899–1985) hopped from job to job before beginning to write for *The New Yorker*, where he would make his name as an essayist.

In 1999, *Time* magazine named *Charlotte's Web* the best children's book of the twentieth century. It has been translated into more than twenty-three languages.

Animals were key to White's storytelling: *Charlotte's Web* was in fact his second children's book, written after the success of *Stuart Little* (1945) and its eponymous mouse as hero.

"Where's Papa going with that axe?" is the first sentence of *Charlotte's Web*. This beginning, worthy of *The Shining*, establishes the story's connection with the realism of ancient folklore. A spider's trapping and eating of bugs is described matter-of-factly by the protagonist: "I have to get my own living" as is her death: "No one was with her when she died," Adults often remember it as a turning point in their reading histories. This beautiful and complex tale, full of unforgettable characters, ministers to a need to understand change, loneliness, animals, family, and death, natural and inflicted. *Charlotte's Web* shows the power of friendship, loyalty, resourcefulness, and courage; it coaches us to keep promises and stand up for the powerless; it opens our eyes and ears to the circle of life and good storytelling.

Elwyn Brooks White was born in Mount Vernon, New York. He wrote more than twenty books of poetry and prose. His satirical sketches, essays, and editorials were published in the prestigious journals of his time such as *The New Yorker*. He co-authored *The Elements of Style* with his former Cornell professor William J. Strunk (1959), the only manual of writing style to appear on bestseller lists, which popularized a motto adhered to by both White and Charlotte: "make every word tell." A great animal lover, White published an obituary for his dog Daisy in *The New Yorker* in 1932.

In 1938 he moved to Maine to run an animal farm. White actively participated in ecological campaigns such as preventing the extinction of bald eagles by the use of DDT. *Charlotte's Web* reveals White's concern for the world around him, in the grip of radical economic, environmental, and social changes during and in the aftermath of World War II. His concerns were industrialization, the growing power of advertisement and propaganda to manufacture gullibility, and people's ever-greater detachment from the animal world.

Charlotte's Web centers on the Arable family and their relatives the Zuckermans, in whose farm most of the story takes place. Whether intended or not, the family's name is eminently suitable. "Arable", from the Latin *arare*, means "plowable". The Arables and the farming community transform their appreciation of a pig from food to sentient animal, thanks to a three-quarters-of-an-inch spider who plows their hardened sensibilities. The protagonists are memorable: Naïve and good to the core Wilbur, a runt of the litter pig whom young Fern Arable rescues from an early death; stuttering geese; Templeton, a conniving rat who, it turns out, is not as rotten as everyone thinks; and above all, Charlotte A. Cavatica, a gray barn spider. White spent one year studying spiders to create her. Weaving texts and textiles, she saves Wilbur for the second time by creating slogans that make him famous ("Some Pig," "Terrific," "Radiant," "Humble").

The book is a love song to farm life composed by a writer who was a farmer and saw the world through children's, and animals', eyes. Even potato parasites and the viscous substance attached to a plant are lovingly described: "In early summer there are plenty of things for a child to eat and drink and suck and chew[...] Everywhere you look is life; even the little ball of spit on the weed stalk, if you poke it apart, has a green worm inside it. And on the underside of the leaf of the potato vine are the bright orange eggs of the potato bug." White's vivid description of the world through Wilbur's eyes even makes a description of pig's food sound appetizing:

> It was a delicious meal—skim milk, wheat middlings, leftover pancakes, half a doughnut, the rind of a summer squash, two pieces of stale toast, a third of a gingersnap, a fish tail, one orange peel, several noodles from a noodle soup, the scum off a cup of cocoa, an ancient jelly roll, a strip of paper from the lining of the garbage pail, and a spoonful of raspberry jello.

The final sentence of *Charlotte's Web* befits both the literary virtues of the protagonist and the book: "It is not often that someone comes along who is a true friend and a good writer. Charlotte was both." In 1999, *Time* magazine named *Charlotte's Web* the best children's book of the twentieth century, and it remains equally worthy of being fed to twenty-first century children.

Details from the 1973 animated film adaptation of *Charlotte's Web*, produced by Hanna-Barbera and starring Henry Gibson as the voice of Wilbur and Debbie Reynolds as the voice of Charlotte.

New Horizons

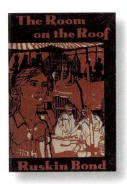

RUSKIN BOND

The Room on the Roof (1956)

Drums, bangles and frogs bring home the brio of the bizarre and the author to his adopted city.

The Room on the Roof won the John Llewellyn Rhys Prize in 1957, an award for young Commonwealth writers, which was won by V.S. Naipaul the following year. It was to be the first of many awards in Ruskin Bond's (b. 1934) long literary career. Bond wrote a sequel *Vagrants in the Valley* in 1956.

Inspired by classics such as *Alice's Adventures in Wonderland*, Bond has had a lasting influence on Indian children's fiction.

Bond has never married, but in 1973 he adopted the family of his household help and still lives with them today in Landour, Mussoorie.

Rusty is a lonely teenager living in a starchy European community on the outskirts of Dehradun in Uttarakhand, India, with his taciturn guardian, Mr. Harrison. There are virtually no other children. The English-style houses all have "neat front yards and name plates on the gates." Life feels empty and meaningless. But the vibrant town center calls to young Rusty, making "his imagination soar."

"India started a mile away, where the bazaar began," writes Ruskin Bond. Exploring his own divided heritage as the child of a British father and an Anglo-Indian mother, Bond wrote *The Room on the Roof* when he was just seventeen. Homesick in a London attic, his personal journal became a novel about India and his love for it. Bond used the money from his advance to travel back to Dehradun. He has lived in India ever since and written stories, novellas, and children's books.

The themes and stylistic elements that make Bond so enduringly popular—simplicity, natural observation, individuality, the power of friendship—are all already here in this youthful account. Bond later called it "a novel about adolescence by an adolescent . . . born out of loneliness." In *The Room on the Roof*, he recaptured: "the sights and sounds, the faces . . . the atmosphere of all that I'd left behind."

Powerful sensory details permeate *The Room on the Roof* and build up the image of life in the wooded Himalayan foothills. "Rusty noticed the sounds, because he was happy, and a happy person notices things," writes Bond. He gives us, sometimes onomatopoeically, the sound of drums, bangles, frogs, jackals, and rain pattering on banyan leaves. There are the smells of citronella oil, cabbage water, jasmine, magnolia.

Bond conjures up spices and sizzling fat from the *chaat* shop, the crowded mayhem of a railroad station, or the force and freshness of an arriving monsoon. There are tastes and sensations too: a spicy salad of potato, guava, and orange, ripe mangoes, soft grass, sticky heat. Above all, Bond's India is exploding with color: the rainbow powders of *Holi*, red and gold chilies, a Flame of the Forest tree "against the blue of the sky," or

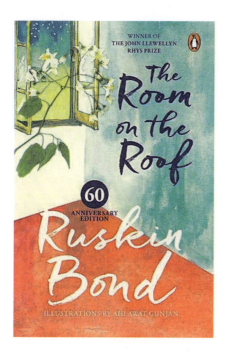
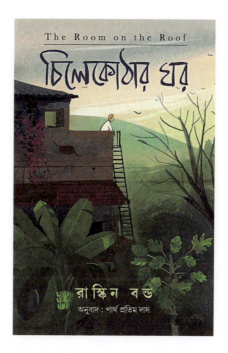

> In his room, Rusty was a king. His domain was the sky and everything he could see.

a shoot of pink bougainvillea. Hindi words like *chaat* (street food) and *barsaat* (rain) help build an evocative picture of the novel's world.

The Room on the Roof is written in a clear, relatable style with a poetic rhythm, but its subject matter can be subtle and complicated. Bond manages to cram surprising depths of passion and compassion, nuance and philosophy into this coming-of-age story.

Watching the lizards in his room, Rusty is fascinated by the way they change color to blend in, a metaphor for his own chameleonic life. He grapples with the sense of "not belonging anywhere," but his friend Somi points out that his inheritance "can also mean that you belong everywhere."

Rusty learns the importance of following his own path to happiness: "Maybe there is more freedom in your little room than . . . all the world," his friend's mother suggests. This basic space becomes symbolic: it is in this room that Rusty starts to talk about becoming a writer just as the novel explores the origins of Bond's own literary career.

Front covers of the 2022 Bengali and 2016 English editions of The Room on the Roof.

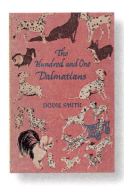

DODIE SMITH

101 DALMATIANS (1956)

The Twilight Barking calls distant friends to the rescue of spotted puppies from the clutches of the evil Cruella de Vil, who is determined to turn them into a new fur coat.

Dodie Smith (1896–1990) trained at the dramatic academy RADA, and was a successful playwright before she turned to novel writing. Her first, the classic coming-of-age story *I Capture the Castle*, was written in the 1940s.

The One Hundred and One Dalmatians was inspired by her own beloved Dalmatian dog, Pongo, and also by a friend, who is said to have remarked: "Those dogs would make a lovely fur coat!"

Smith's novel has spawned two well-known movie adaptations: the 1961 Walt Disney animation and the 1996 live-action remake.

From the very start of *The One Hundred and One Dalmatians*, it is clear we are in the hands of a master storyteller. Dodie Smith's lightness of touch and sparklingly good-natured humor shine through right away, whether it is learning just why our human protagonists, the Dearlys, are so well off (Mr. Dearly "had done the Government a great service (something to do with getting rid of the national debt) and, as a reward, had been let off his income tax for life"), or learning who is in charge in their household: the Dearlys, or their Dalmatians, Pongo and Missis. It's the dogs, of course:

> Like many other much-loved humans, [the Dearlys] believed that they owned their dogs, instead of realizing that their dogs owned them. Pongo and Missis found this touching and amusing and let their pets think it was true.

They are all ably looked after by their butler and cook, Nanny Butler and Nanny Cook (the Dearlys' childhood nannies who have trained in these new roles in order to stay looking after their now-adult charges). This is a happy household, especially when Pongo and Missis learn they are expecting puppies.

But every good story needs a good villain, and Smith dreams up one of children's literature's most compelling, in Mrs. Dearly's old school acquaintance Cruella de Vil. With a shock of half-black, half-white hair, "black eyes with a tinge of red in them" and a rather wimpy furrier husband, Cruella is glorious, terrifying, and desperate to get her hands on those puppies to turn them into "enchanting fur coats."

When the inevitable happens, and the puppies are spirited away by Cruella's minions, the Dearlys fail to help, despite putting advertisements on the front pages of all the papers at great expense, and calling in "one of the Top Men from Scotland Yard" who "promised to Comb the Underworld" to find them (the use of judicious capitals is another of Smith's charmingly humorous traits).

Pongo, Perdita and their puppies in the movie adaptation produced by Disney in 1961.

So Pongo, "one of the keenest brains in Dogdom," and his Missis head out to London's Primrose Hill to rope in the rest of dogdom in their quest to find their babies. What follows is one of children's literature's most delightful inventions, the Twilight Barking: "All dogs know about the Twilight Barking. It is their way of keeping in touch with distant friends, passing on important news, enjoying a good gossip. But none of the dogs who answered Pongo and Missis expected to enjoy a gossip session, for the three short, sharp barks meant 'Help! Help! Help!'"

Their journey, aided by cats, ancient spaniels, sheepdogs, and small boys, dealing with snow, hunger, and sharp stones being thrown, leads them to Hell Hall. Looming and scary, Missis gasps: "It's seen us!" as they arrive, because "it really did seem as if the eyes of the house were staring at them from its cracked and peeling black face."

Fortunately, Pongo, Missus, and their pups are far smarter than Cruella's thieves, Saul and Jasper Baddun, and they sneak their own puppies, and the dozens of others they discover to also have been kidnapped, away into the countryside.

Funny, adventurous, charming, and brimful of heart, this is a tale— or tail—for the ages that will never grow old. As good a read as it was a seminal Disney film.

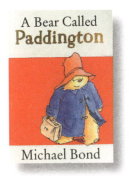

MICHAEL BOND

A Bear Called Paddington
(1958)

Kindness, manners and marmalade make the Peruvian bear a British treasure and an international icon.

Michael Bond (1926–2017) left school at fourteen and worked in a lawyer's office. In 1943 he joined the Royal Air Force and transferred to the army in 1945. After the war, he joined the BBC as a TV cameraman before becoming a professional writer.

There are fifteen books in the Paddington Bear series (ending with *Paddington at St. Paul's*) along with many other short-story collections and picture books.

A Bear Called Paddington was first adapted for the screen in a BBC series from 1976 to 1980. Much later, there have been three high-profile films.

When Paddington Bear drank tea with Queen Elizabeth II and the two shared their secret stashes of marmalade sandwiches—Paddington's in his hat and the Queen's in her handbag—during the "Platinum Party at the Palace" video in 2022, it cemented Paddington's role as a British national icon.

Paddington had already enjoyed over half a decade of being one of the most-loved characters in fiction, having touched the hearts and minds of adults and children since the publication of the first stories about him in *A Bear Called Paddington* in 1958. His appeal was much enhanced by the arrival of a stuffed toy Paddington Bear in 1972, which took him to a market of fans well beyond readers. The well-crafted little bear in his duffel coat, red hat, and yellow Wellington boots was instantly recognizable and eminently collectable. Paddington Bear became so ubiquitous that in 1994 when the U.K. tunnelers linked up with their French counterparts during the building of the Channel Tunnel, they handed over a Paddington Bear figure.

Paddington Bear was so called after he is found by Mr. Brown in Paddington Station having arrived direct from "Darkest Peru" with only a suitcase and a label around his neck with the message "Please look after this bear." Illustrated by Peggy Fortnam, the first title was a collection of seven short stories that build a picture of the charming, accident-prone Paddington by recounting the simple and funny mishaps that he gets himself involved in. Whether it's eating—Paddington loves anything sweet, sticky, or creamy—or shopping, or even just simply having a bath, Paddington can be guaranteed to cause chaos. And whatever he does, long suffering Mr. and Mrs. Brown and their children love him more and more.

The well-crafted drama of the stories and their brevity made them immediately appealing to children, while beyond the easy drama it was Paddington's character with its combination of childhood innocence and adult sophistication that gave the stories their depth. Children could see Paddington Bear as one of themselves but they could also learn from the good behaviors and values he exemplified. These included kindness, exceptionally good manners, and his well-developed sense of right and wrong.

A 1st class British postal stamp commemorating Paddington Bear, first issued in 1994 and designed by Newell & Sorrell.

Both the imaginary Paddington Bear who Michael Bond created and one of the most powerful themes of the books had their origins in reality. When asked about where he got the idea, Michael Bond described how he found "a very tiny bear in a London store one Christmas . . . he'd been left on the shelf all by himself. All the other bears had been sold, and I brought him as a present for my wife. I wrote some stories about the bear, more for fun than with the idea of having them published. Then I found I had a book on my hands. It wasn't written specifically for children, but I think I put into it the kind of things that I liked reading about when I was young."

Describing the influences that had caused him to see Paddington Bear as a refugee, Michael Bond spoke of seeing Jewish children arriving in London and London children being evacuated to the English countryside during World War II. "The evacuees all had a label around their neck with their name and address on and a little case or package containing all their treasured possessions. . . . So Paddington, in a sense, was a refugee, and I do think that there's no sadder sight than refugees."

Following *A Bear Called Paddington*, the next eight Paddington books came out at the rate of almost one a year through the following decade. Published at a slower rate, new stories about Paddington continued through the 1970s and '80s and the books were also adapted for television in 1976 in one of the earliest and most successful examples of animation. In addition to Peggy Fortnum, other illustrators including David McKee and R. W. Alley brought Paddington Bear to life and so did three films from 2014.

Below: Illustration of Paddington by the book's original illustrator Peggy Fortnum.

I daresay you'll be wanting some marmalade.

New Horizons

JAMES VANCE MARSHALL (DONALD GORDON PAYNE)

WALKABOUT (1959)

A plane crash in the desert leads two children to confront different ideas of civilization.

Donald Gordon Payne (1924-2018) worked under various pen names throughout his career, writing his first novel, *The Midnight Sea* (1958), under the pseudonym "Ian Cameron" before settling on "James Vance Marshall" upon finishing *Walkabout*.

Originally published as *The Children* in London in 1959, then as *Walkabout* in America in 1961 and later, in 1971, released as a film that launched the career of the Indigenous Australian actor David Gulpilil.

The word "walkabout" describes the male rite of passage of solitary journeys on foot undertaken by adolescent Indigenous Australians.

Walkabout has polarized critical opinion for two generations. In Australia, critics seemed to willfully forget that it was a novel and not a documentary and severely attacked it as "a hodgepodge of the most incredible misinformation; animal, vegetable, and mineral." Overseas, however, and particularly in America, the book prompted diametric opinion. *The Atlantic* magazine thus saw it as a "luminous and haunting parable" with "nearly tactile descriptions of the endlessly strange flora, fauna, and geology."

The book's journey is undertaken by Peter (aged eight) and his sister Mary (aged thirteen), from South Carolina who travel to Australia to visit their uncle in the southern city of Adelaide. As the sole survivors of their plane crashing in Central Australia's Sturt Desert they begin their own "walkabout." Theirs is a journey in a land "full . . . of terrors all the greater for being unknown." At first, drawing on their own cultural references, they imagine themselves like "Davy Crockett, reconnoitering a new frontier." However, without that backwoodsman's experience and knowledge their naivety seems likely to have fatal consequences as they face what is largely, except for its Indigenous inhabitants, unpopulated territory.

Providentially, a "pure blood" boy who has never encountered white people before and speaks no English finds the children. To him they appear "utterly incapable of fending for themselves" and concludes that they are "perhaps the lost survivors of some peculiarly backward tribe." He is undertaking his initiating rite into adulthood—a walkabout—and equipped with the survival skills honed by his ancestors over millennia, finding water and food on this solitary quest is second nature to him.

In contrast, the white children's "civilized" values have been rendered meaningless since "the basic realities of life were something they'd never had to face." While Mary thus fights to overcome her racial suspicions, her brother is open-minded and life-embracing, and their journey becomes a cultural clash in which all their values will be questioned and forever upset. The book becomes a journey into race relations as Mary is forced to reject her sense of white superiority and its prejudices, and her only hope for survival

Luc Roeg (left), son of Nicolas Roeg, the film's director, and David Gulpilil (right) in the 1971 movie adaptation of *Walkabout*.

is in bridging what initially seems an insurmountable gap between two cultures. On her first confrontation with the native boy, although the physical distance between them "was less than the spread of an outstretched arm," culturally it was "more than 100,000 years." Yet paradoxically it is Indigenous life skills that will raise the children "above the level of the beasts."

What results is a combined journey in which the native boy becomes the children's savior as well as their victim. And this is the tragedy of the book, a journey into ancient Indigenous Australian belief—that a single look, like the evil eye, can transfix and kill. Thus, whether it is this "terror beyond all civilized comprehension" or the cold he catches from Peter or a combination of both, the boy does not survive. Yet even in death his guidance continues because "both children had fallen into his ways" and will thereby reach white civilization, their "promised land."

Ultimately, *Walkabout* depicts their life-changing journey into racial unity, understanding, and self-knowledge. Mary finally rejects all sense of racial division: "the world that she had thought was split in two was one." Significantly, the final word spoken in the book belongs to Peter: it is the word *Kurura*, which they have taken to mean "follow me." Its choice emphasizes the complete reversal in the brother/sister relationship that has occurred: It is the young brother who will take his older sister into the future, one guided by his journey's acquired wisdom and insight.

3 Modern Narratives

1960 to 1984

Blending age-old archetypes with contemporary sensibilities, these books breathed new life into children's fiction for the next generation.

Illustration by Tonke Dragt, The Letter for the King, Leopold 1962.

RENÉ GOSCINNY AND ALBERT UDERZO

ASTERIX THE GAUL
(ASTÉRIX LE GAULOIS) (1961)

One village resists conquest during the Roman occupation of Gaul. Using intelligence, courage, humor, and determination, the warrior Asterix and his friends defy the might of Rome.

Translated by Anthea Bell & Derek Hockridge (1969).

René Goscinny (1926-77) and Albert Udzero (1927-2020) first met in 1951 whilst working at the Paris office of the World Press agency, which distributed French and Belgian bande-dessinée comics.

The Asterix Series has sold over 385 million copies copies across 40 titles.

The first 23 Asterix and Obelix to be published were written by René Goscinny *(below left)* and illustrated by Albert Udzero *(below right)*. After Goscinny's untimely death in 1977, Udzero continued to write and illustrate the next editions alone.

Generations of children have grown up with the adventures of the fearless, flaxen-haired, fun-loving inhabitants of a redoubtable village in Gaul (the region comprising areas of modern France, Germany, and Italy). In the year 50 BCE, despite being surrounded by Roman forts and legionaries, this community alone stood out against Roman occupation.

Initially written as a serial for the Franco-Belgian comic magazine *Pilote*, *Asterix the Gaul* introduces the eponymous hero, a diminutive warrior, and his larger friend Obelix, a menhir delivery man with a bottomless appetite for roast boar and fighting. Perennially pugnacious, the pair relish laying into brigands and Roman soldiers as they go about their daily business, leaving in their wake a trail of broken men nursing headaches and black eyes. Their formidable friendship gathers momentum with its sequel *Asterix and the Golden Sickle* and subsequent titles.

Dumbfounded by the villagers' superhuman strength, Crismus Bonus, the centurion in charge of the nearby camp of Compendium, sends a spy to discover their secret. When he learns that the village druid Getafix makes a potion that renders the drinker invincible, he plots to kidnap him and discover the recipe. After which, he can overthrow Caesar.

In this story, as in all those that follow, there is never any doubt that Asterix and the villagers will prove triumphant. Its pleasure lies not in suspense but in the verve and invention with which it is written.

In the French-Belgian tradition of the *bande-dessinée* (graphic novel), René Goscinny writes with irrepressible humor, lobbing in puns, linguistic gags, and silly anachronisms to keep the narrative bubbling. Anyone learning Latin will enjoy his school book asides—"Vae victo, Vae victis," says one dazed soldier after a bruising encounter, to which his friend replies in the English version, "We decline!"

What makes Asterix exceptional, however, is the fusion of Goscinny's imagination with that of the illustrator Albert Uderzo. Uderzo's vivid and atmospheric depiction of character, place, and mood playfully and sometimes beautifully evokes life in the ancient times. Embellishing his drawings

with incidental detail and visual jokes, his wit dovetails with Goscinny's, enhancing the storyline.

Since Asterix is to ancient history what British sitcom *Blackadder* is to English history, those wishing to learn about the Roman Empire should look elsewhere for rigorous fact. Yet despite its irreverence, *Asterix the Gaul* cleverly conveys a sense of all-pervading threat and embattlement, as the villagers resist oppression and tyranny while trying to live normally. As such, the Gaulish village represents an idyll of contented community living. Indeed, the comic's portrayal of the unbeaten Gauls, and their insistence on holding on to their old way of life, is so powerful it might be read as an allegory of French resistance during France's occupation during World War II.

The villagers' aim is not to win power for themselves, but to be allowed to live in peace and harmony. All they desire is to hunt safely in the forest, for their children to play untroubled in the streets, and occasionally for everyone to gather for a celebratory feast that lasts long into the night.

Above: Still from the animated movie *Asterix in Britain*, produced by Gaumont SA in 1986.

NORTON JUSTER

The Phantom Tollbooth
(1961)

A bored young boy called Milo takes an adventure through the magical and extraordinary Lands Beyond—and takes such delight in discovering things along the way that he is cured of boredom forever.

As an engineer in the United States Navy, author Norton Juster (1929-2021) passed the time honing his comedic sensibilities: on one occasion, he created a fake organization called the "Garibaldi Society," whose sole purpose was to reject potential applicants.

Not all reviews of the book were positive when it came out. *The Library Journal* wrote in 1962 that "The ironies, the subtle play on words will be completely lost on all but the most precocious children."

Illustrator Jules Feiffer lived a floor below Norton Juster in a house they shared in Brooklyn. It was Feiffer's girlfriend at the time who took the book to the editor Jason Epstein, who bought the book for the publisher Random House.

In 1958, Norton Juster was a young architect and won a Ford Foundation grant to write a book about urban planning for children. He couldn't do it—but it was while he was struggling to write this book that he came up with the idea for *The Phantom Tollbooth*.

A chance exchange with a child in a restaurant set Juster thinking about the way he wondered about theoretical questions ("What's the biggest number there is?" for example). Soon, he started to compose what he initially "thought would be a little story" about the way children encounter words and meanings and numbers and the other "strange concepts" that are imposed on them as they learn. He later sent a copy of the finished novel to the Ford Foundation, who were reported to be delighted with the result.

The hero is Milo (his age isn't given—a deliberate choice by Juster), a boy allergic to anything educational. He sees the process of seeking knowledge as "the biggest waste of time of all." But then something remarkable arrives, out of nowhere, to help him change his mind. He is sent a "strange package" containing, as the label says, "One Genuine Turnpike Tollbooth." This turnpike turns out to be big enough to drive through in his toy electric car—so, naturally, that's what Milo does. He is immediately transported to the Lands Beyond, a fantastical place that has been thrown into chaos after its feuding kings banished the princesses Rhyme and Reason to the Castle in the Air. Milo finds himself on a quest to rescue these princesses—and to escape his own inertia in the process.

Milo makes friends with a dog called Tock (so called because he has a watch on his back—that's right—he's a watchdog) and the Humbug (so called because he is a humbug). Together they visit the Half Bakery, which produces half-baked ideas. They meet the world's smallest giant, the thinnest fat man, and the fattest thin man. They visit Digitopolis, ruled over by the Mathemagician—a king obsessed by the magic of numbers. They also visit Dictionopolis, where Milo is offered the hospitality of this "kingdom," "country," "nation," "state," "commonwealth," "realm," "empire," "principality."

The inventive wordplay and the book's countless leaps of logic and

Milo, Tock and the Humbug completing a series of endless tasks heaped upon them by the Terrible Trivium, the "ogre of wasted effort." Illustration by Jules Feiffer for the first edition.

imagination result in a story about learning that manages to be fun from beginning to end; not to mention a visual feast thanks to the gorgeous and energetic illustrations of cartoonist Jules Feiffer.

When the book came out, a review in *The New Yorker* by critic Emily Maxwell compared Norton Juster to John Bunyan: "As *Pilgrim's Progress* is concerned with the awakening of the sluggardly spirit, *The Phantom Tollbooth* is concerned with the awakening of the lazy mind."

That's true enough, but the real magic of *The Phantom Tollbooth* also lies in the fact that it encourages this awakening not by talking down to its readers, but by giving them something to enjoy and aspire to. It's quite possible that parents bought the book in the hope that it might encourage their children to want to learn. But children took it to their hearts because it is worth reading for its own sake. Because it is tremendous.

> You must never feel badly about making mistakes [...] as long as you take the trouble to learn from them. For you often learn more by being wrong for the right reasons than you do by being right for the wrong reasons.

The Demons of Ignorance illustrated by Jules Feiffer for the first edition.

MADELEINE L'ENGLE

A Wrinkle in Time (1962)

Meg Murry and her brother travel across time and space in search of their missing father in a sci-fi battle between good and evil.

Despite her commercial success later in life, Madeleine L'Engle almost gave up writing on her fortieth birthday, believing it to be an unsustainable financial endeavor.

A Wrinkle in Time has been adapted into two movies, most recently a 2018 all-star version directed by Ava DuVernay, multiple stage productions including a 1992 opera, and a 2012 graphic novel.

The success of *A Wrinkle In Time* led L'Engle to begin the Time Quintet series, which follows the adventures of Meg Murry and her family across 4 more books.

When we first meet Meg Murry, then age twelve or thirteen, she is not happy. Her father has been away for years and the letters have stopped arriving, and she is "full of bad feeling." Meg knows she is somehow different—and different is definitely not good. If only she could be more like her twin brothers, Sandy and Dennys, who are never in trouble, they're just so socially well-adjusted and so inconspicuously normal. (Her youngest brother Charles Wallace is definitely different, too—but more of him later . . .) But one night, in the middle of a storm, her family is visited briefly by strange old Mrs. Whatsit, who leaves them with these parting words: "by the way, there is such a thing as a tesseract. . . ." What on earth could a tesseract be? And why did Meg's mother go suddenly very pale when she heard that word? (Meg's parents are both scientists, but we don't know what strange things they have been working on.)

Things start happening fast after that. Before you know it, Meg and Charles Wallace—and their new friend Calvin—are no longer sitting around in the apple orchard but are off on a galaxy-spanning adventure, in the hope of finding their father. Because when they find him, well, everything will be okay then—won't it?

The children swirl from world to world, and eventually shimmer into existence on Camazotz, a creepy place whose population is entirely controlled, entirely brainwashed, abdicating every decision to a thing just called IT, which seems to wield infinite power. Even Charles Wallace proves unable to resist. Young Charles is a wonderfully drawn character—precociously grown-up in his speech and ideas despite his very young age, and able to sense and understand things that he really shouldn't be able to. But ultimately it's Meg who needs to step up and be the hero of this story—and all of the things that make her different, her unusual strengths and weaknesses, are what finally allow her to prevail.

A Wrinkle in Time is a very ambitious book for young readers—not in terms of the narrative or the language (some of the slang is dated now, and delightful)—but in terms of the size of its ideas. It's a book about the ultimate

> Life, with its rules, its obligations, and its freedoms, is like a sonnet: You're given the form, but you have to write the sonnet yourself.

high-stakes battle against evil, about free will. It's about the nature of time (the intergalactic travel happens through wrinkles in space and also in time); it's about science, and there's plenty of religion in it, too. These might have been among the reasons for the rejections L'Engle got from all of the first two dozen publishers she sent it to. But it finally did find a publishing home, to our good fortune, and has remained in print ever since. And there's so much in it that countless readers would come to love and remember, not least the great inventiveness to all the secondary characters the children meet along their way, including the three mysterious old women (who aren't really old women)—Mrs. Whatsit, Mrs. Which, and Mrs. Who—as well as Aunt Beast, who is much lovelier than her name suggests.

After various turns, the story ends briskly—between Meg setting off back to Camazotz to resolve things and rescue her brother and defeat IT and get safely back to her own home on Earth is a matter of just eight pages—but this is not really the end of the story. L'Engle would go on to write several more books in the Time sequence—"companion books," she called them, rather than sequels.

A still from the 2018 Disney production of *A Wrinkle in Time*, starring Storm Reid as Meg Murry, and Reese Witherspoon as Mrs. Whatsit.

TONKE DRAGT

The Letter for the King
(DE BRIEF VOOR DE KONING) (1962)

One of the Netherlands' greatest postwar children's books, Dragt's enduring classic is a fast-paced chivalric quest with simple yet evocative writing.

Translated by Laura Watkinson (2013).

During World War II, Tonke Dragt (1930–2024) and her family were interned in a Japanese prisoner's camp in the Dutch East Indies. Without any books to ease her boredom, Dragt wrote her first novel with a friend on sheets of used paper and toilet paper.

While working as a high school art teacher, Dragt would tell her students short stories to keep their attention and provide inspiration for their drawings.

In 2004, *The Letter for the King* was awarded the Griffel der Griffels, the award for the best Dutch children's book of the last fifty years.

Tonke Dragt was born in Indonesia, then a Dutch colony, in 1930, and enjoyed an early childhood that was both ordinary and idyllic. Ordinary in the sense that her family lived in an unremarkable neighborhood among other members of the well-ordered, self-satisfied colonial business-and-administrative class; idyllic because they spent their vacation escaping the heat in the spectacular Indonesian mountains with their volcanoes, pristine jungle, tropical vegetation, waterfalls, and remote lakes. This idyll came to an abrupt end in World War II when the Japanese conquered the archipelago and interned the European population.

In the women's camp with her mother, twelve-year-old Tonke now suffered a stifling environment where food was short and the days marked by roll calls and searches. At home she had been a bookworm who devoured legends, mythology, and fairy tales, in the camp with nothing to read, she found a different escape by writing and illustrating her own stories that merged these literary influences with the idealized, untouched world of her vacations.

After the war the family moved back to the Netherlands; for the young woman Dragt had become, a chilly unwelcoming place. Dragt studied art in The Hague and became a school art teacher, and it was in the classroom that she began developing her fictional process by engaging and stimulating her students with stories rather than trying to dominate them as a disciplinarian, a role that suited neither her character nor her temperament. Her usual practice was to tell a gripping story as the starting point for a drawing or painting, usually with a cliff-hanger that challenged the students' imaginations. Most of these stories were ephemeral and soon forgotten, but the scene that formed the seed for *The Letter for the King*—an account of a squire, Tiuri, whose vigil on the eve of his knighting is interrupted by a stranger calling for help—refused to be discarded.

The book draws on Arthurian legend to create a fictional world of chivalry and betrayal. It tells the tale of the squire's quest to deliver an urgent letter to the king of a neighboring country, a quest that takes him over mountains and through forests influenced by the Indonesian wilderness of

Dragt's childhood. The coming-of-age story is illustrated by the author with evocative black-and-white drawings and told in fast-paced, effective prose, moving quickly through episodes that engage and stimulate. Throughout, Dragt emphasizes not just the virtue of her main character, but also his courage and determination, characteristics that she had identified as indispensable early in her life.

The Letter for the King was first published in the original Dutch in 1962 and has been in print ever since, enjoying at least two subsequent waves of increased popularity, the first in 2004 after it was voted the best Dutch children's book of the last fifty years and the second after the overwhelming critical and sales success of the first English edition, wonderfully translated by Laura Watkinson and published in the United Kingdom in 2013. Both events were noticed abroad and followed by a jump in the number of translations: the book has now appeared in no less than thirty-six languages, ranging from Afrikaans to Mongolian.

Below: Tiuri and his horse on their journey to deliver the letter for the king, illustrated by Tonke Dragt herself for the first edition.

GIANNI RODARI

Telephone Tales
(Favole al telefono) (1962)

Every night at 9 o'clock, Monday to Saturday, traveling salesman Mr. Bianchi calls his little daughter in Varese with a bedtime story lasting as long as the coin allows.

Translated by Patrick Creagh (1965); Antony Shugaar (2020).

Gianni Rodari (1920–1980) began writing children's books in 1948 while working as a journalist for the Communist periodical *L'Unità*. In 1950, the Italian Communist Party installed him as the editor for the new weekly children's magazine *Il Pioniere*.

In 1970, Rodari received the Hans Christian Andersen Medal for his lasting contribution to children's literature, making him the only Italian author to have done so.

Set and composed in a bygone era of pay phones, Gianni Rodari's *Telephone Tales* is a portrait of postwar Italy. No matter where we are now or that corded-telephones are not part of our lives anymore, it still speaks to us today every time we feel the need for peace, justice, equality, truth.

Its author, Gianni (Giovanni Francesco) Rodari, was an elementary school teacher, pedagogue, and poet, and the only Italian writer ever to receive the Hans Christian Andersen Award, the "Nobel Prize for children's literature," in 1970.

"Once upon a time there was . . ."—the book sets sail as every good old fairy tale should, only to startle the reader at once—". . . a man named Signor Bianchi from Varese. He was an accountant." Every night, at 9 p.m., this traveling salesman of pharmaceutical goods telephones the northern Italian town of Varese to tell his daughter a bedtime story: seventy tales that each last as long as a single coin will allow. "He was paying for all these phone calls out of his own pocket. . . . Only occasionally, if he'd wrapped up some very good sales, could he afford a few extra long-distance 'clicks.'" This serves as the book's narrative frame: a modern one, set in the aftermath of the war, a time of struggle and fast economic growth that still required every coin to be frugally employed. Through telephone lines, switchboards, and operators, the stream of storytelling flows as lively as it used to around fireplaces and country barns.

From the very first line, the book reveals its Surrealist roots in the unexpected juxtaposition of unrelated objects, creating a sense of displacement that opens a gap for the imagination. Magic is found in the day-by-day scene and in the polarity between the cozy and the uncanny. The tone is a domestic one, ironic and affectionate.

Rodari's world is one of everyday objects that conceal a magic soul and sometimes—playfully, unconventionally, radically—stop cooperating and simply protest. Giuseppe's rifle talks "like a little kid reading a comic" and , instead of shooting the bullet, says "Boom!". Trolleybus number 75 takes its passengers to "the edge of a cool, sweet-smelling grove of trees" to have a

look at the cyclamens; the traffic lights in Milan's main square turn blue. Alice Tumbledown keeps falling over and has the most splendid adventures (stuck inside a kitchen drawer, trapped in the shell of a yawning mollusk); there is a "country without sharp edges," a "country with an 'un' in front," a "land of the butter man"; a merry-go-round that flies in space and an elevator to the stars; a palace made of ice cream and a building just for demolishing.

The first issue of this collection of stories, published by Giulio Einaudi in 1962, is illustrated by Futurist artist and designer Bruno Munari (1907–1998) with scribbles and doodles "like those . . . you make when you are on the phone. To some extent they refer to the contents but to some extent they are subconscious drawings." On the front cover, a black rotary dial, as was used on old telephones, opens to nine little blank holes that might in turn potentially open toward new stories and threads, as if Munari himself did not want to spoil too many details in a story where the human voice ought to remain in charge.

Admittedly difficult to translate, Rodari's *Telephone Tales* was first partially translated in Britain in 1965 by Patrick Creagh, but the book was slow to enter the United States, prevented in this by the author's political affiliation to the Communist Party. It was newly translated in 2020 by Antony Shugaar.

Above and overleaf: Illustrations by Valerio Vidali for the US 2020 edition.

Gettoni telefonico (telephone tokens) were used in phone booths across Italy throughout the twentieth century.

Modern Narratives 147

CLIVE KING

STIG OF THE DUMP (1963)

When a young boy falls headfirst into a deep pit filled with trash, he finds a caveman living there. Becoming friends, the pair have a series of amusing, sometimes alarming, adventures.

Clive King's (1924–2018), spent much of his postwar career with the British Council in countries such as Syria and Lebanon before returning to England. He was a superb linguist, and his fascination with communication and language is at the heart of Barney and Stig's relationship. His idea for the story was influenced by Kipling's *Puck of Pook's Hill*.

Since its first publication, *Stig of the Dump* has never been out of print and has been adapted into two television programs, theatre productions, and a computer adventure game.

Barney is a bored eight-year-old who often stays at his grandmother's house in the country with his sister. Near the bottom of the back yard is an old chalk pit, gradually filling up as people dispose of their unwanted things, such as televisions, car tires, and carpets. Getting too close one day to the edge of the cliff, Barney topples into the pit, and crashes through the makeshift roof of a ramshackle dwelling into a caveman's home.

Forgetting the blow he has taken to his head, Barney is fascinated that this ageless man, who calls himself Stig, has ingeniously fashioned thrown-away stuff into useful things, such as turning the tube from a vacuum cleaner into a waterpipe. As their friendship grows, he helps Stig make a window from bottles and a chimney from tin cans. With his "horrible club," meanwhile, Stig frightens off burglars attempting to steal Barney's grandmother's jewelry and silver, and faces down an escaped circus leopard.

The new world Barney has discovered straddles his own age and Stig's prehistoric times, yet the gulf between them is effortlessly bridged by their instinctual understanding of each other. Is this a made-up world, and Barney's adventures nothing more than an over-active imagination or the result of a concussion? Certainly, his grandmother and his sister Lou assume his new chum is imaginary. Until, that is, Lou is dragged into one of Barney's escapades, on Midsummer Night's Eve. On that liminal evening, the children find themselves in an alien forested world, unrecognizable from the tame English countryside, and are befriended by Stig's tribe.

King's fictional dump is based on a real chalk pit near Oliver's Farm, his family home in Ash, on the Kentish North Downs in England. At nearby Swansdowne, the skull of a Paleolithic woman had been discovered in the early twentieth century, and as a boy, King enlivened his vacations by pretending someone lived at the bottom of the pit. As he later said, the farm "was a place of childhood boredom. What it needed was something elemental and primitive to wake it up."

Stig of the Dump's instant and enduring success in part reflects the refreshing freedom Barney is given to roam and play unsupervised by adults.

More interestingly, the world Barney and Stig occupy shows how people from entirely different backgrounds can quickly find common ground. Over the years there has been some criticism of King's middle-class assumptions, such as his depiction of a local gang, the Snargets, who speak with cod-cockney accents (as do the burglars)—"What shall we do wiv 'im, fellers?" Initially at least, he implies that Barney is more in tune with a Stone Age hunter-gatherer than with children from another class.

But despite the somewhat stereotyped social distinctions, the ethos of upcycling that infuses the novel is as modern as if it were written yesterday. King, who came from a family of D.I.Y. fanatics, shows Stig's ingenious mind constantly at work. The question this prompts is, which is the more civilized society: one that carelessly chucks things away when they're no longer wanted, or one that is constantly inventing clever new contraptions out of their trash?

Any fool can dig a hole, but it takes a clever one to know when to stop digging.

Three boys playing near Stig's rubbish dump, illustrated by British artist Edward Ardizzone for the first edition.

Modern Narratives 151

JOAN AIKEN

THE WOLVES OF WILLOUGHBY CHASE (1963)

In a period of English history that never happened, timid orphan Sylvia Green and her dauntless cousin Bonnie Green contend with wolves and villains when Bonnie's parents travel abroad and their ship sinks.

Joan Aiken (1924–2004) was born in England into an American-Canadian literary family. Conrad Aiken had won the Pulitzer Prize in 1930 and was a friend of T. S. Eliot. Her mother, Jessie McDonald, homeschooled Joan until the age of twelve.

Aiken was made a member of the Order of the British Empire in 1999 for her services to children's literature. A treasure-trove of information about Aiken's books and life is maintained by her daughter Lizza Aiken.

The Wolves of Willoughby Chase is regarded as a key pioneer of alternative history in children's fiction, with Aiken reimagining English royal history for the setting of her tale.

It is midwinter in England, 1832. Good King James III has just been crowned. Packs of starving wolves from Europe and Russia roam the snow-covered British Isles, driven by harsh winters to migrate through the recently completed Channel Tunnel between Dover and Calais. In London, orphaned Sylvia Green is about to leave her poverty-stricken elderly aunt to go and live with a wealthy cousin in the north of England, Bonnie Green, whose home is Willoughby Chase, a grand mansion set in acres of parkland. After a long and dangerous train journey, Sylvia is warmly received by her generous and loving cousin. The girls do not have long to enjoy themselves together, however: with the departure of Bonnie's parents for a trip abroad, the wicked Miss Slighcarp, a distant cousin employed as a governess, takes charge and Bonnie's and Sylvia's fortunes take a turn for the worse. The girls must face danger from outside and within before good wins over evil.

The Wolves of Willoughby Chase has been in print in Britain and the United States since its publication in 1962. On the book's fiftieth anniversary in 2012, it was described in the *Washington Post* as "the most quietly influential children's fantasy novel of its time"; a film of the book was released in 1989 and it has also been adapted for the stage. The timeless success of this classic (and the other eleven books of the "Wolves Chronicles" series) lies in Joan Aiken's talent for storytelling. The books combine almost countless adventure motifs and fantastic tropes—child heroes pitted against adult villains, loyal friendships, dastardly conspiracies, mistaken identities, and rags-to-riches revelations, wild chases, and sea voyages to distant lands, dangerous animals, descriptions of mouth-watering, and revolting, food—but with a lightness of touch that, along with the fast-paced action, keeps cliché at bay and the reader captivated.

"I love messing about with history. I feel about it the way Alice did about the Looking Glass House. Supposing we could go back, and it was all different," Aiken commented in an interview. Her books blend alternative history with Dickensian settings, fantasy, gothic fairy tale, and a dash of Victorian steampunk. Vividly described physical settings, sharply crafted

dialogue and adroitly chosen names are also crucial to the compelling world that she fashioned. Willoughby Chase, the "warm and welcoming stronghold" set in the "heart of the world" that Sylvia sees first with every window lit up contrasts with the "fearsome fiery glare" of Blastburn, the industrial town where "huge slag-heaps stood outlined like black pyramids against the red sky" and the girls find themselves captive in a poorhouselike school run by Miss Slighcarp's accomplice, the brutal Mrs. Brisket.

Aiken was a prolific writer, publishing not only children's books but also short stories, ghost stories, romances, and several sequels to Jane Austen's novels. She said that she wrote books because she loved reading so much as a child and wanted to give others the same experience.

She reflected at length on the process of writing for children in her nonfiction work *The Way to Write for Children: An Introduction to the Craft of Writing Children's Literature*, first published in 1982 and re-issued in revised form in 1998. "It is the writer's duty to demonstrate to children that the world is not a simple place. Far from it. The world is an infinitely rich, strange, confusing, wonderful, cruel, mysterious, beautiful, inexplicable riddle," she wrote, continuing, "Children need to get from the stories they read a sense of their own inner existence, and the archetypal links that connect them with the unexplored past; of the similarity in patterns between large and small, old and new; they need to receive something that extends beyond ordinary reality."

> Snow lay piled on the dark road across Willoughby Wold, but from dawn men had been clearing it with brooms and shovels. There were hundreds of them at work, wrapped in sacking because of the bitter cold, and keeping together in groups for fear of the wolves, grown savage and reckless from hunger.

Previous page: The original artwork for the cover of the 2012 Vintage edition of *The Wolves of Willoughby Chase*, by Rohan Daniel Eason.

ROALD DAHL

Charlie and the Chocolate Factory (1964)

Charlie Bucket wins a golden ticket to Willy Wonka's marvelous chocolate factory, where chocolate rivers flow and nuts are sorted by trained squirrels.

Six-foot-six in height, hardened by testing wartime service, strong in his opinions and never shy in imparting them, Dahl made an explosive entry into the tranquil world of 1960s British children's fiction. Shunned at first by Puffin Books and other paperback publishers, Dahl's massive sales soon had them all chasing after him.

His second children's story, *Charlie and the Chocolate Factory*, went on to be filmed and made into a musical. Its faultless young hero, Charlie Bucket, lives amicably but in great poverty with his parents and four grandparents all squeezed into a house too small for them. Cold and hungry, Charlie longs each day for the delicious chocolate manufactured in a factory he passes on his way to school. This is owned by the mysterious Mr. Willy Wonka, not seen for the last ten years. But Charlie's luck turns when he and four other children win a Golden Ticket entitling them to a factory tour and all the sweets and chocolates they want for the rest of their lives.

It is soon apparent that Charlie is the only likable kid there. Augustus Gloop is an overweight glutton, spoiled Veruca Salt keeps wanting everything for herself, Violet Beauregarde incessantly chews gum before parking it anywhere she likes, and Mike Teavee keeps rudely demanding to view more television programs. Each disappears after getting their comeuppance, leaving Charlie to complete the tour on his own. Sailing down rivers of chocolate on Wonka's pink boat he visits a series of rooms crammed with gigantic machinery making different, exotic sweets.

The four missing children finally reappear but in poor shape: Augustus is now "thin as a straw," Veruca is covered in trash, Violet's face has turned purple, and Mike has been stretched to ten feet by one of the machines. But as they depart Dahl does add that they should not be entirely blamed for all their faults. In the case of Veruca, for example:

Since first publication, *Charlie and the Chocolate Factory* has sold more than 20 million copies and spawned iconic film adaptations.

Although Roald Dahl (1916-1990) is best known for his rambunctious children's tales, he also wrote over twenty short-story collections for adults, as well as the highly celebrated memoirs *Boy: Tales of a Childhood* (1984) and *Going Solo* (1986).

Quentin Blake's illustration style has become synonymous with the book; Blake collaborated extensively with Roald Dahl and illustrated 18 of his titles.

For though she's spoiled, and dreadfully so
A girl can't spoil herself, you know.
Who spoiled her, then? Ah, who indeed?
Who pandered to her every need?
Who are the culprits? Who did that?
Alas! You needn't look so far
To find out whom these sinners are.
They are (and this is very sad)
Her loving parents, MOM and DAD.

But Charlie, lucky enough to have excellent parents, is given the factory as a gift. It will now also become the new family house.

Dahl loved sweet treats, remembering them as essential comfort food when he was unhappily away from home at boarding school. In later life he kept a permanent selection of chocolate bars on the family table. The idea of having an abundance of food available has always appealed, and to this Dahl adds in his own opinions and prejudices in a text as unruly as the author himself. Print sizes change from page to page, poems share space with prose, and there is never any certainty what is going to happen next.

The four children who are punished represent aspects of modern life Dahl himself hated. But he was equally emphatic about what he most treasured too. A great lover of books, remembering the joys of being read to at school, he urges readers in particular to abandon the screen and return to much loved classics from Beatrix Potter and Kenneth Grahame.

Or, as he put it:

So please, oh please, we beg, we pray,
Go throw your TV set away,
And in its place you can install
A lovely bookshelf on the wall.
Then fill the shelves with lots of books,
Ignoring all the dirty looks.

If most children caught up in this story still continued to ignore this advice they still loved the way it was put across. Dahl's uninhibited and sometimes cruel humor proved very much to their taste at a time when other writers generally preferred a gentler approach in their fiction. But he was used to toughness in his own life, in constant pain after a near fatal plane crash during the war. Children took to his books in droves, earning him millions in royalties.

Dahl was, above all, a wonderfully entertaining writer, generous with jokes and happy to go from one over-the-top excess straight to another. A devoted father who read to his children every evening, some of his subsequent stories arose from versions first heard within the family. Retiring every morning to what sometimes could be a freezing shed at the bottom of

Opppsite: Willy Wonka showing off his Inventing Room in an illustration by Quentin Blake in the 1995 edition.

This is the most important room in the entire factory! [...] All my most secret new inventions are cooking and simmering in here.

his garden, he would write till noon, constantly revising until he was satisfied. As he once said to the novelist Kingsley Amis about writing for children, "Unless you put everything you've got into it, unless you write from the heart, the kids'll have no use for it. They'll see you're putting them on and just let me tell you from experience that there's nothing kids hate worse than that. "

Many more bestsellers were to come, with Dahl constantly pushing boundaries to the delight of his readers, though not always of their elders. Jokes about dog droppings, spit, belching, wee, and poop appeared, with the title character in *The BFG* farting in front of the Queen.

Dahl had the reputation of a verbal bully at school, and some critics find this trait in his subsequent writings. Others choose to concentrate more on celebrating his wild inventiveness and huge success in drawing in so many young readers over the years. The original *Charlie and the Chocolate Factory*

"Greetings to you, the lucky finder of this Golden Ticket, from Mr. Willy Wonka!" Illustration by Quentin Blake.

shows him at his best and, for some, at his worst too. In 2023, four years after Dahl's death, Puffin books announced that they would be revising all of his texts to eliminate derogatory words and passages. In the new version of *Charlie and the Chocolate Factory* Augustus Gloop is now described as "enormous" rather than "fat," and the Oompa-Loompas go from being "tiny" to merely "small." Elsewhere, references to glass eyes, ugliness, old age, disability, and other potentially sensitive topics were removed or altered. Arguments about censorship swiftly broke out, even getting as far as the U.K.'s House of Commons. But Puffin Books' decision to re-issue the original texts in *The Roald Dahl Classic Collection* finally left readers free to choose whichever version they wanted.

RUSSELL HOBAN

THE MOUSE AND HIS CHILD
(1967)

Clockwork father and son survive sleazy dancehalls and animal lowlife as they are chased by the evil Manny Rat.

Before he became a writer, Russell Hoban (1925-2011) was an illustrator, producing covers for magazines like *Sports Illustrated* and *Time*.

The Mouse and His Child was adapted into an animated film bearing the same name in 1977, which featured British actor and director Peter Ustinov voicing the story's devious villain, Manny Rat.

Hoban was incredibly prolific over his lifetime, with more than 40 children's books alone to his name, many of which were illustrated by his wife, Lillian.

"Where are we?" the mouse child asked his father. His voice was tiny in the stillness of the night. "I don't know," the father answered. "What are we, Papa?" "I don't know. We must wait and see."

First words spoken by one of the strangest duos in children's literature: a clockwork mouse attached to his son with outstretched arms and joined hands. When wound up they move in a circle, father swinging his little son up and down. Sold from their cozy toy store they then take their place under a family Christmas tree, their dance much admired. Broken and thrown away five years later, they can now only walk straight ahead, father pushing his son backward. And wandering through the undergrowth they are soon kidnapped by Manny Rat, a criminal operator residing in a dump who reassembles discarded wind-up toys to make them his slaves.

Intent on locating the good friends they had made before they were sold, father and son manage to escape their evil captor. They then set out on an epic woodland journey, briefly joining the Caws of Art Experimental Theater Group, run by Mr. and Mrs. Crow playing to an audience of animals and insects. Future encounters are with a philosophical muskrat, a snapping turtle who talks about infinity, a friendly grasshopper, a kindly bullfrog, and some helpful birds. Manny Rat, carrying a rock with which he intends to smash these two escapees and so re-establish his murderous reputation, is again thwarted. Father, son, and friends finally return to the now also discarded original doll's house they were searching for. And Manny Rat, defeated, old, toothless but momentarily eager to turn over a new leaf, is allowed to join the community. But danger still exists.

Russell Hoban was a writer for all ages. His descriptions of gambling dens and sleazy dance halls teeming with animal low life are expert parodies of contemporary screen thrillers and pulp fiction. He explained, "I believed that the winning of the doll's house was truly a victory and I believed that victory might be a permanent thing. That's why the book is a children's book. Now I know that the winning of a doll's house may be a proper triumph for clockwork mice in a story but for human beings in real life it won't do. Nor can any victory be permanent."

Some hints of this view already exist in this story. But while such thoughts

"Where are we?" the mouse child asked his father. His voice was tiny in the stillness of the night. "I don't know," the father replied. "*What* are we Papa?" "I don't know. We must wait and see."

Illustration by the author's wife, Lillian Hoban, for the cover of the 1976 Puffin Books Edition.

plus occasional excursions into self-questioning philosophy and literary satire can be demanding, young readers still loved the main plot. The idea of finally returning to the security of a treasured home that had previously been lost has always been a powerful one. The way father and son mouse love each other without complication is also reassuring, and other characters show understanding and affection. But such moments never become sentimental; there are, too, vivid descriptions of bloodthirsty deaths as one animal routinely feasts on another for its own survival.

"What about the ultimate truth?" asks father mouse at one point. "Nothing is the ultimate truth," replies the wise bullfrog Serpentina. Older children will have plenty to think about reading this extraordinary story. Younger ones, caught up in the couple's constant battle for survival, may simply want to rush to the end to find out what finally happens. Both will have been royally entertained.

MARIAN ORŁOŃ

Detective Nosegoode and the Music Box Mystery
(Ostatnia przygoda detektywa noska) (1968)

A detective story starring a talking dog from a teacher turned librarian who sought to inspire and amuse.

Translated by Eliza Marciniak (2017).

Marian Orłoń (1932-1990) worked with Płomyczek and Swierszczyk, two of the leading Polish publications for children.

The book originally appeared in Poland in 1968 and was only published in English in 2017.

Although the Polish title, *Ostatnia przygoda Detektywa Noska*, means "Detective Nosegoode's Final Adventure," its success prompted Orłoń to write two more books starring Nosegoode and Cody, published in English as *Detective Nosegoode and the Kidnappers* and *Detective Nosegoode and the Museum Robbery*.

Elderly detective Ambrosius Nosegoode comes out of retirement to investigate the disappearance from the local clockmaker's store of a mysterious music box that was in for repair. Despite evidence of a break-in, nothing else has been stolen. Assisted by his dog Cody—who can talk, but only speaks to his master—Nosegoode follows various leads, questioning a series of suspicious characters. In fact it's a double enigma—before he can identify the thief, he has to find out what's special about the music box, which apparently hides the clue to missing treasure. Meanwhile Cody is convinced he has recognized the criminal, but he's barking up the wrong tree. As a more dogged investigator, with a better nose for scenting criminals than his canine companion, Nosegoode persists until he has solved the mystery.

This well-constructed, fluent plot provides for several episodes in various settings and a colorful assortment of characters. They range from a level-headed hero to his excitable dog, via eccentrics such as Mrs. Hardtack the neighbor, her creepy lodger "Blackbeard," Ignatius Blossom the clockmaker, his naughty assistant Joey, Boniface Swallowtail the pharmacist, and more. There's lots of entertainment for the reader, a crime puzzle to work out, hair-raising moments of danger, suspense, lessons to be learned, plenty of jokes, and even some magic.

The funny character and place names are from the seamless English translation by Eliza Marciniak to retain the comedy. She captures the charm and humor of the original text perfectly. Both are complemented by Jerzy Flisak's cartoon-style illustrations, which also appeared in the first Polish publication.

Marian Orłoń combined his career as a children's writer with work as a teacher of Polish and religion, and later as a librarian. He began by writing for children's magazines, and published his first full-length story in 1962. The Nosegoode series, written at intervals, were bestsellers in Poland, and have since been translated into six languages. In 1981 he won Poland's highest literary honor, the Council of Ministers award, for his life work.

Detective stories weren't typical for Orłoń's work. As his main audience was elementary-school children, he wrote about first friendships, school, and family life, and also set his heroes the problems his readers might encounter in real life. In an afterword to this book, by Ewa Niewczas, we learn that Orłoń took a responsible approach to writing for children, showing them the importance of values such as honesty, courage, and dedication. He stressed that writing for children took "the courage of an elephant that has risked entering a china shop." He saw the importance of children's books in shaping the readers' life choices and attitudes, helping them to form their characters, and prompting their curiosity about the world.

Illustrations by Jerzy Flisak for the Polish editions of *Detective Nosegoode and the Music Box Mystery* and *Detective Nosegoode and the Museum Robbery*.

"Ambrosius!" Cody said. "I bow my nose to you. You are the most brilliant detective and I'm the stupidest of all dogs. But is it my fault that there are more things on Earth than are dreamed of by dogs?"

URSULA K. LE GUIN

A Wizard of Earthsea (1968)

In a world of sorcerers and healers, Ged unleashes powers that may destroy him, but also reveals Taoist and Jungian philosophies.

Ursula K. Le Guin (1929–2018) was the first woman to win a Hugo award for best novel. Her literary career spanned nearly sixty years and produced more than twenty novels and over one hundred short stories.

A Wizard of Earthsea is the first novel in a six-part epic fantasy series.

Le Guin based this novel, first published by Parnassus Press in 1968, on two short stories she had written earlier: "The Rule of Names" (1964) and "The Word of Unbinding" (1964).

A Wizard of Earthsea has all the vital aspects of a heroic journey. The world in which it is set has magic as a part of daily life—it is "a land where sorcerers come thick." Magic is respected, its users trained to be a vital part of society, be it as healers of the sick or engineers of safe boats and ships. Earthsea has its own creation myth; it has a political system; there is an economy; a social hierarchy even where the "wizard born" consider themselves superior; there is disease, piracy and warmongering that endangers lives; a shipping trade; smiths who work in bronze and iron; livestock and farming. There are also dragons to fear, huge ancient magical beasts that sound like an avalanche when they speak and "have their own wisdom [and] they are an older race than man." Earthsea is a classic example of Le Guin's strong world building, rock-solid yet never heavy-handed.

The journey the of central character Ged begins in a way that is now standard for a hero's epic fantasy journey. He is a lonely young goatherd who doesn't have much, he lives in a poor village, is motherless but has magical abilities greater than he can perceive. He is partly trained by his aunt who is a witch, but her skills are far less than his, and she has only a superficial understanding of the craft. Ged eventually reaches a school for wizards, where he finds himself among other young men with similar abilities. In attempting to impress them with his power, he sets free an evil that nearly kills him, one that he then has to struggle to find and face among the islands of Earthsea.

Earthsea is a large archipelago; three of the islands are named for Le Guin's children's pets, the others named in ways that sounded "right" to her. Earthsea's civilization is preindustrial but literate, with an inbuilt, accepted system of magic as part of its history and culture. The magic system is such that knowing the true name of something or someone in "Old Speech" gives you power over it or them. It is not possible to lie in true speech, so to speak a truth is to make it happen, though of course only those with powerful abilities can force such transformations, and each have repercussions. Earthsea's magic isn't without its checks and balances.

Language is important. The idea of words as power and that of true

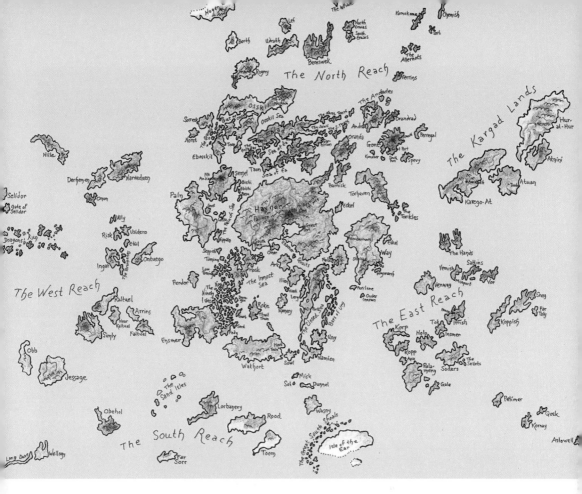

A map of Earthsea drawn by Ursula K. Le Guin and used with permission of her estate.

names can be traced back to many real-world tribal societies and to Le Guin's interest in anthropology. The people of Earthsea are genuinely multiracial and multicultural, without any implication that the few who are of lighter skin are superior in any way. Le Guin has openly criticized the common assumption that sets much Western fantasy in a Eurocentric version of the Middle Ages. Earthsea is, in a way, the anti-Middle-earth. It's an archipelago, it is home to many people of color, and, in it, Le Guin is more focused on the personal development of its individual residents than large-scale wars. Ged isn't in a constant battle with a large army—his battle is with his shadow self and, along the way, he must complete tasks that fade in comparison to his ultimate quest.

Magic may be a part of Earthsea's culture, but so is spirituality. Le Guin has based the spiritual systems of her world more on psychology and anthropology than on a monotheistic religious model. Through the entire series, there is a very strong element of Taoism, especially in regard to the magical balances required. In *A Wizard of Earthsea*, Ged's battle with his shadow self is clearly Jungian, though he, too, believes in the Taoist idea of Dynamic Balance. As he is taught, to light a candle is to throw a shadow.

Overleaf: Illustrations by David Lupton for the Folio Society edition, 2023.

Modern Narratives

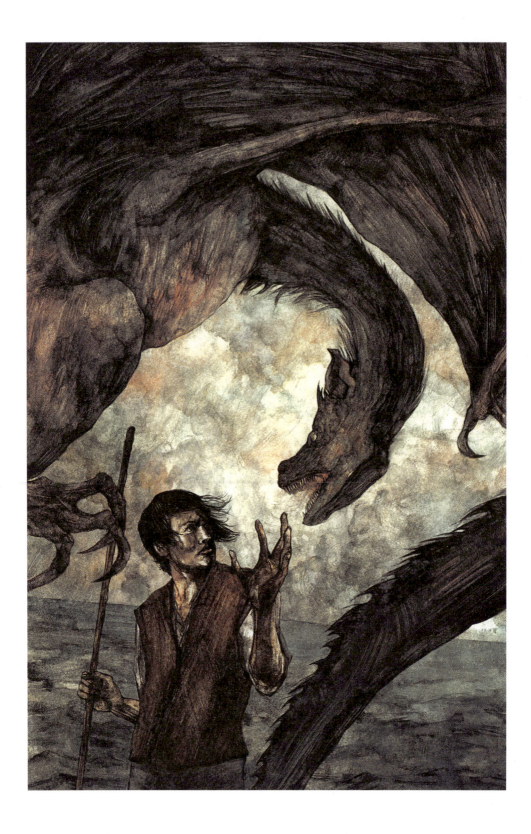

ANNIE M. G. SCHMIDT

The Cat Who Came in off the Roof (Minoes) (1970)

A cat woman and reporter tackle the big polluter and kick back against conservative repression.

Translated by David Colmer (2014).

In 1988, Annie M. G. Schmidt (1911–1995) was presented with the Hans Christian Andersen Award by Astrid Lindgren, who lamented the relative lack of translations of Schmidt's work. "Annie," she said, "I love you so much, where have you been all my life?"

The Cat Who Came in off the Roof has been translated into thirty-one languages.

Miss Minoes, the English title of the novel's movie adaptation, was filmed in 2001 with a young Carice van Houten in the lead role. Van Houten has gone on to star in movies and TV series like *Game of Thrones* (Melisandre).

With a status in the Netherlands that compares to Astrid Lindgren's in Sweden or Roald Dahl's in the United Kingdom, Anna (Annie) Maria Geertruida Schmidt is considered the queen of twentieth-century Dutch children's literature. Born into a Calvinist minister's family in Zeeland in 1911, her literary career took off in Amsterdam after the war when she was employed as an archivist by the former resistance newspaper *Het Parool*. There she began writing and publishing poems and stories for children. Her work stood out for its strong sense of humor, its stylistic control and originality, its sympathy for and understanding of children, and its irreverent, no-nonsense anti-authoritarianism.

The collections of the *Jip and Janneke* stories she published in the newspaper with the now iconic Fiep Westendorp illustrations are bestsellers to this day and helped, with their celebration of children's mischievous creativity, to reshape not only Dutch children's literature, but also attitudes to child-raising and early-childhood education. Because of the limitations of cheap postwar newspaper printing, Westendorp drew the characters as silhouettes that recall the paper-cutting style popular in the eighteenth and nineteenth centuries. These figures can still be seen on many children's products in the Netherlands.

The Cat Who Came in off the Roof is Schmidt's most popular work for older children. The eponymous heroine—Minou in the current English translation—is a young woman, or rather, a young cat who has been transformed into human form by a mysterious contamination. This transformation, however, is far from complete, as Minou retains many catlike qualities, including the ability to walk on rooftops, sing the Yawl-Yowl Song, and speak fluent Cattish. Rejected by her sister and driven out of the garden she calls home, Minou is facing life as a stray, before being taken in by Tibble, an ineffective reporter who is about to be sacked for being too shy to ask questions. (He first encounters her just after she has been treed by a large dog.) Minou repays Tibble's hospitality by saving his job with scoop after scoop from her wide network of feline informants, the Cat Press Agency. The book is rich with situational comedy, such as the scene in which Tibble sends Minou to a psychiatrist to try to resolve her behavioral problems.

"Perhaps you can start by telling me your name," the doctor said, holding a pen over a card for his files.

"Minou."

MINOU, he wrote down. "Is that your first name? Or your last name?"

"It's the name they gave me."

"Ah, Minou is your given name. What's your family name?"

She was silent for a very long time, watching a fly buzz past the window. Then she said, "I don't think I have one."

"Really? What's your father's name?" the doctor asked, holding his pen ready again.

Minou thought for a moment, trying to remember, then said quietly, "He was a tom . . ."

TOM, wrote the doctor.

"At the back of a house . . ."

BACKHOUSE . . .

"Near one of the parks."

PARKES . . .

"Tom Backhouse-Parkes," said the doctor, reading what he'd noted down. "That's your name too then. Miss M. Backhouse-Parkes. Now tell me, what's bothering you?"

Illustration by Carl Hollander for the Dutch third edition, printed in 1971.

Superficially the story is about Minou and Tibble's attempt to expose the villainous businessman and developer Mr. Ellmore and prevent him from expanding his polluting factory, but the essential story is one of identity and change and Minou's struggle to reconcile her new human state with her cattish qualities. *The Cat Who Came in off the Roof* is a warm, funny book that proves especially irresistible for cat lovers.

Besides children's books and her many published poems for children, Schmidt also wrote poetry for adults and musicals for both adults and children, often working in long-term collaboration with illustrators and composers. With its skillful deployment of meter and rhyme, her poetry is also much loved and even now, up to seventy years later, many Dutch people can quote at least a line or two from one of her poems or songs. Her work captured the public imagination not just for stylistic reasons, but also because of the way its rejection of the repressive conservatism of traditional Dutch society resonated with the liberalization of society and the postwar generation's longing for individual freedom.

JUDY BLUME

Are You There God? It's Me, Margaret (1970)

A compelling portrait of the everyday trials of tween life that pioneered realism in fiction for generations.

Judy Blume (b.1938) is an American author whose honest depictions of teenage life in the American family have propelled her total book sales to over 82 million copies worldwide.

In 1970, *Are You There God? It's Me, Margaret* was named New York Times Outstanding Book of the Year and chosen by Scholastic for 100 Greatest Books for Kids.

Blume has constantly updated the book to keep ahead of product trends in female hygiene.

Blume refused to sell the movie rights for almost fifty years. When the 2023 film adaptation came out, she described it as a "dream come true."

Generations of readers have grown up with Judy Blume, finding themselves engrossed in *Tales of a Fourth-Grade Nothing* as children, *Deenie* as middle schoolers, and *Forever...* as young adults. Her books have been translated into more than thirty languages, and more than 80 million of them have been sold worldwide. And Blume—who lives in Florida, where she cofounded Books & Books independent bookstore—has been an enduring presence in U.S. culture as a writer and an outspoken opponent of censorship.

In 1970, Blume was living with her first husband and two elementary-school-aged children in New Jersey and only beginning to establish herself as an author when she published her third and arguably most beloved novel, *Are You There God? It's Me, Margaret*.

Although his name comes first in the title, this isn't really a book about God. Instead, it follows Margaret Ann Simon through her sixth-grade year after her parents decide to move from New York City to suburban New Jersey. Over the course of the novel, Margaret—whose nonpracticing Jewish father and Christian mother have not raised her in a faith tradition—does talk to God about her problems and sets out to learn more about religion for a school project. Just as importantly, though, she navigates her new friendship with confident, know-it-all Nancy Wheeler; develops her first crush; meets her estranged maternal grandparents; turns twelve; and worries about whether she and her body are "normal." Near the end of the novel, the increasingly angst-ridden Margaret wonders,

> What was wrong with me anyway? When I was eleven I hardly ever cried. Now anything and everything could start me bawling. I wanted to talk it over with God. But I wasn't about to let him know that, even though I missed him.

Though she gets no closer to choosing a religion, when her last day of sixth grade coincides with the arrival of her longed-for first period, Margaret enthusiastically and gratefully reaches out to God again.

Margaret Simon (Abby Ryder Fortson) and Sylvia Simon (Kathy Bates), in a still from the film adaption of *Are You There God? It's Me, Margaret* (2023).

While she does grapple with some weighty concepts, the book also takes seriously the more mundane aspects of leaving childhood and entering adolescence. In one of the novel's most famous sequences, Margaret and her friends chant "We must, we must, we must increase our busts" while doing an exercise that Nancy insists will help them develop more quickly; this moment, while funny, offers commentary on the demands that beauty standards place on girls and women. Along the way, without ever becoming preachy, Blume introduces subtle but important insights about believing rumors, forgiving ourselves for our worst behavior, and finding our own voices in the face of pressure to conform.

A compelling portrait of the everyday trials of tween life, *Are You There God?* has, like many of Blume's books, been the subject of controversy. For decades, it appeared in the American Library Association's list of most frequently challenged books because of both its straightforward discussions of puberty and the fact that Margaret is given the chance to choose a religion (or no religion) for herself. Whether being celebrated for its authenticity or condemned for its commitment to being honest with child readers, *Are You There God?* had an undeniable impact on literature and culture, the effects of which can be traced through much of the realistic fiction for young readers that has emerged in the years since its initial publication.

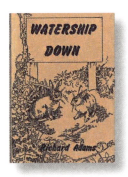

RICHARD ADAMS

Watership Down (1972)

A rural tale of danger, deceit, and redemption played out among rabbits in their burrows, nestled among the fields of southern England.

Watership Down was Richard Adams's first book, which he developed from stories improvised for his daughters on long car journeys.

Watership Down was first adapted into a feature-length animation by Martin Rosen (1978) and second, into a four-part CGI miniseries in a BBC/Netflix collaboration (2018).

Adams invented a rabbit lexicon for the novel, examples of which include: *hrair* (a lot, or a thousand) and *hrududu* (tractor or any motor vehicle). His depiction of rabbit culture was supplemented by factual details drawn from Ronald Lockley's *The Private Life of the Rabbit* (1964).

"Come where the grass is greener / And the lettuces grow in rows / And a rabbit of free demeanor / Is known by his well-scratched nose." So sings Bluebell, the would-be rhymester and jester rabbit within *Watership Down*'s band of breakaways who abandon their home at the beginning of the novel to find a new warren—one, unlike Sandleford, which will be safe from human interference and *elil* ("rabbit enemies"). Richard Adams's richly lyrical narration envelops readers in a "great, indestructible flood of Rabbitry," which he imagines as an elaborately anthropomorphized rabbit culture, with its own proverbs and Lapine language.

The titular Watership Down, where the rabbits settle, is a real place situated at Ecchinswell in Hampshire, England, near where Adams lived: an Edenic promontory of soft earth, lit up on first sight "like a gold rind." It is a world astir with the small whispers, dancing wind, flickering light, and sensuously minute movements of the countryside. A haven for Hazel (the judicious and self-sacrificing leader of the group), Bigwig (its strong but occasionally hot-headed defender), Blackberry (the cleverest), Dandelion (the storyteller), and miscellaneous other members undefined by archetype, the Down offers them safety, comfort, and the company of would-be friends of the sky and undergrowth.

Whimsical but also, in places, brutal—as anyone who has watched the Martin Rosen 1978 animated adaptation will know—*Watership Down* is "a novel that pulls children toward adulthood," as Nicholas Lezard observes, representing the conflict within the rabbits' fragile social world, as well as the human violence that threatens a more comprehensive devastation to rabbit environments. While it is a tale of suspense, adventure, survival, and jeopardy, marked by the very human discourses of power and class (particularly evident in the representation of the fascist regime at the warren *Efrafa*), it is also a mythically proportioned work of literary ambition and poetic sensitivity.

Each chapter is paired with a highbrow epigraph, with the tone set by the first choice, Aeschylus's *Agamemnon*, which establishes Fiver as a kind of rabbit–Cassandra. The field, he glimpses in a premonition, is "covered in blood!" Subsequent chapters draw on moments in the works of Shakespeare, Dostoevsky, John Bunyan, Robert Browning, Walter de la Mare, W. H. Auden, and even Napoleon Bonaparte to consolidate the sense that this modest children's story belongs to a long, self-consciously gilded tradition of western literature. Steeping the book in an invented mythos of rabbitry, which includes the fables retold by Dandelion about the rabbit sun-god Frith and the heroic trickster "El-ahrairah" (from whom "Odysseus himself might have borrowed a trick or two"), Adams establishes his novel as a kind of rabbit epic, noticeably nostalgic for a rural past.

> "Animals don't behave like men," he said. "If they have to fight, they fight; and if they have to kill they kill. But they don't sit down and set their wits to work to devise ways of spoiling other creatures' lives and hurting them. They have dignity and animality."

Indeed, Adams's book articulates an anti-modern stance whose reactionism is only more pronounced for a modern-day reader. Many will find the Orientalism that marks the rabbits' depiction offensive, as evident in the close resemblance between Lapine and Arabic, in the characterization of El-ahrairah as "The Prince with a Thousand Enemies" and "so many wives that there was no counting them," and in the repeated comparisons between rabbits and "primitive people." While the protagonists are exclusively buck rabbits, females only enter the story only to solve the problem of "breeding stock" for the warren; they lack substantial characterization, and no doe speaks until two-thirds of the way through the book.

Adams's book enchants as a sensorily minute picture of the North Hampshire fields: this is a chorus of "ubiquitous restlessness," of smells, noises, shadows, and weeds ("all growing in the green gloom") as well as tenderly noticed flowers ("such pink lousewort with its sprays of hooked flowers, bog asphodel, and the thin-stemmed blooms of the sun-dews"), and "creatures that have neither clocks nor books [but] are alive to all manner of knowledge about time and the weather." As a paean to the nervous and fleet-of-foot, *Watership Down* beguiles readers with its alertness to the "hesitant approaches, silences, pauses, movements, crouchings side-by-side" of "the rabbit awake" who is watchfully perceptive. It brims with a warm-hearted curiosity for creaturely worlds so easily overlooked.

The rabbits of Watership Down on a hillside, illustrated by Paolo D'Altan for the 2008 Young Reader edition.

SUSAN COOPER

THE DARK IS RISING (1973)

A group of children are recruited into the epic battle between Light and Dark in an ode to the English village and the layers of magic, myth and folklore that underpin even the most ordinary-seeming places.

Susan Cooper (b. 1935) was a student at Oxford University while both J. R. R. Tolkien and C. S. Lewis were teaching. She attended lectures by both.

The Dark Is Rising is the second of five books in the titular *The Dark is Rising* sequence. The books were published over a decade (1965–77) and won numerous awards, including a Newbery Medal (*The Grey King*) and a Newbery Honor (*The Dark is Rising*).

The first book in the series, *Over Sea, Under Stone* (1965), was meant to stand alone. Cooper began writing *The Dark Is Rising* and realized they were connected: she then plotted out the rest of the series.

The Dark Is Rising, the second, and most famous, of the series, begins on the eve of Will Stanton's eleventh birthday. Will lives in the village of Huntercombe, nestled in the Thames Valley. At the start of the book, he learns he is the last of the Old Ones, a group of near-immortals that secretly protect humanity from the Dark. The Light and the Dark have been jockeying for position since the dawn of humanity; a brutal competition that can read more realpolitik than ideological. The Dark are, as the title indicates, on the verge of power, and Will is essential to holding them at bay.

Despite this heroic set-up, Will's role is more witness than champion. Events have been centuries or more in the making, waiting for his presence to trigger. He is important, but as a catalyst. Will is immensely significant and wildly powerful, but he is also only eleven years old. This balance—between the ageless and the now—is also a recurring theme in *The Dark Is Rising's* sense of place.

That place is remarkably confined, at least, geographically. From the opening pages, Will's village is "the world." Everything significant that has happened, and will happen, takes place within the boundaries of Huntercombe.

The village is quaint, but that charm conceals hidden depths, a strata of mythology underfoot. The paths that Will walks down are ancient roads, imbued with their own powers. The local church conceals ancient, pagan magic. The town blacksmith represents a timeless order. The local gentry conceals a long occult tradition. Every object in the village—and seemingly every resident—is merely the most recent representative in an unbroken chain. Will frequently blinks backward in time, and these episodes reinforce that magic is everywhere; beneath us and behind us.

Well, not everywhere, because the focus is on the specific importance of rural England. The rest of the country, and planet, exists—there are mentions of Slough, Eton, and London, with family members off at school and in the military. There is also one tantalizing reference to an Old One in Kingston, met by Will's brother in the Navy. But even that encounter ends

> If you were born with the gift, then you must serve it, and nothing in this world or out of it may stand in the way of that service, because that is why you were born and that is the Law.

with a powerful artifact being shipped back to England where it belongs in an act of inverse colonization. At eleven years old, it is understandable that Will's universe exists only as far as he can see. However, beyond that, this vast cosmic dispute is being resolved in a cozy corner of Buckinghamshire.

The Dark Is Rising is an ode to English rural life. Hunterscombe is a myth in and of itself; a self-contained world where everyone knows everyone and young children wander freely. It is demographically homogeneous and undeniably picturesque, but, despite its seeming Anglocentricity, the story alludes to a different future. Hunterscombe is, subtly, changing. The ancient Saxon church is crumbling and the lordly manor has been refurbished. The bus conductor is from Trinidad. The schoolteacher who taught the whole family is now retired—and lives in genteel poverty. And, of course, the last of the Old Ones has been born. Change is coming: it is neither good nor bad in and of itself, but the reader can sense that another layer of myth is about to be laid to ground in Hunterscombe.

Herne the Hunter, one of the folkloric figures Will encounters in the novel, startles Henry VIII. Illustrated by by British cariacaturist and illustrator George Cruikshank.

Modern Narratives

MARGARET MAHY

THE GREAT PIRATICAL RUMBUSTIFICATION (1978)

Wildness and silliness abound when group of happy pirates take over a family home to host the best party ever, in Margaret Mahy's hilarious, high-energy story.

Before becoming a full-time writer, Margaret Mahy (1936–2012) trained and worked for 20 years as a librarian, during which time she wrote more than thirty short stories and children's books.

In 2006, for her lasting contribution to children's literature, Mahy won the prestigious Hans Christian Andersen medal, sometimes nicknamed "the Little Nobel."

In her home country of New Zealand, the Margaret Mahy Award has been given out every year since 1991 in recognition of significant contributions to children's literature, publishing, or literacy.

Margaret Mahy was the most internationally successful of New Zealand's many great children's writers, with an extensive and highly decorated career (including being awarded the prestigious Hans Christian Andersen Award in 2006). Though she wrote close to two hundred books for various ages, and is probably best known today for *The Changeover* and *The Haunting* (two fantasy novels that made her a rare double-winner of the Carnegie Medal) one of the most popular Margaret Mahy books is unquestionably *The Great Piratical Rumbustification*. Which also has—I'm sure you'll agree—pretty much the best title of any book by anyone ever.

It is a short book—a few dozen pages, just "thirteen lucky chapters," it says, and it's for younger readers. It's a very funny book, too—all of which perhaps makes it easy to dismiss by some. But it is a book of sheer brilliance, and the perfect demonstration of this New Zealand writer's apparently effortless gifts.

The book begins with a group of aging pirates. Though they have now retired to the seashore, old habits die hard, and they're starting to get restless —it's been too long since they've had a big piratical party. But they're not the only ones—the Terrapin family (Mr. and Mrs. Terrapin and their three wild sons: Alpha, Oliver, Omega) are getting restless, too. They've just moved into a brand new home—which is all very promising, even if Mr. Terrapin is apt to go green and limp at the very thought of how much he had to pay for it.

When Mr. and Mrs. Terrapin decide to go out one evening for some important soup, they call for a babysitter, but it doesn't take long to notice that the sitter who arrives—Orpheus Clinker, with his wooden leg and hook hand, and the bottle of rum in his pocket—is, undeniably, a pirate.

The moment their parents are out the door, the boys learn that their visitor has exciting plans. After all, he says, "I'm not the only pirate in the city, and this house is crying out for festivity and rumbustification." Before long a flare has been sent up to notify the other pirates, and Orpheus Clinker is in the kitchen cooking up some Pirate Stew and wearing Mrs. Terrapin's

"I don't think parties are what they were," he said as he drove. "I remember parties that went off with a bang and seemed to fill the air with rainbows and parrot feathers."

Illustration by Quentin Blake for the cover of the first edition of *The Great Piratical Rumbustification*, originally published alongside another of Mahy's stories, *The Librarian and the Robbers*.

apron. Soon the party has begun, and all the pirates have come over. Even the 105-year-old pirate called Terrible Crabmeat is here. The boys, naturally, are delighted.

But how will their parents feel when they get back home from an extremely disappointing dinner (the most important guest never showed up, *and* none of the food had enough salt in it) only to find a Great Piratical Rumbustification in full swing in their lovely new house?

The set-up is a joy, and the simple but cleverly constructed plot brings the story to a satisfying denouement for all concerned. (Well, at least until the next rumbustification, which we are promised won't be long in happening). The whole world of the book is patently ridiculous, but it's also sort of sidelong to the recognizable real world. It shows Mahy's real relish in language, a pleasure that is uncompromised—it's full of of juicy, interesting, high-voltage words. (Impulsive! Despondency! Metropolis! Disgruntled! Ominously! Delicacy! Doubloons!)

Oh, and if that weren't enough, Mahy's publisher paired her story with the perfect illustrator. Quentin Blake—known for his collaborations with Roald Dahl and others, as well as his own astonishing picture-book creations—has just the right spiky anarchic energy to enhance Mahy's superb text.

The Great Piratical Rumbustification was originally published in a volume with another story, *The Librarian and the Robbers*, in which a group of robbers are outsmarted—obviously—by the clever librarian they attempt to kidnap. Needless to say, the robbers are no match for a resourceful librarian and her stories (and her shelving classification system). The great Margaret Mahy had been a librarian herself, and knew what she was talking about.

Maurice Gee

Under the Mountain (1979)

A compelling and thought-provoking fantasy-cum-science-fiction novel about eleven-year-old twins from New Zealand who are tasked with saving the world from menacing, mud-dwelling aliens.

Following in the footsteps of J. R. R. Tolkien's Middle-earth and C. S. Lewis's Narnia, *Under the Mountain* by Maurice Gee is set in a convincing and chilling 1970s otherworld beneath the dormant volcanoes that dot the real-world landscape of Auckland, New Zealand. The story centers around Auckland harbor, Mt. Eden, and the volcanic island of Rangitoto—which, as Gee presciently points out, means "bleeding skies" in Māori.

Into this vibrant city, Gee introduces an underbelly of giant slugs from another planet, dangerous shapeshifters, and a lonely wizard with telepathic and telekinetic powers. Below the mountains, craters, lakes, forests, and suburbs of Auckland, the menacing Wilberforce family are carving out a subterranean world riddled with glass-lined tunnels for speedy escapes and yawning caverns housing giant, mud-sucking alien slugs. These creatures are about to launch an attack on an unsuspecting world by drowning it and its inhabitants in a sea of mud.

While the book was originally published in 1979, the message it carries is still pertinent. In describing the Wilberforces, the alien Mr. Jones comments:

> They're creatures of tremendous will—no imagination, no feeling, no conscience. They remind me of some of the leaders of your race.

Gee also explores the power of opposites, as the enigmatic Mr. Jones tutors the red-headed twins, Theo and Rachel Matheson, in how to fulfill their destiny and stop these alien creatures. Like Dr. Who, Mr. Jones is the last of his race, and he needs the children's help to destroy the Wilberforces and their army of giant slugs.

Starting with the conceit of "linked twins," Gee takes their ability to communicate with one another through what he calls "pebbling"—dropping thoughts into one another's minds so they can speak without sound. He also gifts them enchanted stones that only they can use against the enemy. Rachel's empathy and intuition, combined with Theo's practical and analytical approach, help them escape from the implacable Wilberforces.

Maurice Gee (b. 1931) was brought up in the Auckland suburb of Henderson, New Zealand. After studying English at the University of Auckland, he became a schoolteacher for a short time, before becoming an award-winning writer.

Since first publication, *Under the Mountain* has never been out of print and in 2004, it won the Gaelyn Gordon Award, which recognizes much loved New Zealand books that did not win awards at the time of publication.

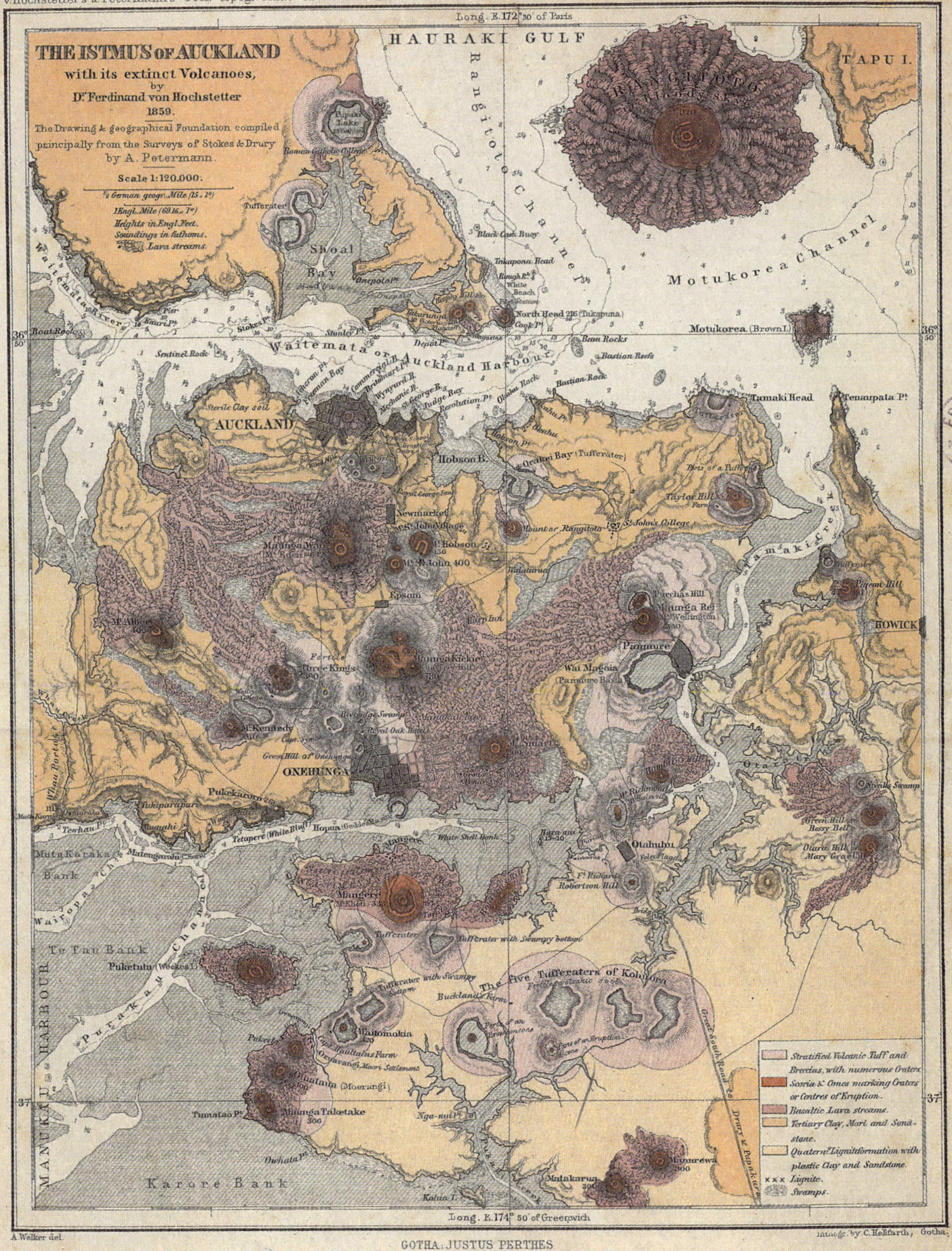

THE ISTMUS of AUCKLAND
with its extinct Volcanoes,
by
Dr Ferdinand von Hochstetter
1859.
The Drawing & geographical Foundation compiled
principally from the Surveys of Stokes & Drury
by A. Petermann.
Scale 1:120.000.

Through the twins, Gee also subtly explores the moral culpability of those who must destroy another race, albeit an alien one, to save themselves and their world. It is unusual—and at times unsettling—to find the question of genocide at the heart of a children's book.

Under the Mountain has been compared to the first book in Susan Cooper's *The Dark is Rising* sequence, in which children are also taught how to fight against an ancient evil. The fact that *Under the Mountain* has become a New Zealand classic is a testament to the quality of Gee's writing and craftsmanship, and his ability to deal with difficult moral questions in a non-didactic way. It is a case of heart-stopping adventure first and ethical navel-gazing second.

The book's rather abrupt and bleak ending ensures that the child reader is in no doubt that victory does indeed come at a cost. Luckily for the twins, the Wilberforces are amoral beings who do not have a better nature to appeal to, and in some ways this makes the children's choices easier. However, Gee provides neither his characters nor his readers with an easy way out—there is no happily-ever-after ending here. Good does finally triumph over evil, but at a cost to all involved—including Gee's otherworldly version of the city of Auckland.

Opposite: A map of the Auckland Volcanic Fields produced by Ferdinand von Hochstetter in 1859.

> An old man stood beside the sleeping children. He knelt and touched their faces. "Twins," he murmured, "twins." He touched their red hair. "Yes, yes, our colour." He looked into their minds. "And with the gift. They will be the ones."

MICHAEL ENDE

The Neverending Story
(Die Unendliche Geschichte) (1979)

The Nothing is fueled by people losing interest in books and imagination, but Bastian's stolen tome may be a way to stop it.

Translated by Ralph Manheim (1983).

The first edition of the novel was printed with red text for the events that take place in the real world inhabited by Bastian and green text for the parts of the story that occur in Fantastica.

Michael Ende (1929–1995) disliked the 1984 film adaptation of his novel so intensely that he launched legal action that delayed the release of the sequel until 1990.

Ende's father, Edgar, was a German surrealist painter and his art is believed to have influenced his son's writing.

Bastian Balthazar Bux is a lonely boy who steals an unusual book from Mr. Coreander's antiquarian bookstore. He becomes enthralled as he reads about the events taking place in Fantastica, a magical land that is being consumed by a sinister force called The Nothing and in which the ruling Childlike Empress has fallen ill. A green-skinned boy warrior named Atreyu has been chosen to find a cure for the Empress, aided by a protective medallion known as AURYN.

Numerous characters aid Atreyu, including a giant turtle named Morla the Aged One, a flying luckdragon called Falkor, and Uyulala, an invisible oracle. Uyulala explains that the only way to save the Empress is for her to be given a new name by a human being who lives outside of Fantastica. When Atreyu looks in the magic mirror gate at the Southern Oracle, one of the tests he must face, he views an image of Bastian in the human world. Bastian, in turn, becomes aware that the characters in Fantastica can see or hear him.

There are other threatening characters, such as the werewolf Gmork, but the real danger comes from The Nothing. It is fueled by humans losing interest in books and imagination, gradually consuming the fantasy world and the Fantasticans themselves. After Falkor and Atreyu return to the Childlike Empress having evaded Gmork, they are fearful that they have failed in their quest as most of Fantastica has already disappeared.

Bastian is skeptical that he can influence the story but is eventually convinced when the Old Man of Wandering Mountain reads aloud from a book called *The Neverending Story*, which begins with Bastian stealing the book from Mr. Coreander and sitting in the attic to read it. Bastian calls out the name "Moon Child" and is transported to Fantastica. Having been brought to the Empress by Atreyu he uses his imagination to restore the beings and places that have disappeared.

The second half of Ende's story involves Bastian's time within Fantastica after the Empress has given him AURYN, on the back of which is inscribed the words "Do What You Wish." Unlike the fearless Atreyu, Bastian is not an ideal hero. With every wish he progressively loses his memories, abuses

Die Begegnung (*The Encounter*, 1933) by the surrealist painter Edgar Ende, Michael's father.

magic objects to cater to his vanity, and causes havoc by creating beings so that he can conquer them. Eventually Bastian loses almost all of his identity and the evil sorceress Xayide is able to urge him to seize the role of the emperor of Fantastica. The human boy is reduced to an empty husk with only two memories: that of his father and of his name.

Children's literature often clearly rewards good characters and punishes evil ones, yet *The Neverending Story* suggests that both good and bad are essential elements of life and storytelling. The Childlike Empress considers all her subjects to be equal and does not interfere in their actions: "Every creature, whether good or bad, beautiful or ugly, merry or solemn, foolish or wise—all owed their existence to her existence." AURYN, a powerful medallion comprised of entwined black and white snakes consuming each other's tails that is often depicted on the book's cover, symbolizes the way in which light and dark must coexist in Fantastica.

Aided by Atreyu and Falkor, Bastian is eventually reunited with his father in the real world with his memories restored. His father is relieved to see his son, who has only been missing for one night in the real world. Bastian's journey to Fantastica brings to light the qualities that he already possessed. Much as the characters in *The Wizard of Oz* (1900) make the journey down the yellow brick road to be rewarded with the traits of courage, wisdom, and heart that they have already demonstrated during their adventures, so too does Bastian finally realize that he had always possessed the qualities of courage and faithfulness.

MICHAEL MORPURGO

WAR HORSE (1982)

Farm-horse Joey and farm-boy Albert grow up together. But at the outbreak of war, the horse is sold into the army and sent to the trenches, recounting the good and evil on both sides of the carnage he observes as he searches for Albert.

Michael Morpurgo (b. 1943) taught in a primary school in Canterbury, England, before beginning a writing career in children's literature that would see over 50 of his books published.

Since its publication in 1982, War Horse has been translated into over 40 languages and sold 1.4 million copies in the UK alone.

The stage adaptation of War Horse opened at the National Theatre, London, in October 2007 and was rapturously received by critics and audiences. In December 2010, the play was named "the theatrical event of the decade" by The Times. In 2011, a film adaptation of the novel was released, directed by Steven Spielberg.

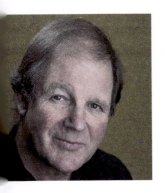

War Horse is a raw and emotional story told simply and powerfully. Carrying an antiwar message that was close to Morpurgo's heart, *War Horse* captures all the familiar ingredients of World War I stories from the sociopolitical, including the scale of the disaster in terms of lives lost and the chaos of the military and political leadership, to the domestic details of the mud, the wire, and the pain. It is designed to shock but that shock is ameliorated for young readers by Morpurgo's original storytelling touch: the narrator is a horse called Joey.

Joey is a Devon, England, farm horse sold into the army. Uprooted from his peaceful life on a Devon farm he spends his time on the Western Front and elsewhere searching for Albert, the young farmhand who, like his horse had been conscripted into the army. As a narrator, Joey has the great advantage of being neutral in his views of all those involved. He "sees" the war from both sides and he even works for both sides—first the British Army and then the Germans. He finds that the work and the human qualities are very much the same in both camps. Specifically, with no historic hatred of Germans his interpretation is that the German soldiers are just young boys—more like his beloved Albert than different.

In his storytelling, Morpurgo largely uses Joey's perspective as a fresh way of reporting the familiar. But, in his most original touches, as in a scene set in No Man's Land, he creates invented scenes in which Joey's views become more human, giving a picture of Morpurgo's own views on the futility of war.

After much drama and jeopardy, which Morpurgo captures well, Joey is reunited with Albert. Morpurgo eschews the sentimentality that could offer. In general, the horses are not well-served by the war and it is only through a later twist of fate that Joey gets home to Devon.

Morpurgo's immediate inspiration for *War Horse* came from conversations he had with World War I veterans in the Devon pub near to his home. They shared their stories of the fighting and also highlighted the destructive impact of the war on the animals who were unwilling

> This one isn't just any old horse. There's a nobility in his eye, a regal serenity about him. Does he not personify all that men try to be and never can be?

participants. These view on war chimed with Morpurgo's own, which were forged by his experience of growing up surrounded by the devastating effect of the bombing of London in World War II.

War Horse embodies many of the themes for which Morpurgo's subsequent novels rightly became famous. The special bond between humans and animals; the importance of the countryside and the joy it can bring humans; the human folly in fighting wars and the waste they cause. Morpurgo writes lyrically about Joey and Albert's peaceful Devon life, setting it in sharp contrast with the viscerally imagined horrors of the trenches.

From the outset, *War Horse*, with its ambitious storytelling and its moving observation of war and its effects, was hailed as a book for all ages. Its enduring appeal and its successful reimagining on stage and screen is a testimony to its original and imaginative storytelling.

Joey (Finder) and Albert (Jeremy Irvine) in the 2011 film adaptation of *War Horse*, directed by Steven Spielberg.

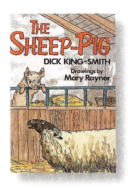

DICK KING-SMITH

The Sheep-Pig (1983)

This soft power parable starts at the fair, where Babe is won by Farmer Hogget and befriends a kind-hearted sheepdog called Fly, who will teach him the art of sheep-herding.

Ronald Gordon King-Smith (1922–2011) was a soldier in World War II and a farmer for 20 years, before becoming an elementary school teacher. It is not until 1978, while he was teaching in Somerset, U.K., that he published his first book, *The Fox Busters*.

The Sheep-Pig was inspired by King-Smith's career in farming. Pigs are unique in character, he reveals in his memoirs: " The other beasts think, 'This human is looking at me.' The pig thinks, 'I am looking at this human.' There is all the difference in the world."

The book would later go on to be adapted into the 1995 film *Babe*.

The Sheep-Pig is a warm-hearted adoption narrative in praise of self-determination and escaping the butcher's block of destiny. Accompanied by the fine black-and-white line drawings of Mary Rayner, it is the story of a pig who saves his bacon through hard work, intelligence, and kindness. Central pig protagonist, Babe, becomes a skilled and precious assistant for his human master, moving herds of sheep from place to place.

Won at a fair by a kindly man of few words, Farmer Hogget, the piglet is adopted by skilled but aging sheepdog, Fly. Brave, observant, emotionally intelligent Babe not only fits into farm life under Fly's care but soon excels. His success is rooted in his unwavering commitment (this is a pig who not only trains but diets!) and his instinctive faith in kindness and decency. He takes opportunities to get to know the sheep viewed contemptuously and treated brutally by dogs. Babe's secret—eventually adopted by Fly too and borne out by his faultless performance at the televised sheepdog trial that closes the book—is simply to ask nicely.

The depiction of English farm life is much more feel-good than that of Orwell's *Animal Farm* almost forty years earlier. But it doesn't ignore tough questions and big topics altogether. Babe loses no less than two mothers in the course of the story: first his biological mother and later his sheep friend, Maa, whose name suggests both her species and her maternal role. Like his piggy predecessor Wilbur in the acclaimed *Charlotte's Web* (1952), Babe also spends much of his time dicing with death. There is a powerful scene in which he literally looks down the barrel of a gun. But Babe is saved by the (telephone) bell, and the overall tone of the story is much more optimistic than Orwell's satire. While King-Smith brilliantly makes room for the fear and misunderstanding that groups feel toward each other (sheep and dogs alike are convinced that their opponents are totally stupid), his story shows that division can be overcome. In this soft-power parable, common decency triumphs over brute force and domination.

As in *Charlotte's Web*, correct use of words is key. Sometimes they are not needed at all: Babe and the supremely taciturn Farmer Hogget immediately

Two early, unpublished sketches by illustrator Mary Rayner for *The Sheep-Pig*.

and instinctively understand each other. But Dick King-Smith also takes huge pleasure in words in this book, as with the talkative Mrs. Hogget—whose rambling regional speech he delights in setting down. The author has immense fun with sheep-related figures of speech e.g., getting things done in the "shake of a lamb's tail," and the flock walking through a gate "like lambs." There is also a Lewis Carroll–esque reveling in sound and wordplay, including the confusion of homonyms "ewe" and "you," and the expert use of "bah" as both onomatopoeia and expression of contempt.

If *The Sheep-Pig* is a celebration of English wordplay and rural life, it has also had a significant global impact. Translated into more than a dozen languages, the story has equally been adapted to both stage (in an adaptation by David Wood) and screen. Released in 1995, motion picture *Babe* actually transfers the story to an American setting, as well as introducing new episodes and characters. But while this may sound like a recipe for disaster, *Babe* is in fact one of the rare cases of a film adaptation that fully lives up to its source. With exceptional human and animal performances enhanced by animatronics, *Babe* is a successful film in its own right. Although there are differences between the two works, the film conveys many of the key features of King-Smith's book, most especially its finely drawn characters, humor, and warmth.

Book and film alike advocate for respectful communication, kindness, intelligence, and understanding. In other words, with its simple morality in which good turns and bravery are rewarded, *The Sheep-Pig* offers a much-needed balm for our times.

4 Contemporary Classics

1985 TO PRESENT

Whether imagining worlds of magic and mystery or fictionalizing historical reality, these diverse tales have fast become children's favorites.

Concept art by Nick Keller for the film adaptation of *Mortal Engines* (2018), depicting the traction city of London.

EIKO KADONO

Kiki's Delivery Service
(Majo no Takkyūbin) (1985)

Following family tradition, the young witch Kiki travels to a new city to make a life for herself, with only her cat Jiji for company.

Translated by Lynne E. Riggs (2003).

Like Kiki, Eiko Kadono (b.1935) had experience of living in an unfamiliar place as a young woman, having left Japan in her mid-twenties to spend two years in Brazil.

Kiki's Delivery Service met with immediate success in Japan, winning both the Noma Award for Juvenile Literature and Shogakukan Award for Children's Literature. In 2018, Kadono was awarded the Hans Christian Andersen Award, recognizing her lasting contribution to children's literature.

Kiki's Delivery Service (the Japanese title of which translates literally as "Witch's Delivery Service") may be best known to Western audiences through Hayao Miyazaki's 1989 Studio Ghibli film of the same name. However, the novel on which the film is based is a classic in its own right, and its author, Eiko Kadono, is one of Japan's most distinguished children's writers. Her story of a teenage witch's attempts to make a life for herself in a new city is both a psychologically astute coming-of-age tale and a charmingly comedic take on witch stories and traditions.

Eiko Kadono was already a prolific author when, aged fifty, she published the novel that would make her internationally famous. Her first children's book, which had appeared fifteen years earlier, had drawn on her years living in Brazil, particularly her friendship with the Brazilian boy who taught her Portuguese. That was a nonfiction work, but it signaled Kadono's interest in the experience of cultural dislocation—of trying to find one's bearings in a new environment and making friends in a place where assumptions and expectations are very different from what one is used to. That interest is displayed in full in *Kiki's Delivery Service*.

The story begins with Kiki, the daughter of a witch and now on the cusp of her teenage years, about to follow the family tradition, mount her broomstick, and seek out a city where she can make a living using her magical gifts, with only her cat Jiji for company. In her hometown, where her mother Kokiri has practiced for many years, the existence of witches is warmly accepted; but the city of Koriko, where Kiki eventually settles, has not had a witch for a long time, and she finds it hard to make people appreciate the benefits of having her in their midst. However, she slowly makes friends—beginning with the owners of the bakery where she finds lodgings—and builds a business based on her ability to make airborne deliveries. The episodic narrative tells of her adventures as a one-woman delivery service, including her growing friendship with Tombo, doyen of the local Aviation Club. By the time she visits her parents at the end of her first year away, Koriko has become her home. Although a Japanese novel, its witches and witchcraft

Above: Kiki and her cat, Jiji, in the 1989 Studio Ghibli anime adaptation of *Kiki's Delivery Service*, directed by Hayao Miyazaki.

draw on Western witchcraft traditions: broomsticks, black clothes, black cats.

Kadono was initially inspired by a picture of a witch drawn by her twelve-year-old daughter, combined with the memory of a bird's-eye photograph of New York City that Kadono had seen in *Life Magazine* as a student. But the witchcraft of this world is not frightening or even particularly powerful. Kiki's is a world where witches have been gradually losing or forgetting their powers as modern life and its distractions encroach on nature. Kokiri's magical abilities are flying and making Sneeze Medicine; Kiki herself can only fly. For all the Western appearance of this book's world, it is Japanese in its minimalistic approach to magic, which, while important at the level of plot, is less central than the story of Kiki's emotional development.

When Miyazaki adapted Kadono's novel into a film, he kept many of these elements, basing the architecture of Koriko on various European locations, most prominently Stockholm and the Swedish island of Gotland; however, he reshaped the episodic plot, notably through the addition of a climactic episode involving an airship.

Kadono later wrote five sequel volumes (the final book in the series was published in 2009), following Kiki's progress into adulthood, her marriage to Tombo, and her own children's lives.

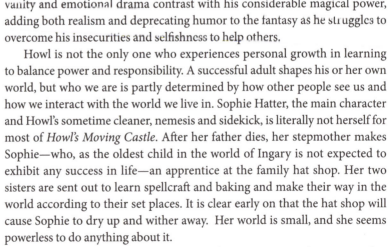

DIANA WYNNE JONES

HOWL'S MOVING CASTLE (1986)

The titular castle lurches on command around the countryside of Ingary and features magical doors that open on to different landscapes as Wizard Howl and his household battle the Witch of the Waste.

Diana Wynne Jones (1934–2011) studied English at St. Anne's College, Oxford, where she attended lectures by C. S. Lewis and J. R. R. Tolkien. Their influence is clear in her approach to fantasy—though she often parodied their seriousness.

Jones wrote the novel after a child at a school visit asked her to write about "a moving castle." That offhand suggestion stuck, and she built the story around it.

In 2004, the book was adapted into a popular movie by Studio Ghibli, directed by Hayao Miyazaki.

The world of Diana Wynne Jones's *Howl's Moving Castle* (1986) is a semi-Victorian society interwoven with familiar fairy-tale tropes and a wild assortment of characters with different magical gifts (and curses). The story is set primarily in the fictional kingdom of Ingary, where magic is a part of everyday life. Pseudo-English villages such as Market Chipping, Kingsbury, and Porthaven all have distinctive atmospheres that blend ordinary details with mysterious undercurrents. However, Howl's castle, powered by his fire demon, Calcifer, includes a portal to modern-day Wales, and Howl's home (his real name is Howell Jenkins), suggests a multiverse-like structure where magical and actual worlds coexist. The fantasy world is often accented with tongue-in-cheek practicalities and realistic personalities. For example, Howl's vanity and emotional drama contrast with his considerable magical power, adding both realism and deprecating humor to the fantasy as he struggles to overcome his insecurities and selfishness to help others.

Howl is not the only one who experiences personal growth in learning to balance power and responsibility. A successful adult shapes his or her own world, but who we are is partly determined by how other people see us and how we interact with the world we live in. Sophie Hatter, the main character and Howl's sometime cleaner, nemesis and sidekick, is literally not herself for most of *Howl's Moving Castle*. After her father dies, her stepmother makes Sophie—who, as the oldest child in the world of Ingary is not expected to exhibit any success in life—an apprentice at the family hat shop. Her two sisters are sent out to learn spellcraft and baking and make their way in the world according to their set places. It is clear early on that the hat shop will cause Sophie to dry up and wither away. Her world is small, and she seems powerless to do anything about it.

When the Witch of the Waste turns her into an actual crone, Sophie becomes further limited in her mobility, eyesight, and strength—but at the same time, when she is seen as someone very different from who she actually is, Sophie is forced to develop heretofore unknown skills and boldly make mistakes. Sophie's "curse" becomes a liberation—a metaphor for women

"'I must thank you', it said... 'I would have lain in that hedge forever if you had not come and talked life into me.'" Sophie and the Scarecrow, illustrated by Janelle Carbajal for the Folio Society's 2019 Book Illustration Competition.

feeling freed and emboldened once they are past the burden of youth and the expectations of appearance and behavior. The trope of the "loathly lady," seen in medieval stories such as The Wedding of Sir Gawain and Dame Ragnelle and Chaucer's Wife of Bath's Tale, usually involves an ugly crone who teaches a handsome hero a lesson, causing him to fall in love with her and break her curse of ugliness and old age. In a rewriting of the trope, Sophie's own power and initiative changes her world and herself (and enables Howl to defeat the Witch of the Waste). She eventually breaks her curse and finds her equal and romantic partner while not conceding any of her agency or abilities.

Sophie's journey—from self-effacing young woman to a powerful, confident figure who reframes her world out of necessity and a love for others —reflects many elements of Diana Wynne Jones's growth and challenges in her own world. She grew up in a chaotic, neglectful household during World War II. Jones was in her early fifties when she wrote *Howl's Moving Castle*, and she later commented that aging had made her stronger and more assertive in her own appearance, speech, and relationships.

Howl's Moving Castle had become a staple in children's fantasy literature, inspiring two sequels: *Castle in the Air* (1990) and *House of Many Ways* (2008), which expand on the world and its rules.

Overleaf: A still from the 2004 Studio Ghibli adaptation of *Howl's Moving Castle*.

Contemporary Classics 195

WITI IHIMAERA

The Whale Rider (1987)

A young Māori girl is excluded by her chieftain grandfather from becoming the next leader of the Whangara tribe, but proves herself worthy by rescuing and riding an ancient whale.

Witi Ihimaera (Te Whānau-a-Kai, Te Aitanga-a-Māhaki, Rongowhakaata, Ngāti Porou, Tūhoe) (b.1944) is emeritus professor of English at the University of Auckland, with more than 20 novels, memoirs and short story collections to his name. In 2017, he was the recipient of the New Zealand Prime Minister's Award for Literary Achievement.

The Whale Rider is one of the most translated books by a New Zealand author, published in more than fifteen languages. In 1995, it was translated into Māori by Tīmoti Karetu as *Kaieke Tohorā*; in 2002, it was adapted into a successful movie directed by Nikki Caro and filmed on location in New Zealand.

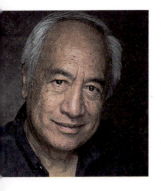

Ancestors are of particular importance to Māori in defining their identity and their connections within and between communities. The key legendary *tipuna* (ancestor) for the Whangara clan is Paikea, who is believed to have traveled from Hawaiki to New Zealand on the back of a whale. The name represents strength, endurance, and an enduring connection to the sea; a name appropriate for the Whangara, a coastal Māori community based on the East Coast of the North Island of Aotearoa New Zealand—and not coincidentally the home of Ihimaera's own community.

The Whale Rider opens with a retelling of this myth, using the narrative voice of the ancient bull whale himself. Chapters told from the perspective of the whale and his herd are interspersed with the contemporary story, bringing a sensitive interweaving of myth and reality to the novel.

A succession crisis looms for Koro, the head of the Apirana family and the Māori chieftain of the Whangara. The leader had traditionally always been male and Koro wants that tradition to continue. However, a family tragedy means that the only possible family descendent is his granddaughter, Kahu.

Koro will not accept Kahu and is intent on finding a future leader from one of the boys in the clan, while repeatedly excluding her from leadership activities. The recurring pattern in their relationship is exemplified by a key scene in the novel. Koro, at work on the outboard motor, shows Kahu a frayed rope and tells her that the interwoven strands are like the generations and must be kept strong for future survival; telling her in Māori to "weave together the threads of Paikea so that our line remains strong." But when Koro uses the rope to start the boat's engine, it breaks and he storms off. Kahu manages to mend the rope, twisting the strands tightly together but instead of thanking her, Koro scolds her.

Kahu has inherited a special connection to whales. When a pod of whales is stranded near their *marae*, she plays a key role in their rescue. It is through this special connection that she finally makes her grandfather see that, despite being a girl, she is indeed the next leader of their tribe, the next Paikea. Kahu changes Koro's entrenched ideas of leadership and evolves Māori tradition.

Still from the 2002 movie adaptation of *The Whale Rider*, featuring Keisha Castle-Hughes as the lead character Kahu Paikea Apirana.

Part of the beauty of *The Whale Rider* lies in its setting; the movie adaptation was also filmed in location on the North Eastern Cape. The book also highlights the important links to *mātauranga Māori*—Māori knowledge systems—along with the intergenerational relationships between Kahu and her grandparents who raise her. The use of the Māori language (Te Reo Māori) is woven into the mostly English text of *The Whale Rider*, reflecting the way in which the two languages and two cultures sit beside each other in New Zealand. Significantly, the novel's publication in 1987 coincided with the year that Te Reo Māori was given official status after decades of activism.

The book was conceived when Ihimaera was working as a diplomat in New York in the 1980s. A whale was spotted in the Hudson River, which affected Ihimaera deeply; he believed his ancestor Paikea had come from the Pacific to greet him and was inspired to start writing. The book was, fittingly, written for his two young daughters.

> And the whale herd sang their gladness that the tribe would also live, because they knew that the girl would need to be carefully taught before she could claim the place for her people in the world.

SALMAN RUSHDIE

Haroun and the Sea of Stories (1990)

A postmodern fairy tale and political allegory, young Haroun finds himself in a world where he must fight against a terrifying cult of silence to save the Sea of Stories—and his family—from deadly pollution.

Salman Rushdie (b.1947), grew up in Bombay (now Mumbai) and has also lived in London and New York. "Cities' stories were my story too, . . . my preferred ocean, this story-sea of concrete and steel in which I had always preferred to swim."

Rushdie has been awarded numerous literary prizes and honors for his 22 published books, and in 2023 he was one of the *Time100* list's most influential people in the world.

In 2022, Rushdie was violently attacked while on stage at a literary event in Chautauqua, New York. He describes the attack, and the remarkable recovery he made subsequently, in *Knife: Meditations After an Attempted Murder* (2024).

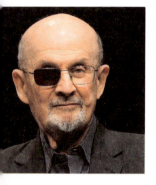

"What's the use of stories that aren't even true?" is the terrible question that young Haroun Khalifa hurls at his father, a professional storyteller (the "Ocean of Notions" to admirers, the "Shah of Blah" to jealous rivals), when his mother stops singing and runs off with the clerk upstairs, and Rashid Khalifa's previously endless stream of tales suddenly dries up. A romance-infused, journey-quest ensues. Haroun is accompanied on his adventures by Iff (a sky-blue-bearded, story-supplying Water Genie), Butt (a mechanical hoopoe-bird), two Plentimaw fish called Goopy and Bagha who speak alternately in rhyme, and Mali (a floating gardener of the First Class responsible for weeding the Sea of Stories).

The structural and thematic core of *Haroun and the Sea of Stories* is the fundamental matter of language, of free of speech versus its suppression. The world that Rushdie creates, and that Haroun inhabits, signals this overtly and subtly in different ways. The land in which Haroun lives is called Alifbay (Alif and Bay are the first two letters of the Hindustani alphabet and the word itself means "alphabet"—one of many names derived from Hindustani and glossed at the end of the book). But a pervading sorrow has seeped into people's lives and affected their memory: Haroun's home is a city "so ruinously sad it had forgotten its own name." Things aren't much better elsewhere, though up in the Mountains of M the most spectacular view on earth is still to be found—a vista of the Valley of K, "spread out like a magic carpet, waiting for someone to come and take a ride." Rashid has been booked by Valley of K politician Snooty Buttoo to tell stories ("up-beat sagas only. None of your gloompuss yarns") at a campaign rally and Haroun accompanies him.

An exuberantly funny journey by bus is just the beginning of Haroun's adventures to the Lands of Gup and Chup (separated by the Twilight Strip) and all around the Sea of Stories. In the Land of Gup, King Chattergy's army is led by General Kitab ("book"). This military "Library" is formed of Pages who are organized into Chapters and Volumes, and whose uniforms are rectangular garments covered in writing. War has been declared but before the armed Library can set off, the process of pagination and collation must be

Previous page: Haroun is carried across the Sea of Stories by Butt the Hoopoe, illustration by British cartoonist Martin Rowson.

completed. Haroun is chastized by sharp-tongued Page Blabbermouth when he comments on an apparent lack of discipline: "You shouldn't judge a book by its cover." The Guppees are up against a sinister, shadowy force led by a dark sorcerer who rules over the Land of Chup, a region of Perpetual Night. Cultmaster Khattam-Shud ("The End") "eats light raw with his bare hands" and eats words, too, having imposed fanatical Silence Laws on his subjects. Khattam-Shud's ultimate victory will be the total destruction of the Sea of Stories, which he is poisoning and whose source he plans to block.

At the heart of *Haroun and the Sea of Stories* and Rushdie's writing more widely are questions as old as time and storytelling themselves: Where do stories come from? What purposes do they serve, singly and combined? How do they help us to understand the world? Rushdie's Ocean of the Streams of Stories is an utterly mesmerizing and beautiful creation.

It is made up of "a thousand thousand and one different currents, each one a different color, weaving in and out of one another like a liquid tapestry of breathtaking complexity." Each colored strand contains a single tale and the whole liquid body is alive: the stories' fluid form means that they have the "ability to change, to become new versions of themselves, to join up with other stories and so become yet other stories".

Stories—whether intended for children or for adults—are a playground or testing ground where life and its hardest questions can be faced up to, contended with, studied, queried, overturned, rewritten. Rushdie has spent his life considering the purposes and possibilities of story, urging most recently in his autobiographical work *Knife* that "Above all, we must understand that stories are at the heart of what's happening." Rushdie's position is resolute and hopeful: "Art is not a luxury. It stands at the essence of our humanity, and it asks for no special protection except the right to exist. It accepts argument, criticism, even rejection. It does not accept violence. And in the end, it outlasts those who oppress it." The suppression of story and language is something that Rushdie knows more about firsthand than most writers, and that he has experienced at great personal cost. *Haroun and the Sea of Stories*, he stated in an essay, was conceived as a "fable about language and silence, about stories and anti-stories, written, in part, to explain to my young son the battle then swirling around his father about another novel, *The Satanic Verses*." Published in 1988, *The Satanic Verses* was banned in Pakistan and in 1989, a death-order or *fatwā* was issued by Iranian Ayatollah Ruhollah Khomeini who decreed the book blasphemous against Islam.

Perhaps one of the most appealing things about the novel is its humor and gentle arguments for balance. Haroun marvels at the opposites in the battle between Chup and Gup: "Gup is bright and Chup is dark. Gup is warm and Chup is freezing cold. Gup is all chattering and noise, whereas Chup is silent as a shadow. . . . Guppees love Stories, and Speech; Chupwalas, it seems, hate these things just as strongly." But the boy realizes that "it's not as simple as that" since "silence ha[s] its own grace and beauty (just as speech could be graceless and ugly)." This revelation builds on another discovery Haroun

Haroun speaks with the excitable mail courier, Mr. Butt, illustration by Martin Rowson.

makes at the beginning of the book when, working hard to keep his father's depressed spirits from failing utterly, he sees that just as the real world is full of magic, so too could magical worlds also be real. The book's epitaph similarly imparts this message:

> Z embla, Zenda, Xanadu:
> A ll our dream-worlds may come true.
> F airy lands are fearsome too.
> A s I wander far from view
> R ead, and bring me home to you.

In his own essays and in media interviews Rushdie has pushed back against critics' use of the label "magical realism." His writing is a kind of magic, though, and its expression makes our world a richer and more beautiful place. Children who read *Haroun and the Sea of Stories* have a strong chance of growing up knowing what Rushdie has described as the "joyful thing that happens in the act of reading, that happy union of the interior lives of author and reader." Adults who take up the book will delight in, and appreciate, the value that good storytelling brings to our lives.

PHILIP PULLMAN

THE GOLDEN COMPASS
(NORTHERN LIGHTS) (1995)

Pullman's multiverse-spanning fantasy tale is the start of the story for Lyra Belacqua, a young girl on a quest to save her friend and the choices she makes that will save or doom worlds.

Sir Philip Pullman (b.1946) is a celebrated English author of fantasy and children's literature, who first honed his narrative talent as a primary school teacher whilst reading Homer's The Iliad and Odyssey to his students.

The Golden Compass is the first book in Pullman's His Dark Materials trilogy and was originally entitled *Northern Lights* the UK and Australia.

The series has been a publishing phenomenon, selling more than 17 million copies worldwide and translated into more than 40 languages. Pullman has subsequently written additional works set in the same world as *The Golden Compass*, including The Book of Dust trilogy (2017-2025).

The Golden Compass begins in Oxford, England. It is not the Oxford University of our own world—for one thing, people in this alternative world are accompanied by daemons, physical manifestations of their souls in animal form—but one that is close enough that we can almost recognize it. It is this feeling of being somewhere that is almost recognizable—almost known, yet not quite home—that characterizes the worlds of the entire series.

Lyra is an eleven-year-old girl who has been growing up in the care of the professors at Jordan College with her daemon Pantalaimon, a shape-shifting creature that is sort of spirit animal and the representation of a person's soul. Lyra is naughty, brave, curious and clever and fate has something big in store for her though she doesn't know it yet. The book opens with Lyra hiding in a room that is forbidden to her. She creeps into a wardrobe that is "bigger than she'd thought"—echoing the wardrobe that leads to Narnia—but Lyra's wardrobe doesn't open to a new world. Instead, it is Lyra's curiosity and quest for knowledge that broadens her world. When her friend Roger goes missing, she is, at first, comforted by the appearance of the charming Mrs. Coulter—that is, until Lyra discovers that Mrs. Coulter may be complicit in her friend's kidnapping.

With the aid of the alethiometer, the titular golden compass, Lyra sets out in search of Roger. And, as she journeys to the wildness of the North, she discovers that hers may not be the only world there is.

Place is inherently tied to knowledge in the book. The witches who live in the north of Lyra's world do so because the veil between worlds is thin and their knowledge comes from this proximity. Place is also inherently tied to perspective: "Is this a new world?" one character asks, and is answered, "Not to those born in it." Things look different, depending on where they are seen.

The Subtle Knife (1997), the second book of the trilogy, begins in our world, but protagonist Will Parry soon discovers a portal to the world of Cittàgazze. Here he meets Lyra, and becomes the guardian of the subtle knife—the blade that can cut doors through universes. Yet travel between worlds is not without consequences. *In The Amber Spyglass* (2000), yet more worlds are explored.

Lyra and Pantalaimon, her daemon, meet the armored bear, Iorek Byrnison in the 2007 film adaptation directed by Chris Weitz.

From the land of the dead to that of the elephantine mulefa, Lyra is forced to make her fated choice. But once Lyra's choice is made, the doors between the worlds must be closed—never to be opened again.

The Golden Compass, and the trilogy as a whole, is loved by many for its rich characters and the subtle complexities of its plot, as well as for its engaging re-readability. Pullman's prose is exhilarating, and the scope of his storytelling is staggering. It can be read on many levels; an exciting and compelling adventure story full of new and beautiful worlds, while simultaneously offering an underlying treatise on free will along with a sharp critique of religion. In Pullman's own words: "My books are about killing God."

> The idea hovered and shimmered delicately, like a soap bubble, and she dared not even look at it directly in case it burst. But she was familiar with the way of ideas, and she let it shimmer, looking away, thinking about something else.

LUIS SEPÚLVEDA

The Story of a Seagull and the Cat Who Taught Her to Fly (Historia de una gaviota y del gato que le enseñó a volar) (1996)

A dying seagull lays an egg and asks a nearby cat to make three promises: take care of the egg, don't eat the egg, and teach the hatchling to fly.

Translated by Margaret Sayers Peden (2006).

Luis Sepúlveda (1949–2020) called *The Story of a Seagull and the Cat Who Taught Her to Fly* his "thank you to Hamburg," the city he moved to after becoming politically exiled from his home country of Chile.

The novel's main character, a cat named Zorba, was named after Sepúlveda's own cat.

The Story of a Seagull and the Cat Who Taught Her to Fly has been translated into more than 40 languages and has sold over five million copies.

A seagull named Kengah is living the blissful life of a bird, when she gets trapped in a man-made oil slick in the waters outside of the port of Hamburg. All birds know that oil is lethal—they call it the "black plague"—and Kengah is lucky enough to unstick her wings just long enough to fly back to shore, where she lands on a balcony occupied by a black cat named Zorba.

Zorba's human family is away on vacation, and he's just settling into what he thinks will be a relaxing few weeks when the gull lands in front of him, changing his life in an instant. Kengah is grateful to have landed, but she knows that with her body covered in oil she's not long for this world. With her final moments, and last bits of energy, she resolves to lay an egg and asks Zorba to make her three promises in the process: "Promise me you won't cat the egg.... Promise me that you will look after it until the chick is born.... Promise me that you will teach it to fly." Zorba accepts all three promises, and soon finds himself in charge of a small blue-speckled white egg.

Not knowing what to do with the egg, Zorba recruits the help of the whole community of Hamburg port cats, who work together to learn what is needed to keep an egg safe, and a chick healthy once it's born. The cats are determined to teach the chick to fly too, even if their purely four-legged existence means they need to do a whole lot of work to figure out how to pass along that skill.

Sepúlveda imagines an animal world in which species talk to one another and coexist in a kingdom imbued with the realities of human existence, but entirely separate from them too. In Sepúlveda's imagination, cats not only understand the language of humans but can speak it—though it's the ultimate taboo to let humans in on that little secret. This slim chapter book, originally published in Spanish, shares many philosophies about human impact on the world, particularly on the lives of animals. "Cats were aware, of course, of the sad fate of the dolphins, who had displayed their intelligence to humans who had in turn condemned the dolphins to acting like clowns in aquatic spectacles." Not to mention the fact that the entire, rather sad, story of this book is precipitated by the harmful effects of man-made pollution.

Lucky and Zorba with a copy of *The Story of a Seagull and the Cat Who Taught Her to Fly*, illustrated by Camilla Cerea for her 2020 *Audubon* article about the novel.

Ultimately, here is a larger moral; one that is about finding love and common ground in spite of differences. "The necessity was to put two very different characters, like a cat and a seagull, together," Sepúlveda once shared in an interview. "I wanted to show people that they could discover that even if you are different you can still understand one another and have feelings for someone who is different."

And so he does. "We've given you all our affection without ever thinking of making a cat out of you. We love you as a gull," Zorba the cat says to the baby seagull who the cats decide to name Lucky. "It's very easy to accept and love those who are like us, but to love someone different is very hard, and you have helped us do that." And so the story seems to enter the reader's consciousness with a mission: to teach young readers to love those who are different. And to remind older readers that oftentimes it is those very differences that spark the most meaningful relationships of our lives.

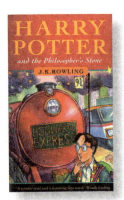

J. K. ROWLING

HARRY POTTER AND THE SORCERER'S STONE (HARRY POTTER AND THE PHILOSOPHER'S STONE) (1995)

Platform 9¾, Charing Cross Station, Hogwarts School, Voldemort, muggles and the boy who lived.

After her publisher suggested boys would not want to read a book written by a woman, Joanne Rowling (b.1965) adopted the middle name "Kathleen"—after her paternal grandmother—to form her more well-known moniker "J.K. Rowling."

The series has sold more than 450 million copies worldwide and has been translated into more than 70 languages.

The Harry Potter series has spawned multiple additional books, including Hogwarts textbooks, the fables read by wizard children (*The Tales of Beedle the Bard*), a short online story by Rowling, and a stage play (*Harry Potter and the Cursed Child*).

When J. K. Rowling wrote *Harry Potter and the Sorcerer's Stone* in 1997 (originally published as *Harry Potter and the Pihlosopher's Stone*), she sparked one of the greatest and largest franchises in history. The world of Harry Potter extends beyond the books themselves. The blockbuster adaptations are the second highest- grossing film series of all time, and Harry Potter pervades popular culture.

Perhaps the greatest appeal of the Wizarding World is that it is one both familiar and unfamiliar. Our world is translated into another, parallel world, which operated on rules sometimes similar, sometimes different. Rowling's creation expands through the seven books to reference wizards in different parts of continental Europe (and the world, in the afterlife of the Harry Potter fandom universe). However, a global presence is not necessary to be transported to a mirror image of our own universe made fantastical: The place is suburban England; travel is on English trains; schools have classrooms and dormitories. The familiarity of each of these locations is made fresh—sometimes strange—as the reader delights in the intersection—sometimes collision—of the wizarding and Muggle (non-wizarding) existences. The word "utopia" does not quite apply here, but neither is this the "dystopia" popular in contemporary fiction. The neologism "contopia" might suit this world alongside our own, sometimes even within our own, but still functioning successfully on its own. As Hagrid explains to Harry, wizards keep their world secret because "everyone'd be wantin' magic solutions to their problems."

Harry actually begins his life in a wizarding home, but is ushered out of that world and into the life of Muggles with his aunt and uncle, not through a change of location or consciousness, but a traumatic event that he only remembers in dreams. Rowling at first merely suggests the happenings of that night celebrated by every wizard in England: Voldemort has gone into hiding after spectacularly failing to kill the one-year-old Harry. As Voldemort does manage to kill his parents, Lily and James Potter, "the boy who lived" must be hidden away in the Muggle world. He is subjected to eleven years

Rupert Grint, Daniel Radcliffe, and Emma Watson play Ron, Harry, and Hermione in the Warner Bros' 2001 film adaptation of *Harry Potter and the Sorcerer's Stone*.

Previous page: "Not to worry," she said. "All you have to do is walk straight at the barrier between platforms nine and ten." Platform 9 3/4, illustrated by Jim Kay, winner of the 2012 Kate Greenaway Medal, for Bloomsbury's 2015 illustrated edition.

Page 209: Hogwarts School of Witchcraft and Wizardry, illustrated by Jim Kay.

of privation on Privet Drive with the Dursleys, who are not just aggressively Muggle (partly in response to Aunt Petunia's embarrassment over her sister's magical abilities) but also petty and mean.

As in the Chronicles of Narnia, readers are acquainted with the space and environment of wizard life through the eyes of a newcomer. Harry does not understand the flood of letters that are so determined to be opened only by him that hundreds of them follow the Dursleys' escape to a deserted island. The letters are missives that can fly, squeeze under doors, come down chimneys and change address at will if the recipient changes locations. Sentient letters are only part of Rowling's versatile system of communication technology—owls are the major means of communication for all wizards. Simple oral instructions from their owners send owls off to carry letters and packages back and forth between wizards, anytime, anywhere. Photographs, newspaper illustrations and paintings are also forms of communication, conveniently allowing their occupants to move about and even move between frames to convey information to their viewers.

A fundamental distinction between our existences is the markedly different capabilities of Muggles and wizards to master, and then manage, the knowledge required to make technology or magic work. We have developed complex mechanical and electronic products and systems external to our beings that control our lives probably more than we like to acknowledge. If a car coughs and stalls, many are helpless in the face of the blinking lights on the dashboard. If a computer screen is suddenly blue and blank, a visit to the electronics store is in store. Witches and wizards, trained for seven years in the magical arts, learn to control certain forces with their own minds and talents to accomplish similar tasks. We flip a switch on a flashlight; illumination springs from a wizard's wand at the sound of "*Lumos!.*" After a big meal Molly Weasley waves her wand at the dirty dishes, and they quietly begin to wash themselves in the sink. A mirror does not reflect one's own face, but, as Dumbledore says to Harry, the Mirror of Erised "shows us nothing more or less than the deepest, most desperate desire of our hearts."

It may be assumed that the potential scope of a wizard's abilities would bestow unlimited powers, but Rowling has not resorted to that easy way out. For instance, they choose not to exercise complete control over their world. One question raised by magical skill is the creation of wealth: Why not conjure up endless supplies of money? Some wizards are wealthier than others (the rich, haughty Malfoys versus the poor but good-hearted Weasleys), but they do not generate gold out of thin air, despite the Sorcerer's Stone. Neither is the handling of their wealth what we might expect. One of Harry's first visits in the magical world is with Hagrid to Gringotts Bank, a Dickensian-looking establishment staffed by goblins so nasty they even intimidate Hagrid. We might expect wizards merely to render their money invisible, or enchant it to prevent theft. Instead, Harry enters an institutional setting organized vaguely like Muggle banks, but with special features: Gringotts sits above enchanted passages hundreds of miles beneath London, reached by a goblin driving a sort of miner's cart, with dragons guarding the most precious vaults.

> "There are all kinds of courage," said Dumbledore, smiling. "It takes a great deal of bravery to stand up to our enemies, but just as much to stand up to our friends."

This existence is imbued with magic, but is not effortless, uncomplicated, or free from evil. The world envisioned in *Sorcerer's Stone* raises numerous questions addressed throughout the series: How does one negotiate with nonhuman creatures who also have powers? Can wizards create life? What happens if they try to control Muggle lives?

To Rowling's credit, she has conceived rich possibilities, not just for plot purposes, but to explore how we interact with nature, exert power over others, and cooperate in a diverse and sometimes dangerous world.

HANS MAGNUS ENZENSBERGER

THE NUMBER DEVIL
(DER ZAHLENTEUFEL) (1997)

Robert, a mathematically anxious young boy, encounters the mysterious Number Devil across twelve dreamy nights. Each dream is a mathematical adventure where The Number Devil inspires Robert's creativity.

Translated by Michael Henry Heim (1998).

Hans Magnus Enzensberger (1929–2022) was one of Germany's most celebrated poets, writers, and thinkers. A request from his 11-year-old daughter inspired *The Number Devil*, his most commercially successful work.

The Number Devil has been translated into more than 30 languages and has sold well over 1 million copies.

Despite suggestions from his publisher, Enzensberger declined to write a sequel to *The Number Devil* on the basis that he never likes to repeat himself.

It hardly comes as a surprise when anyone says that mathematics is boring and hard. The struggle to correct this impression is an uphill one, as is the task of showing that mathematics can, in fact, be very exciting! In the mid 1990s this task was taken on by Hans Magnus Enzensberger who, in a diversion from his usual work, entered the world of children's literature with the publication of *The Number Devil*.

In press interviews Enzensberger made no secret of the fact that he disapproved of how mathematics was being taught in school and so his contribution was never destined to join the mountain of mathematical textbooks. Instead, Enzensberger kept it simple. His work delivers Robert to us, a twelve-year-old boy who finds math boring and hard. He also delivers the Number Devil, Robert's personal mathematical mentor and, best of all, he crafts out dreamworld landscapes, where, night after night, the pair are able to join up to explore mathematical topics with playful creativity.

By setting the adventures in a dreamworld, Enzensberger can dispense with factual plausibility and create fun. Lewis Carroll, who also enjoyed a degree of unreality, is certainly channeled. In Robert's first dream he finds himself sunk in tall grass, with a giant beetle and a caterpillar for company. Hovering below, sitting on a leaf we meet the Number Devil, a small red-faced old man with devil horns, a pointy beard, and a cane. The cane, as it transpires, allows the Number Devil to write mathematical expressions in sky, sand, and water.

In their first encounter the Number Devil, whose character is by no means a friendly one, ponders how many sticks of chewing gum have been chewed. Robert suggests a number in the trillions, but the Number Devil can always take a stick from his pocket and add one more, and so the concept of infinity is explored . . . that numbers never end. Similarly, by convincing Robert that his special stick of gum can be shared with every living being (and with whoever else should come along) the concept of the infinitesimally small is explored.

The next adventure is set in a forest where all the trees are replaced by number ones and where we find the Number Devil sitting on a mushroom—a direct nod to *Alice's Adventures in Wonderland*.

The reader following Robert's journey here will understand just why we count in tens (and why Roman numerals failed to take off). At this juncture we see a breakthrough as Robert confidently demonstrates his knowledge to his mom the next morning.

Illustrations for the 1997 first edition of *The Number Devil*, by Rotraut Susanne Berner.

Still in a daze the next morning, Robert said to his mother, "Do you know the year I was born? It was 6 x 1 and 8 x 10 and 9 x 100 and 1 x 1000." "I don't know what's got into the boy lately," said Robert's mother, shaking her head. "Here," she added, handing him a cup of hot chocolate, "maybe this will help. You say the oddest things." Robert drank his hot chocolate in silence. There are some things you can't tell your mother, he thought.

The book continues with more exciting dreamland settings serving as the host for the Number Devil's mathematical revelations. With each dream Robert's curiosity and confidence grows; one night the Number Devil reveals patterns of prime numbers (the prima-donnas) in an ancient cave, another night he unearths the numbers that lie between fractions (the unreasonable numbers) on an isolated sandy beach.

The big finale sees Robert gifted with a guided tour of Number paradise, the Number Devil's natural habitat. Here he brushes shoulders with a host of famous historical mathematicians, feasts on slices of delicious pie (π), and is awarded a golden prize from the General Secretary of Number paradise.

MALORIE BLACKMAN

PIG-HEART BOY (1997)

An early novel by Malorie Blackman, the author of Noughts & Crosses, *that invites young readers to consider some big questions alongside Cameron, a thirteen year old making a life-or-death decision.*

Since writing her first collection of stories in 1990, Malorie Blackman (b.1962) has had more than 60 books, plays, and television scripts published to date, including the successful *Noughts & Crosses* (2001).

Pig-Heart Boy was shortlisted for the U.K.'s Carnegie Medal literary award, and quickly adapted to television by the BBC in 1999. In 2000, the newly produced TV show won the BAFTA Award for Children's Drama.

In 2013 Blackman was named UK Children's Laureate, in recognition of outstanding services to children's literature.

Cameron is facing a big decision—bigger than most thirteen year olds will ever need to make. A couple of years ago, he caught a viral infection that damaged his heart. Now, thanks to the pioneering research of one Dr. Byrne, there's suddenly the chance for a heart transplant. If Cameron doesn't have it, he probably has less than a year left to live—but it comes with risks. Should he do it? The alternative is to spend what little life he has left on the side-lines, hanging out with his well-meaning friends at the park and just *watching* them play soccer; hanging out with them at the pool and just *watching* them play Daredevil Dive. What kind of a life is that, he wonders. Maybe the risks of a heart transplant would be worth it?

Of course, it's more complicated than that, because what he's being offered is a brand-new procedure (Cameron gets annoyed when they use that word), which hasn't been successfully tested on a human before—to receive the heart of a genetically modified pig. A genetically modified pig *called Trudy*, to be precise. Dad thinks he should do it, Mom is against. Ultimately, the choice is Cameron's.

It's a controversial procedure (for one thing, animal rights groups are fiercely opposed, and some of them show their displeasure very aggressively), so it's got to be kept quiet. I mean, it's surely got to be okay for Cameron to tell his best friend Marlon, but that's it. People at school might treat him differently if they knew—and what happens if the press find out?

This isn't just a book about the science, and about the dilemma that Cameron faces, it's also about privacy—because the press *does* find out and they can be shamelessly invasive in their pursuit of a story. Cameron will learn this to his cost.

Pig-Heart Boy was one of Malorie Blackman's earliest books. And though she would go on to be better known for things like *Noughts & Crosses*, an excellent series for teenagers set in an alternative world of racial segregation, she shows here that she's not nervous about challenging younger readers with some big ideas. Not to mention with an ending that might surprise. . . .

 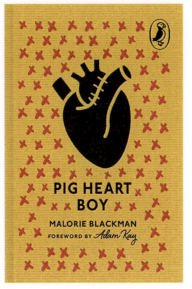

Front covers of the 2015 Farsi and 2025 English editions of *Pig-Heart Boy*.

> I closed my eyes and stood up slowly. If I had to emerge, it would be at my own pace and in my own time – no matter how much my body screamed at me to take a breath as fast as I could. I was the one in control. Not my lungs. Not my blood. Not my heart.

Blackman has always been interested in science. She reveals the processes around transplants and the language to describe them—including xenografts (animal organ transplants). And while the procedure that Cameron gets, based though it is on some scientific research, is not exactly a reality. She says in her introduction that she prefers to describes this book as not science fiction but "science possible," or "science probable." Since the novel's appearance in 1997, many advances have been made that have led to the first pig-heart transplants actually being carried out.

A successful TV series was made not long after the book was published, and in 2025 it was adapted into a stage production, testament to the book's enduring appeal. As the story progresses, Cameron learns that his mother is pregnant, and though he dearly *hopes* to live long enough to meet his little brother or sister, he starts to keep a sort of video diary by way of a message for them to watch when they're old enough. Because besides being about all those complicated things—science and medical ethics and privacy and more . . . this is also a brave story about friendship and loyalty and family, about testing oneself and living life on one's own terms.

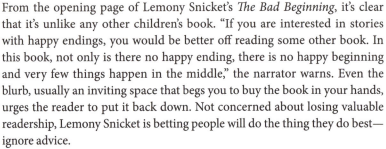

LEMONY SNICKET (DANIEL HANDLER)

The Bad Beginning (1999)

The first in A Series of Unfortunate Events, which follows the lives of Violet, Klaus and Sunny Baudelaire, and their recent orphanhood which has delivered them into the hands of the wicked Count Olaf.

A Series of Unfortunate Events has sold 60 million copies, not counting the extra material and companion books that came out alongside the thirteen in the series.

Daniel Handler's early books got rejected from publishers so many times that he began hosting a reading series called "Great Writers Who Can't Get Published".

The pseudonym "Lemony Snicket" came about while Handler was doing research for his first novel. He needed to contact a right-wing organization for the book, but didn't want to reveal his identity. So, he called himself "Lemony Snicket."

From the opening page of Lemony Snicket's *The Bad Beginning*, it's clear that it's unlike any other children's book. "If you are interested in stories with happy endings, you would be better off reading some other book. In this book, not only is there no happy ending, there is no happy beginning and very few things happen in the middle," the narrator warns. Even the blurb, usually an inviting space that begs you to buy the book in your hands, urges the reader to put it back down. Not concerned about losing valuable readership, Lemony Snicket is betting people will do the thing they do best—ignore advice.

The Bad Beginning follows Violet, Klaus, and Sunny Baudelaire, three siblings who learn that their parents have died in a fire that has destroyed their entire home. They are sent to live with Count Olaf, a distant relative and actor who is loathsome and cruel. He sets up an elaborate plot to try to steal their family's enormous fortune, but the very smart kids manage to foil him at the last minute. Each one has a special skill: Violet is an inventor, Klaus is a reader, and Sunny has very sharp teeth for biting. As the rest of the series unfolds over thirteen books, we follow the siblings as they come across secret organizations, fires, and guardians of varying evilness.

Violet, Klaus, and Sunny do not live in a world of magic or fairies or talking animals. They are snatched cruelly from a life of privilege and wealth by grief and dropped into a world of bankers, neglectful adults, and complicated legalese as they navigate Violet's impending marriage to the evil Count Olaf. These are real problems, if heightened, and the only magic they have to solve them is their own talent and limited resources.

But Daniel Handler, writing under the pseudonym Lemony Snicket, makes these problems thrilling, in part with his world-building. *The Bad Beginning* is not set now, nor is it in the future or past. It is not really set in any one place, either. People have simple computers, but they also send telegrams. The children dress like Victorian orphans. By removing the series from any recognizable place or time, Snicket builds a fantastical world that feels exciting even as the orphans' problems are so often real, even banal. He

Sunny Baudelaire (Kara Hoffman), Count Olaf (Jim Carey) and Klaus Baudelaire (Liam Aiken) in the 2004 movie adaptation of the first three novels in the series, entitled Lemony's Snicket's A Series of Unfortunate Events.

creates a space wherein a secret organization, VFD, can flourish and schism. There are magical-feeling touches as A Series of Unfortunate Events unfolds, but in *The Bad Beginning*, we only have hints of bad things to come.

Those hints, though, are scattered masterfully. The themes and the narrative threads that will later be explored are already present in *The Bad Beginning*. Lemony Snicket is far from an impartial narrator but a character in his own right, hinting that he is on the run. Eye motifs feature throughout Count Olaf's home, nodding to the VFD symbolism that's to come. More than that, though, are the themes that made children fall in love with the series. There are just a few types of adults. Some are flat-out evil, like Count Olaf. Others, like his henchmen, will gladly serve at the side of evil. Others, like Mr. Poe, are so useless and cowardly that they allow evil to flourish. Just a few, however, are truly good, attempting to help the orphans at great personal cost. Their fate is rarely a happy one.

Snicket's rich world is brought to life by illustrator Brett Helquist, with simple drawings in his signature crosshatch style. Sunny dangles helpless from a tower; Violet clutches a bouquet; the skeleton of their home stands still smoking. The detailed monochrome is unflashy and unpretentious, leaving enough room for interpretation of the Baudelaires' harrowing experience.

The final book in the series, *The End,* was released in 2006. Count Olaf, Snicket, Klaus, Violet, and Sunny compelled readers to keep buying not only the series, but also the supplemental material, like *The Beatrice Letters* and *The Unauthorized Autobiography*. *The Bad Beginning* introduced us to a world of characters who are still keeping readers hooked.

Contemporary Classics   219

ANDRI SNÆR MAGNASON

The Story of the Blue Planet
(SAGAN AF BLÁA HNETTINUM) (2000)

In a modern, poetic parable, children Brimir and Hulda fly farther than they intended: to get out of trouble, they must learn how to appreciate each other and the magical beauty of the natural world just as it is.

Translated by Julian Meldon D'Arcy (2012).

Andri Snær (b.1973) is known internationally as one of Iceland's leading writers of fiction and nonfiction for children and adults.

In 1999, *The Story of the Blue Planet* was the first children's book to win the Icelandic Literary Prize. It has been translated into more than 30 languages and adapted for the stage.

In 2016, Andri Snær ran for office as President of Iceland, campaigning on environmental and cultural matters; in 2019, he helped to organize a funeral for a deceased Icelandic glacier.

Andri Snær Magnason's "saga" begins "on a little island in a deep ocean, shortly before the annual awakening of butterflies"—but the idyllic existence of young friends Hulda and Brimir (who live in a community of nature-loving children) is disrupted when a spaceship comes crashing down nearby. What seems to be a monster emerges out of it. The monster is, in fact, a grown-up (there are no adults on the island): Mr. Gleesome Goodday, "stardust vacuum cleaner traveling salesman but chiefly DreamComeTrueMaker and Joybringer." Learning of the island's butterflies, and the children's dreams of flying over mountains and wilderness, Mr. Goodday hoovers up all the hibernating insects' magical dust and shows the children how a sprinkling of it makes them light as a feather and able to take to the skies.

The effects of the powder wear off when the sun sets. Back on the ground, the children resent all the time that is not spent in the air. They are quick to agree to pay the price of a tiny bit of youth for more of the precious dust. And, so they can fly around the clock, Mr. Goodday rests a gigantic ladder on the end of a white cloud when the sun is at its highest. Climbing up the ladder, he drives a stupendous nail into the sun, pinning it to the sky. Night is banished from the island as are rain clouds. However, when Hulda and Brimir are blown by a gust of wind far out to sea and off into the blue, they discover that on the other side of the world there is now only darkness, with all the dire consequences that perpetual shadow brings for the children who live there.

The Story of the Blue Planet asks moral and philosophical questions of its readers about responsibility and sustainability, friendship, and inequality. Its apparent simplicity (a directness complemented by Áslaug Jónsdóttir's colorful, cartoon-style illustrations) encourages conversations about the children's world—and, of course, about our world and our place in it. Published in 1999, *The Story of the Blue Planet* was the first of several fiction and nonfiction books by Andri Snær that address environmental matters with increasingly urgent, lyrical intensity. These books build on themes and motifs (butterflies!) that underpin *The Story of the Blue Planet*, drawing too on structures from

"Mr. Goodday nails the Sun in place," illustrated by Áslaug Jónsdóttir for the first edition.

mythology and fairy tales. Underscoring the importance of fiction in educating readers on the climate crisis, Andri Snær describes an encounter with a professor of climate science in his most recent book, *On Time and Water*, who tells him: "people don't understand numbers and graphs, but they do understand stories. You can tell stories. You must tell stories."

Andri Snær is an eloquent spokesperson for the health of our planet and the vital role that poetry and storytelling can play in this context, believing that "poetry is the silver thread of the human spirit; without it, human existence is unthinkable." *The Story of the Blue Planet* is a wise and charming tale, simultaneously fierce and gentle, and founded on hope.

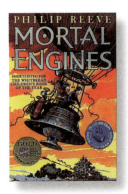

PHILIP REEVE

Mortal Engines (2001)

Rampaging cities eat up rivals and enslave their inhabitants in post-apocalyptic future England dominated by machines.

Philip Reeve (b.1966) trained as an artist and worked as an illustrator before writing his first novel in 2001. Since then he has written more than 10 books, including a trilogy of Victorian space adventures and a standalone novel set in fifth-century Britain, *Here Lies Arthur*, which won the Carnegie Medal in 2008.

Reeve employs the principles of "Municipal Darwinism" in the book meaning that the bigger moving cities "eat" the smaller ones.

A film adaptation, directed by Christian Rivers and produced by Peter Jackson, was released in 2018.

Philip Reeve, who trained as an illustrator, doesn't dismiss modernity entirely, but he finds little to interest him post-1946. He believes that "stuff" from the past, such as machines and especially steam trains, had more character. His inspiration for the story of *Mortal Engines*, his first novel, was in part the massive road building program of the 1990s that allowed roads, and then housing, to eat up the countryside. To reimagine the technology of the time, he drew on his detailed knowledge of nineteenth-century machines and his affection for them.

He planned *Mortal Engines* as "a great big rambling story with lots of characters" without any thought of it being specifically a children's book—though it was exactly the kind of book he would have enjoyed as a teenager. *Mortal Engines* is certainly big and rambling and full of action, but without any loose ends. In this alternative future, London gets moving; it has been lying low to avoid the other towns that are bigger and more predatory, but now it's up and off. With all speed behind it, it is chasing a small mining town across the dried-up bed of the old North Sea. On board is Tom Natsworthy, a mere Third Class Apprentice with a naïve and hopeful attitude, who he is as excited as anyone by the movement of the top-heavy, old city as it lurches off on its quest. This is the beginning of a fabulous adventure for Tom and for Hester Shaw, a refugee from the Out-Lands with revenge in her heart, following an accident in which she has become disfigured. She meets Tom after both have been pushed out from the speeding city.

Hester would happily stay hidden and away from the world of power that the moving London represents but Tom is determined to get back on board; this is so he can unravel the sinister mystery that he knows lurks deep in the city. Intrigue is everywhere, and unraveling the many strands is difficult, but Tom's eye is firmly fixed on the Medusa Plot that he knows he must crack. The stakes are high. Tom's quest for the truth causes him to blunder into great danger, putting his own and Hester's lives at risk.

Tom and Hester are just two of a huge cast of Dickensian characters created by Reeve. Although easily recognizable by their characteristics, both teenagers

Previous page: Illustration by David Wyatt for the cover of the 2009 edition of *Mortal Engines*.

are rounded and convincing. Against the traditions of fantasy, Reeve creates characters with uncertain status who may behave villainously or virtuously, depending on the circumstances.

In terms of place, Reeve seems to be able effortlessly to whisk up confections: entirely credible cities with ladders and walkways and unfurling sails and dangling ropes, as well as complicated dramas with cascading subplots. But, saving the book all from the weightiness that this might imply, is Reeve's sense of humor: his wordplay on the names of characters and places; his references to "goggle-screens" around which people gather in shop windows; the glittering circular "seedy," which is an archaeological find; and rumors of a mysterious piece of ancient technology, known as an "eye-pod."

> London will never stop moving. Movement is life. When we have devoured the last wandering city and demolished the last static settlement we will begin digging.

Reeve wrote *Mortal Engines* as a standalone title but following its success he continued the series with *Predator's Gold*, *Infernal Devices*, and *A Darkling Plain*, forming a quartet that he called *The Infernal Engines*. The sequence includes the same characters, and the dramatic action grows considerably in scale, picking up developing concerns about the physical survival of the planet, and the importance of conserving resources. Tom Natsworthy becomes middle aged, and the small, almost domestic skirmishes between the cities are replaced by an all-out struggle between the Green Storm and the Traction League, with the threat of the bomb created by the Ancients always lurking in the background.

CORNELIA FUNKE

INKHEART
(TINTENHERZ) (2003)

Mortimer Folchart possesses the ability to call characters out of books. In doing so he releases a pair of robbers into the contemporary world, where they create problems that he and his daughter must attempt to resolve.

Cornelia Funke's Inkheart trilogy is not only a celebration of the love of books and reading, but also a meditation on, and warning about, the potential power of words, blending the grit of the real world with the fantasies that are encased in fictions. The page-turning excitement of this action-packed hybrid has won the series a global audience, selling more than twenty million copies worldwide.

Funke had already established her writing career with her previous titles, and her first novel *The Thief Lord* (entitled *Herr der Diebe* in its original German, 2000) almost succeeded in topping the *New York Times*' bestseller list. However, it is her award-winning Inkheart series for which she is best known. Here Funke pursues the notion of being "lost in a book" or "living in a book" to its logical extremity with her creation the Inkworld, the world within the pages of *Inkheart*, a book written by one Fenoglio that is itself a story within Funke's own novel.

At the beginning of the novel, twelve-year-old Meggie discovers that her father, Mortimer "Mo" Folchart, has the ability to bring fictional characters to life when he reads aloud. Having learned to his cost that for every character fetched from the page, a person from the real world must enter the book in return, Mo has sworn never to read aloud again. Yet the characters of *Inkheart* that Mo once read into the contemporary world are not content to let him forget the past. Dustfinger seeks to return home to the pages of his story, while the villainous Capricorn and his accomplice Basta attempt to take control by destroying all the existing copies of *Inkheart*. Books, we understand, are powerful objects in both the right and wrong hands.

The tension between the roles of reader and writer becomes ever more apparent in the later titles *Inkspell* (2005) and *Inkdeath* (2007) as the author Fenoglio, living in the fictional world he has created, finds it is constantly changing from his memory of it, while Orpheus, a "silvertongue" like Mo, having written himself into the story, endlessly tinkers with it, creating interpolative pastiche texts, what we might call fan

Translated by Anthea Bell (2003).

Prior to becoming an author, Funke (b.1958) worked as a social worker, then as an illustrator of children's books. It was in part her work with children that inspired her to start writing.

Funke has written more than 30 novels, including the second and third books in the Inkheart trilogy, *Inkspell* and *Inkdeath*, and her work has been translated into more than 28 languages.

In 2007, *Inkheart* was voted one of the Teachers' Top 100 Books for Children by the U.K.'s National Education Association. The book was made into a movie in 2009.

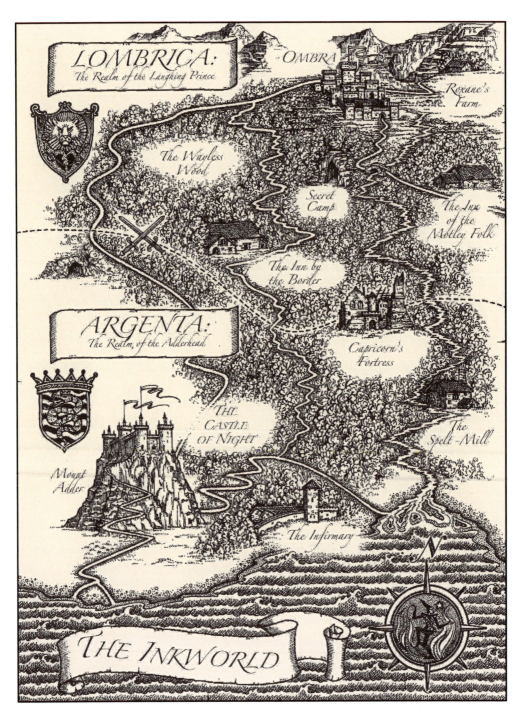

A map of The Inkworld, in which *Inkheart* is set, from the book's sequel, *Inkspell* (2006).

Perhaps there's another, much larger story behind the printed one, a story that changes just as our own world does. And the letters on the page tell us only as much as we'd see peering through a keyhole. Perhaps the story in the book is just the lid on a pan; it always stays the same, but underneath there's a whole world that goes on developing and changing like our own.

Mo reads *Treasure Island*, illustrated by Alice Cao for the 2023 twentieth anniversary edition of *Inkheart*.

fiction, in which he plays increasingly significant roles. The implication is that, as the theorist and philosopher Roland Barthes suggested, once a novel is published, the original author is supplanted by myriad reader-authors. Critics have argued that, although she raises intriguing questions about the metafictional nature of text, Funke cannot properly answer them because the Inkworld is itself too insubstantial to support a full-scale enquiry into the nature of fiction. Regardless, the series continues to win favor around the world.

MORRIS GLEITZMAN

ONCE (2005)

A young Jewish storyteller with his trusty notebook struggles to survive in a divided Poland during the Second World War.

Morris Gleitzman (b.1953) was Australian Children's Laureate for 2018 and 2019.

Gleitzman's Jewish grandfather lived in Krakow in Poland. He left Europe before the Holocaust; however, many of his family members were killed by the Nazis during World War II.

First published in 2005, *Once* has never been out of print. It has been translated into numerous languages, including German, Czech, Portuguese, Japanese, Brazilian, and Chinese. It has also won many awards, both in Australia and overseas.

The narrator in *Once* is a ten-year-old boy called Felix, the son of Jewish booksellers. Through Felix's first-person narrative, the reader is introduced into a world where the wonders of childhood are constantly challenged by the realities of war. However, despite the often harrowing subject matter, at its heart *Once* is a life-affirming book about hope, resilience, survival against the odds, and the importance of friendship.

Felix has lived in a Catholic orphanage in Poland since his parents deposited him there more than three years ago when they were looking for somewhere safe for their son. Unaware of what is happening out in the real world, Felix is convinced that his parents will be coming back soon to take him home.

When a whole carrot miraculously appears in his watery soup, Felix takes it as a sign that his parents are on their way. Unfortunately, the only people who arrive at the orphanage are a troop of German soldiers intent on burning books. Afraid that his parents and their bookshop are in danger, Felix heads off on a quest to find his family and save their books.

Young Felix knows the power of words and is not afraid to use them, especially for getting out of difficult situations. Storytelling is his superpower. Through his words, we experience Felix's world in real time—journeying with him, watching events unfolding through his innocent eyes, empathizing with him when things go wrong, and marveling at his often overly optimistic interpretation of what is happening.

On his journey, Felix befriends a young girl whose parents have been killed as collaborators by partisan forces, not the Nazis, as Zelda's father was a collaborator. The children develop a friendship that is strong enough to weather anything. At times confronting, the story pulls no punches as Felix and Zelda go on a long march into the city of Warsaw. They are saved by a dentist, who hides them in a cellar along with five other traumatized children.

When the children's hiding place is discovered, they are forced to march to the railroad station where, along with hundreds of others, they are herded into boxcars on a train destined for the death camps. Again, it is Felix's

At last, the river.

After walking such a long way, it's so good to kneel on the cool stones, stick my face in the water, and have a drink. This river is beautiful. The water is gleaming gold in the sunset, and the warm air smells damp and fresh, and there are millions of tiny insects turning happy floating cartwheels in the soft light.

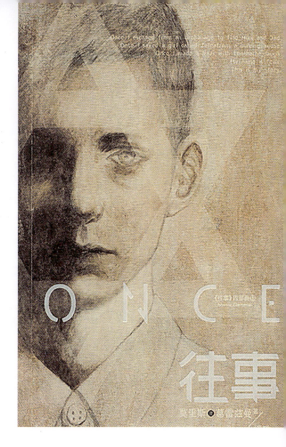

Cover for the 2013 Chinese edition of *Once*, illustrated by Voider Sun.

kindness and thoughtfulness—and his trusty notebook with its wonderfully exaggerated stories—that save the day.

The cliffhanger ending leaves Felix and Zelda battered and bruised but alive, their future still uncertain. Despite this, the irrepressible Felix ends his story on an optimistic note. Luckily for his readers, Gleitzman does not abandon Felix and Zelda beside those railroad tracks. After the success of *Once*, he wrote six more books in the series ending with *Always* (2021).

Gleitzman shows that history is about the day-to-day lives of ordinary people trying to survive as best they can in extraordinary situations. With its endearing main characters and surprisingly ebullient sense of humor, *Once* shows that friendship, kindness, and empathy can flourish even in the most troubled of worlds.

CAO WENXUAN

Bronze and Sunflower
(QĪNG TÓNG KUÍ HUĀ) (2005)

Stuck in the Cultural Revolution, a boy learns to speak again thanks to his friend Sunflower.

Translated by Helen Wang (2017).

Cao Wenxuan (b.1954) is the Director of the Institute for Literature and Creative Writing at Peking University. He has published many novels and more than 80 picture books.

Bronze and Sunflower by Cao Wenxuan has been translated into more than 40 languages.

Wenxuan has won more than 50 literary awards including the National Book Award and the Song Qingling Literature Prize.

Set in rural areas of Southern China during the Cultural Revolution in the 1960s and '70s, a young city girl, Sunflower, accompanies her artist father when he is sent to the countryside to labor among farmers. After her father is drowned in an accident, Sunflower is adopted by an impoverished local family with hardworking parents, a loving grandma, and Bronze, a smart and kind-hearted young boy who cannot speak after a high fever in early childhood.

Since the family can only afford to send one child to school, they give the opportunity to Sunflower. Bronze spares no effort to support Sunflower; he tries his best to sell reed flower shoes during heavy wind and snow storms and he makes a firefly lamp for Sunflower to study in the evening since the family have no money to buy oil lamps. In return, Sunflower saves every penny to buy paper and pens to teach Bronze to read and write. Fires, floods, locust plagues, and various other hardships come one after another. However, the whole family support each other and make it through all the difficulties.

A strong trust in human nature's goodness is written and felt in all of Cao's writings. With signature "hardship aesthetics," Cao Wenxuan creates a literary world where people help each other to overcome difficulties with dedication and self-sacrifice. In this literary world, action always speaks louder than words. The voiceless boy can brave any challenges to support his sister and family, while his family will do the same for him. Sympathy and kindness are shared by the villagers even though they all live a hard life. People are kind not because they are pragmatic but because kindness is part of the true human nature.

In Cao's works, kindness, good faith, and self-sacrifice are pathways to self-redemption, which can work miracles. When Sunflower is sent to the city at age twelve, Bronze stays on top of a high haystack for many days to wait for her, until he sees Sunflower running back and Bronze finally begins to speak.

Cover art for the 2015 English edition, illustrated by Meilo So.

Bronze shouted again, "SUNFLOWER!"

The sound wasn't perfectly clear, but it had definitely come out of Bronze's mouth. Gayu left the ducks and ran to Bronze's house, and as he ran he shouted out so all the villagers could hear, "Bronze can speak! He can speak!" Bronze ran like crazy from the haystack to the fields.

Sunshine spilled over the boundless fields of sunflowers, filled with thousands and thousands of stems, whose big round heads were turning, just as they should, to face the golden body of heaven as it rolled across the sky.

The plot and characters of are inspired by Cao's own childhood. Born in 1954 and the son of a principal for rural elementary schools, he grew up in a poor village in Southern China. He often had little to eat and would look forward to having rice gruel once a month. He wrote, "My home village was well known for its poverty. Day in and day out, my family lived with deprivation." However, the poverty of childhood life does not bring despair or disappointment to this young boy; instead, the childhood hardships helped to develop his unique outlook, in which people could live a difficult yet genteel life.

From his own accounts, we can find two things. First, the beauty of the vast and free view of the countryside fields remains an inexhaustible source of inspiration and joy to him as a writer in future years. Secondly, that the human spirit can be elevated through hardship. He holds that the history of human beings was never, is never, and will never be free of hardship. What we need is calmness and gracefulness in the face of any hardship. That's why, in his afterword, titled "Beautiful Hardship," he writes, "In the Hedonistic world of today, *Bronze and Sunflower* is an alternative. It follows a reverse way of thinking, for it serves not only as a confirmation but also an interpretation of hardship and pain."

MARKUS ZUSAK

THE BOOK THIEF (2005)

The girl who steals books to sage them from the Nazis meets Death himself, cast as a jovial, philosophical soul with a sense of humor.

Markus Zusak was born in Sydney, Australia, in 1975. After studying at the University of New South Wales, he became a teacher for a short time, before writing his first book and going on to become a professional writer.

In writing *The Book Thief*, Zusak was influenced by the firsthand accounts of life in Nazi Germany told to him by his parents, who emigrated to Australia in 1950.

First published in 2005, *The Book Thief* has been translated into over 60 languages. It has won numerous literary awards and was made into a feature film in 2013 and a musical in 2023.

Many authors have explored the dystopian world of Nazi Germany, but Markus Zusak recreates that world from an unusual perspective. The central theme is the transformative power of words and storytelling, explored through the experiences of teenager Liesel Meminger. It is narrated by none other than Death himself.

However, in Zusak's recreation of this all-too-familiar world, Death is not a grim reaper skulking in the shadows. Nor is he the berobed skeletal figure who brings black humour to Terry Pratchett's *Discworld* series in his role as psychopomp. Zusak's Death is a sympathetic and philosophical soul with a wry sense of humour, whose epitaphic observations on people, places, and events punctuate the text.

As in nineteenth century novels like *Alice's Adventures in Wonderland*, the narrator directly addresses the reader, taking them into his confidence as he interprets Liesel's experiences through his own colourful prismatic view in which entities such as the sky, the earth and himself are sentient beings.

This coming-of-age tale begins with Death documenting the traumatic death of Liesel's younger brother on a train. At his funeral, Liesel commits her first act of book-thievery, before she is fostered out to the gentle and caring Hans Hubermann and his irascible, foul-mouthed wife, Rosa, who live in the fictional German town of Molching.

Liesel becomes a compulsive book thief, but she only steals unwanted or abandoned books, snatching them from graveyards, book-burnings, and the neglected libraries of the rich. Ultimately, she is not stealing books but saving them from a fate worse than incineration—not being read.

As well as documenting Liesel's burgeoning interest in books and reading, Death also explores her relationships with her foster parents, her mischievous school friend Rudy Steiner, the lonely and bereaved wife of the town mayor, Isla Hermann, and the Jewish refugee Max Vandenburg, hiding from the Nazis in the Hubermanns' basement.

Ultimately, Liesel loses almost everything she has grown to love when Molching is bombed by the Allies, but her obsession with the written word saves her. She goes on to live a fulfilling life in Australia—just like Zusak's

Liesel (Sophie Nélisse) sits on a step reading, in a still from the 2013 film adaptation of *The Book Thief*.

parents, who migrated from Europe and inspired Zusak's storytelling with their memories of that terrible time.

Zusak highlights the plight of ordinary German families, who in their own way fought back against the Nazi regime. Just as Hitler weaponized words through his speeches and propaganda machine, Liesel and her family and friends use words to fight against persecution, putting their own stories down on paper and validating their existence.

The refugee Max makes a particularly telling statement when he creates his autobiography. He rips pages out of Hitler's *Mein Kampf*, obscuring the Fuhrer's rantings with white paint and replacing them with his own words and images. The pages of his book are interspersed throughout *The Book Thief* in the form of black-and-white illustrations by Trudy White, providing both social commentary and graphic representations of the "books" created by Max and Liesel.

Commenting on the world he created in *The Book Thief* and his unusual narrator, Zusak says: "I knew that [Death] should be telling this story to prove to himself that humans can be worthwhile, and beautiful, even in the ugliest times." Fittingly, it is Death who has the last word.

Contemporary Classics 233

SHAUN TAN

The Arrival (2006)

An extraordinary graphic narrative depicts the hopes and fears of newcomers to a strange city in pencil drawing alone.

Shaun Tan (b.1974), artist, writer and film maker, has won numerous awards for his work, including the Children's Book Council of Australia Picture Book of the Year award, the Astrid Lindgren Memorial Award and the Kate Greenaway Medal.

The Arrival was first published in Australia in 2006, has since sold over 500,000 copies worldwide, and is frequently cited as one of the most unique children's books in recent history.

For the making of *The Arrival*, Shaun Tan drew inspiration from photographs that he took in his garage, using empty boxes and lamps to create dioramas from which to base the cityscapes that make up the book's settings.

A utopian version of immigrant experience, *The Arrival* depicts an unnamed man who travels to a foreign land to establish a new life, in which he is eventually joined by his family. Drawn entirely with pencil, the illustrations employ either sepia or grayscale tones according to shifts in temporality or mood.

That Tan's story is told only in visual images often creates an ambiguity of meaning and places readers in the same position of uncertainty as the protagonist when faced with the surreal depiction of the new country, where technologies, modes of transport, animals, and foods take alien forms. Although many depicted objects are familiar, they are nevertheless subject to interpretation. The first page, for example, consists of a grid of nine panels that are fragments of a domestic scene. The panels depict three kinds of readily recognizable objects that may be combined to articulate the motive for migration. First, a specific social norm (the nuclear family) is evoked by a family portrait, a child's drawing of a happy family, and a man's hat and woman's headscarf hanging together on a wall. Second, some domestic objects indicate the family is under economic stress: their teapot is cracked and a cup badly chipped, and a saucepan with lid askew suggests that food may be scarce. Third, a packed suitcase and a picture of a steamship lying next to the cup allude to travel. The first image in the grid is an origami paper crane, which has come to symbolize resilience, strength, and peace. The suggestion is that someone, prompted by economic stress and hope, will travel to support the family. The images of the crane, hat, suitcase, boat, and domestic utensils then recur as motifs throughout the book and trace the protagonist's efforts to understand and adapt to the forms taken by everyday life in the new country. When a new version of the opening grid is introduced in the book's final section, the reunited family is shown living happily, enjoying the no longer alien food and artifacts.

The motivation for migration is symbolic; the family walks through streets and images of shadows cast by dragon-tails overhead. The society seems oppressed by a reign of terror. The micronarratives of other immigrants the man meets in the new country also involve various forms of oppression.

It is about escape from tyranny and deprivation and travel to a land where individuals may strive to build their own happiness.

The images are varied in size, function, and drawing techniques. Panels can be connected by a gesture or an eye-line, or by zooming or panning to narrativize a sequence of panels to express an activity or the passage of time. The book's narrative tempo is further related to two different functions of panel images, either action panels or conceptual panels. An action panel's main function may be to unfold the story, so that a sequence may express temporal or spatial progression, and the spectator moves quickly from one image to the next, while conceptual images require pause and analyze.

A key strategy is the presentation of perceptions as focalized by the protagonist. The significance of the illustrations depends less on what is on the page than on how he responds to it. Readers share his struggle with meaning, just as they share how his growing understanding of his new country enables a reconstituted family life. The book closes with the positive image of the daughter embarking on an unaccompanied shopping trip, guiding another newly arrived immigrant to a destination in a society that is both empathetic and multicultural.

The New Country, inspired by images of immigrants arriving in New York, illustrated by Shaun Tan with graphite pencil.

JUAN VILLORO

The Wild Book
(El Libro Salvaje) (2008)

Welcome to Unle Tito's magic library, where books choose their readers and seek out those who need them.

Translated by Lawrence Schimel (2017).

In addition to authoring short stories for both children and adults, Mexican writer and journalist Juan Villoro (b.1956) was also once made the cultural attaché of Mexico to the German Democratic Republic.

The Wild Book has sold over 1 million copies in its original language, Spanish.

Villoro's journalistic work is equally celebrated, and he has received numerous prizes including the King of Spain International Journalism Award.

The Wild Book begins with bad news. Juan is thirteen years old and his parents are splitting up. His father jetted off from their home in Mexico City to Paris, and his mother is grief-stricken and falling apart. It is the start of summer vacation and Juan's mother makes the decision that he and his younger sister, Carmen, are better off spending the summer away from home: Carmen is sent to a friend's house, but Juan is sent to live with his strange Uncle Tito.

Uncle Tito lives in a sprawling old house in the middle of Mexico City. The house is filled with books; and not just filled with books, but bursting with books: "There were bookshelves and books piled in columns that stretched up to the ceiling everywhere." The house is so labyrinthine that Juan is instructed to carry a bell with him to ring in case he gets lost in the endless library. Uncle Tito spends all of his time reading, and so committed is he to his reading that he shuts himself in his library for most of his life. "Uncle lived without any company other than his books and his cats." Juan is surprised of his uncle would tolerate his company for an entire summer, but as his uncle quickly reveals he has an ulterior motive. Juan, we learn, is a Lector Princeps, which means that books respond magically to him. There is one book in the library that Tito has never been able to catch, the Wild Book, and he thinks his Lector Princeps nephew may be the one to find it.

The world inside Uncle Tito's house is filled with quiet magic, the magic of books. Books move from shelf to shelf on their own, the words inside them changing depending upon who is reading. The books also play an active role in who reads them, finding the right reader at the right moment and intervening in their lives. "Every book is like a mirror," Uncle Tito explains. "It reflects what you think." Hunting down the Wild Book is harder than anyone ever imagined and it takes Juan both knowing the library inside out and staying open to the wisdom and whims of books to find what he is searching for. It also takes the help of a teen girl who works at the pharmacy across the street; in tandem with the book-hunting adventure, a love story blossoms.

Villoro's text, originally written in Spanish, is a decadent swim through the power of books. It is hard to pin down and articulate the magic of books, and what the experience of reading really feels like. As Uncle Tito says,

> You will always find a book that supports you. The books are loyal.

Cover illustration for the 2015 Spanish language edition by Mexican designer and illustrator Gabriel Martínez Meave.

Previous page: Juan in Uncle Tito's library, illustrated by Gabriel Martínez Meave.

"When you read you never see the letters; you see the things the letters are about, like a forest, a house turned into a library, or a pharmacy. Books serve as mirrors and windows—they're full of images." It's the truth, and it's also magic. Villoro takes that inherent literary magic and evolves it into magical realism; books flutter through the house while no one is looking, books create staircases to lead Juan where they need him to go.

Designated as a young adult book, *The Wild Book* teeters in between the worlds of stuffed animals and childhood, and adulthood and regret. It breathes magic into a thirteen-year-old character who is just on the edge of the age where childhood magic gets lost. And in the way the story is told, *The Wild Book* also breathes magic into whoever reads it, its lesson being that books find readers who need them. With that in mind, this book is needed by anyone who picks it up and gazes at the mirror of its words.

SACHIKO KASHIWABA

Temple Alley Summer
(KIMEIJI-YOKOCHYO NO NATSU) (2011)

Fifth-grade pupil Kazu helps a ghostly classmate fulfill her greatest wish by tracking down the author of an unfinished fantasy novel written decades earlier.

Temple Alley Summer is a novel about a Japanese fifth grader who learns about a statuette that can give the dead a second chance at life. After he meets a new classmate who might just be a ghost, a forgotten forty-year-old fantasy story inspires an unlikely bond between the pair and an elderly woman in their neighborhood who firmly believes no one deserves to live again.

Kazu is both the protagonist and the narrator of Temple Alley Summer. After an evening spent watching scary movies on TV, he spies a girl leaving his home in traditional Buddhist funeral garb. The next day, the girl appears in his fifth-grade classroom. Everyone else claims to have known Akari for years. Kazu is the only one who suspects her secret—she's a ghost brought back to life by a secret neighborhood religious relic.

Kazu's investigation of Akari draws attention. He is afraid he may have cost her the second chance she so clearly wants. He tries to make it up to her by helping her fulfill at least one wish before she disappears from this world—to read the final installments of The Moon Is on the Left, a serial novel she enjoyed during her first life. (Serial storytelling has lasted far longer in Japan than it did in the English-speaking world, so Akari's experience isn't surprising.) To help her, Kazu has to track down the story and, eventually, the now-eighty-two-year-old author.

The story-within-a-story is what makes Kashiwaba's novel such a testament to the power of imaginary worlds. Set in a fantasy land of witches, magicians, and missing princes, it stars a little girl descended from a ghost who returned to life. Her ancestry grants the girl, Adi, certain powers that an evil witch wants to use as a part of a spell to bring her own dead son back.

In the parts of the story written in the 1970s—the parts Akari read during her first life—the witch's ghostly son is a sinister figure. His mother promises he'll have his chance to "fill this land with hatred and fighting."

But by the time the author finishes the story for Kazu and Akari, real human relationships built over a shared fantasy world have changed the way all three think about life and death. The author has had time to reconsider why someone might cling so hard to life. Some characters "have an especially

Translated by Avery Fischer Udagawa (2021).

Sachiko Kashiwaba (b.1953) is a Japanese author of children's and young adult fantasy literature, whose books have often been adapted into animated films. Most notably, her novel The Marvellous Village Veiled in Mist (1975) was used as inspiration by director Hayao Miyazaki for his 2001 movie Spirited Away.

Following its translation into English, Temple Alley Summer received the American Library Association's Mildred L. Batchelder Award in 2022, which recognises the "most outstanding" work of children's literature each year.

strong attachment to life" and "[wish] to live, no matter what." Even the once-sinister prince becomes an object of pity. After he is defeated, his ghost lingers. "What does it mean to embrace life?" he asks Adi, as though he has never known.

Throughout, Kashiwaba's discourse about death is strikingly sophisticated for a children's novel. Even though Kazu fights for a second chance for his new friend, the words of his elderly neighbor ring no less true:

> Everybody in this world gets one lifetime, Kazu. One chance. We all try to live in such a way that we have no regrets [...] People have to live as if there is no second chance—so they'll make the most of every day.

The main narrative is a contemporary Japanese school story, but the older text of *The Moon Is on the Left* reflects the influence of European fantasy traditions on Japanese children's literature—in particular those of C. S. Lewis, one of Kashiwaba's acknowledged influences. The story also echoes the work of one of Lewis's most important influences, the nineteenth-century Scottish fantasy writer George MacDonald, author of works like *The Light Princess*.

Notably, Sachiko Kashiwaba is from the Tohoku region of Japan, the area most affected by the Triple Disasters of March 2011—the earthquake, tsunami, and meltdown at the Fukushima Daiichi Nuclear Power Plant. *Temple Alley Summer*'s 2011 debut made it a cultural touchpoint for children mourning the dead in the aftermath of the disasters. Kashiwaba paid homage to the 20,000 people who lost their lives with her later novel *The House of the Lost on the Cape* (also translated by Udagawa) in 2015.

PATRICK NESS

A Monster Calls (2011)

Struggling with his mother's terminal diagnosis, Conor wakes at 12:07 to a recurrent nightmare: the yew tree has transformed into a monster. The monster's cure for Conor's grief is to unlock the truth—through stories.

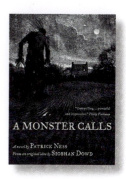

Dramatic, poignant, funny and profound, *A Monster Calls*, an exceptional novel written for children but engaging for readers of all ages, is the story of thirteen-year-old Conor O'Malley's struggle as he lives through his mother's terminal illness and faces up to her death with guidance from an imaginary storytelling monster. "Stories are wild creatures," the monster tells Connor and the four that he tells provide emotionally honest truths in an imaginary framework that help Conor to confront what he is avoiding.

The origin of *A Monster Calls* is as poignant as the story itself. Patrick Ness, already an award-winning author for his Chaos Walking fantasy sequence, was invited to write a novel inspired by a story fragment left by Siobhan Dowd, also an award-winning novelist, who died from cancer before she could write it herself. Having read the fragment, Ness had complete freedom to write his own story. He didn't try to write mirroring or imitating what Dowd would have done. Instead, he followed a principle that he felt was in tune with Dowd's own approach. "She would have set it free, let it grow and change." He said. "I was merely following the same process she would have followed, which is a different thing."

Patrick Ness fuses two narrative strands. In the first, Conor copes with the hope and despair brought on by his mother's treatment and the way that he is told about it, his challenging relationship with his grandmother, being bullied at school for his "situation" but also being curiously invisible because of it, is told in painfully sharp, everyday detail. In the second, Conor's nightmares lead to his meetings with the monster in a fantasy world inspired by nature in which everything from the monster himself and the emotions he allows Conor to explore are wild and tactile. Physically linked to the gnarled yew tree, known for its medicinal powers, outside Conor's bedroom window, the monster always appears at 12:07. He is powerful and loud but his intention is not to scare Conor. Instead, much to Conor's initial fury, he has come to tell Conor stories that will help him to understand how imprecise the world is and how hard it is to find answers. By telling his stories, all of which have mythological overtones, and by demanding Conor to tell his own story in

British-American author Patrick Ness (b.1971) won the Carnegie Medal, awarded for excellence in children's literature, both in 2012 for *A Monster Calls*, and the year before for the last book in his Chaos Walking series, *Monsters of Men* (2010).

On publication, *A Monster Calls* was garlanded with awards in the United Kingdom and the United States, including both the 2012 Carnegie and Greenaway medal.

A Monster Calls was adapted into a 2016 movie, starring Liam Neeson and Sigourney Weaver, and a 2018 stage play.

return, he forces Conor to express the "truth" as a way of unlocking his own complex feelings.

Unusually for a book for this age group, *A Monster Calls* was published with illustrations. Jim Kay's atmospheric illustrations, in particular his skilful blurring of the tree and the monster, are fundamental to the fantasy elements of the story. They bring life to the monster and augment Conor's internal struggles that are at the heart of the story.

By interweaving his wild fantasy stories into the everyday observations of Conor's struggle, Ness has created a profound story about death that pushes Conor to explore the emotional complexity of grief.

The monster sitting on the shed, illustrated by Jim Kay for the first edition.

It does not matter what you think, your mind will contradict itself a hundred times each day. Your mind will believe comforting lies while also knowing the painful truths that make those lies necessary. You do not write your life with words, you write it with actions. What you think is not important. It is only important what you do.

R. J. PALACIO (RAQUEL JARAMILLO)

WONDER (2012)

Ten-year-old Auggie, born with a facial abnormality, faces cruelty at school in a tale that has inspired a classroom movement to fight prejudice against disfigurement.

Since its publication in 2012, *Wonder* has been translated into 50 languages and has become a staple of middle-grade fiction. The novel started a global movement called "Choose Kind," through which children signed a kindness pledge.

Wanting to keep her "day job" identity as a book designer separate, Jaramillo published *Wonder* under a nom de plume, R. J. Palacio, derived from her initials and her grandmother's surname

Jaramillo later published the spin-offs *Auggie & Me* (2014), including an additional chapter from the perspective of Julian, the bully who victimizes Auggie, and *White Bird* (2019).

Raquel Jaramillo was working as a book designer in New York City when a trip to an ice cream store with her two sons changed everything. A girl with a significant facial disfigurement walked by. Jaramillo's younger son spotted her and started to cry. Unsure what to do, Jaramillo rushed him off so the girl would not have to witness his response. Afterward, Jaramillo felt haunted by the episode and by her own response, wishing she had instead stayed and talked to the girl, demonstrating by example that the child's facial difference was nothing to be scared of, and showing kindness to someone no doubt accustomed to being avoided and shunned.

Jaramillo, who grew up as the child of bookish Colombian immigrants, had always written fiction in her spare time. Soon after the ice cream store incident, she began waking up in the dark as her family slept to work on a story about a boy born with craniofacial deformities. August Pullman, as Jaramillo called her protagonist, has undergone years of reconstructive surgeries while being homeschooled by his mother, and is about to start middle school. Auggie, as he's known, is filled with dread at the prospect, having spent his life bearing up while people who see him for the first time do "that lookaway thing," watching the friends from his early childhood slowly drift away and avoid him. Now, every day at school, he will face the potential for casual cruelty that lurks in the pre-teen psyche.

While Jaramillo's younger son's encounter at the ice cream store sparked the idea that became *Wonder*, it was her older son's experience navigating the fifth grade social environment that gave the book its rocket fuel. "It's beautiful and painful watching kids that age transform into the adults they're going to be," Jaramillo has said, "doing and saying things, at times, that you know they might come to regret." She was determined that her story of a child whose very face shocks and frightens his peers would not simply reinforce the prevailing cultural narrative that all kids go through a mean stage, "as though that's a rite of passage." What if, she thought, the presence of a child like Auggie also, eventually, stirred up the other children's innate nobility? What if the adults around them, rather than looking away or throwing up their hands at the brutality of adolescence, managed to facilitate an ultimately positive experience for all the children involved?

Wonder was more than just the right message at the right time, however. Jaramillo wove realism, humor, and heart into her story, populating the novel with recognizable people who wrestle with conflicting feelings and don't always do the right thing. Short first-person chapters alternate between Auggie's point of view and those of his classmates, his teenage sister, Via, and Via's friends, each one distinctive and poignant. Together this symphony of young voices moves forward a classic plot that employs suspense, surprise, and emotional crescendo.

Auggie's first year at Beecher Academy is marked by a painful, slow-burning social ostracism engineered by a boy named Julian, including a secret game called "The Plague" requiring anyone who touches Auggie to wash their hands. But as time goes on, others find ways to protect Auggie from the worst of the blows. After another boy named Jack Will, whom Auggie initially took for an ally, unaccountably betrays him, the two forge an honest and genuine friendship. A girl named Summer withstands social pressure to sit at his lunch table every day ("Let's just say he's not the neatest eater in the world," she says. "But other than that he's pretty nice.") And when a school outing takes a scary turn involving bullies from another school, Auggie's ingenuity saves the day, and even results in a boost to his social standing. While no one ever quite sees him as "normal," most of his classmates, more often than not, learn to focus on Auggie's personal qualities like his sense of humor and his deep loyalty. At the year-end school celebration, Auggie receives a special award for bravery and a rousing standing ovation. By then everyone around him has grown as much as he has.

As for Auggie's family, there, too, Jaramillo created a heartbreaking yet ultimately uplifting portrait of winning characters faced with the unimaginable who, rather than despairing, choose to stick together and shore each other up. His parents may sometimes argue about how best to prepare Auggie for all the disappointments of his life, but they also reliably fall back on humor to stay sane. (When they learn the principal of Beecher Prep is named Mr. Tushman, for example, they let fly a torrent of posterior-oriented one-liners). Auggie's sister Via wrestles with her resentment about all the attention and resources Auggie has drained over the years, as she navigates her own tentative steps toward independence from this close-knit family, but she never wavers in her defense of her brother from the careless arrows of strangers.

Two promotional posters for the 2017 movie adaptation of *Wonder*, designed in the style of the book's original cover.

About The Contributors
Index & Credits

ABOUT THE CONTRIBUTORS

DANIEL HAHN – GENERAL EDITOR
Daniel Hahn is a writer, editor and translator. His translations have won the International Dublin Literary Award and the Independent Foreign Fiction Prize and been shortlisted for the International Booker Prize, among others. He was the editor of the most recent edition of *Oxford Companion to Children's Literature*, and is currently translating a Guatemalan novel, co-editing (with Padma Viswanathan) an anthology of Brazilian short stories, and writing a book about Shakespeare.
Winnie-the-Pooh (page 78), *The Adventures of Tintin: The Secret of the Unicorn* (page 102), *A Wrinkle in Time* (page 140), *The Great Piratical Rumbustification* (page 176), *Pig-Heart Boy* (page 216)

JULIA ECCLESHARE – FOREWORD
Julia Eccleshare MBE is a journalist, writer and former Children's Books editor at *The Guardian* and recipient of the Eleanor Farjeon Award for distinguished service to the world of children's books. She is the editor of *1001 Children's Books You Must Read Before You Grow Up* and has been Director of the Hay Festival Children's Programme since 2014
A Bear Called Paddington (page 128), *War Horse* (page 186), *Mortal Engines* (page 222), *A Monster Calls* (page 241)

JOHN BATCHELOR
John Batchelor is the Joseph Cowen Professor of and Head of Department for English Literature at Newcastle University. Formerly a Fellow of New College, Oxford and editor of the Modern Language Review, he is a celebrated biographer of John Ruskin, Joseph Conrad, and Alfred Tennyson.
The Jungle Book (page 48)

CATHERINE BUTLER
Catherine Butler is Professor of English Literature at Cardiff University, UK. Her books include *Reading History in Children's Books* (2012) and *British Children's Literature in Japanese Culture* (2023). She edits the journal *Children's Literature in Education*.
The Hobbit (page 97), *Kiki's Delivery Service* (page 192)

DAVID COLMER
David Colmer is a writer, editor and translator of Dutch literature in a range of genres. His translations of children's literature include works by Annie M.G. Schmidt, Toon Tellegen, Anna Woltz and Edward van de Vendel.
The Letter for the King (page 142), *The Cat Who Came in off the Roof* (page 166)

NICOLA DALY
Nicola Daly is a sociolinguist and Associate Professor at the University of Waikato, Aotearoa New Zealand, specialising in children's literature.
The Whale Rider (page 198)

SARA K. DAY
Sara K. Day is an independent scholar and editor with a background of research in children's and young adult literature. She is the author of *Reading Like a Girl: Narrative Intimacy in Contemporary American Young Adult Literature*.
Are You There God? Its me, Margret (page 168)

MARIANNE ELOISE
Marianne Eloise is a journalist and the author of the essay collection *Obsessive, Intrusive, Magical Thinking* (2022).
The Bad Beginning (page 218)

JOSEPH FARRELL
Joseph Farrell is an Emeritus Professor of Italian at the University of Strathclyde, biographer of Dario Fo and Franca Rame, author of works on Sicily, Italian theatre, duelling, R L Stevenson in Samoa, as well as translator of several plays and novels from Italian.
The Adventures of Pinocchio (page 40)

ALISON FINCHER
Alison Fincher is the founder of *Read Japanese Literature* and co-editor for Japanese fiction at the *Asian Review of Books*.
Temple Alley Summer (page 239)

ALISON FLOOD
Alison Flood is comment and culture editor at the New Scientist and former books writer at the Guardian. She chairs the British Book Awards' Crime and Thriller Book of the Year award and was a judge for the 2024 Baillie Gifford Non-Fiction Prize.
Heidi (page 37), *The Hundred and One Dalmatians* (page 126)

ROSEMARY GORING
Rosemary Goring is a columnist and reviewer with the *Herald*, where she was literary editor for many years. Her books include the novels *After Flodden* and *Dacre's War*, and *Homecoming: The Scottish Years of Mary, Queen of Scots*.
Asterix the Gaul (page 134), *Stig of the Dump* (page 149)

ROBERT HOLDEN
Lecturer, historian, and the author of over thirty books, Robert Holden has received awards from the Literature Board of the Australia Council, held a Mitchell Library Fellowship, and spoken at numerous conferences in Australia and at the Universities of Oxford and Cambridge.
Walkabout (page 130)

KAT HOWARD
Kat Howard is a writer of fiction and comics, including the Alex Award-winning novel, *An Unkindness of Magicians* (2017).
The Golden Compass (page 204)

SIMON HUBBERT
Simon Hubbert is a Reader in Mathematics at Birkbeck, University of London. He is the author of *Essential Mathematics for Market Risk Management* (2012). He has previously worked as a risk analyst for HM Treasury and has conducted advisory work for IBM.
The Number Devil (page 214)

JON HUGHES
Jon Hughes is Reader in German and Cultural Studies at Royal Holloway University of London, and has published widely on modern German literature and film.
Emil and the Detectives (page 82)

PETER HUNT
Peter Hunt is Professor Emeritus in English and Children's Literature at Cardiff University, UK, and holds the Anne Devereaux Jordan Award for Distinguished Service to Children's Literature. He has lectured widely and has written and edited 36 books, the latest of which is *Alice's Oxford: the People and Places that Inspired Wonderland* (2025).
The Wind in the Willows (page 66)

ROSEMARY JOHNSTON
Rosemary Johnston is the author of *Australian Literature for Young People* (2017). She was previously the Director of the International Centre for Youth Futures at the University of Technology Sydney, Australia. She has sat on the board of the Australasian Association for Children's Literature and Research, as well as numerous other international literary organisations.
Seven Little Australians (page 45)

SAM JORDISON
Sam Jordison is the co-director of the independent publisher Galley Beggar Press, a journalist and literary critic, and the author of several works of nonfiction, including *Enemies of the People* (2017).
The Phantom Tollbooth (page 136)

REYES LAZARO
Reyes Lázaro teaches language, cultures and literatures of Iberia at Smith College Massachusetts, USA, where she also directs the Translation Studies Concentration.
Charlotte's Web (page 122)

EMILY LETHBRIDGE
Emily Lethbridge is a writer and researcher at the Árni Magnússon Institute for Icelandic Studies at the University of Iceland, Reykjavík.
The Wolves of Willoughby Chase (page 146), *Haroun and the Sea of Stories* (page 200), *The Story of the Blue Planet* (page 220)

ANTONIA LLOYD-JONES
Antonia Lloyd-Jones is a translator of Polish contemporary literature. She is a former co-chair of the UK Translator's Association,

and in 2018 received Poland's Transatlantyk Award for outstanding ambassadorship of Polish literature abroad.
Detective Nosegoode and the Music Box Mystery (page 160)

SARAH MESLE
Sarah Mesle is a professor of writing at the University of Southern California. A frequent contributor to the Los Angeles Review of Books, her writing on gender, literature, and culture has also appeared in venues ranging from Studies in American Fiction to InStyle to The New York Times Magazine. She is the co-editor of the NYU short book series Avidly Reads and the author of Reasons and Feelings: Writing for the Humanities Now (Chicago UP, 2025).
Anne of Green Gables (page 62)

LAURA MILLER
Laura Miller is currently books and culture columnist for Slate and the author of *The Magician's Book: A Skeptic's Adventures in Narnia* (2008). She was co-founder of Salon.com and her work has appeared in *The New Yorker*, *The Guardian* and *The New York Times Book Review* amongst others.
The Lion, the Witch and the Wardrobe (page 116)

MAHVESH MURAD
Mahvesh Murad is an editor, critic and voice artist. She is the co-editor of the World Fantasy Award- nominated short story anthologies *The Djinn Falls in Love* and *The Outcast Hours*.
A Wizard of Earthsea (page 162)

ABIGAIL NUSSBAUM
Abigail Nussbaum is a reviewer and critic, winner of the Hugo and BSFA awards. She is the former reviews editor of Strange Horizons, and her writing has appeared in the Guardian and New Scientist. Her review collection, Track Changes, was published in 2024 by Briardene Books.
The Moomins and the Great Flood (page 113)

MARGARET J. OAKES
Margaret Oakes is a Professor of English at Furman University in Greenville, South Carolina. She holds a PhD from Stanford University in English and Humanities, and is the author of *To Gender or Not To Gender: Casting and Characters for 21st Century Shakespeare* (2024).
Howl's Moving Castle (page 194), *Harry Potter and the Philosopher's Stone* (page 208)

STEPHANIE OWEN REEDER
Dr Stephanie Owen Reeder is an award-winning author of books for children. She has worked as a teacher, a critic, and as a Hansard editor at the Federal Parliament of Australia.
Under the Mountain (page 178), *The Book Thief* (page 232)

JESS PAYN
Jess Payn is a writer and editor whose essays and reviews have been published in *The Times Literary Supplement*, *The London Magazine*, *The i Paper*, and *theartsdesk*, among others.
Watership Down (page 170)

ERIC RABKIN
Eric S. Rabkin, University of Michigan Professor Emeritus of English Language and Literature and of Art & Design, includes among his books works on fantasy, science fiction, literary theory and pedagogy.
The Little Prince (page 108)

KIM REYNOLDS
Kimberley Reynolds OBE is Professor Emerita of Children's Literature, School of English Literature, Language and Linguistics at Newcastle University, UK. She helped found the UK Children's Laureate and Seven Stories, the National Centre for Children's Books. Recipient of the Children's Literature Association Book Award (twice) and the International Brothers Grimm Award for contributions to children's literature research (2013).
Ballet Shoes (page 95)

MARIA RUSSO
Maria Russo is Editor-at-Large at Union Square Kids, an imprint of Hachette Book Group, where she acquires and edits children's picture books. A longtime cultural journalist, she served for several years as Children's Books Editor for the New York Times, and she is the co-author of How to Raise a Reader (Workman, 2019). Russo holds a Ph.D. In English and Comparative Literature from Columbia University and a B.A. in English from Georgetown University.
Wonder (page 244)

ELENA SHEPPARD
Elena Sheppard is an author and critic based in New York, whose work has been featured in *The Cut*, *The New York Times*, *Catapult*, and *The*

Guardian. She holds an MFA in non-fiction writing from Columbia University.
Little Women (page 24), Mary Poppins (page 92), The Story of a Seagull and the Cat Who Taught Her to Fly (page 206), The Wild Book (page 236)

JARED SHURIN
Jared Shurin is the editor of The Djinn Falls in Love, The Best of British Fantasy series, The Big Book of Cyberpunk, and many others, including the pop culture website Pornokitsch.
The Sword in the Stone (page 100), The Dark is Rising (page 174)

DREW SMITH
Drew Smith is an award-winning food writer and former editor of The Good Food Guide. He is the author of Oyster: a Gastronomic History (2015) and translator and editor of La Mère Brazier (2016). He also runs the literary blog 101greatreads.com
The Little Mermaid (page 18), Fattypuffs and Thinifers (page 84)

MICHELLE SMITH
Michelle J. Smith is Associate Professor in English at Monash University, Australia. She is author and editor of many books about children's and Victorian literature, including Literary Cultures and Nineteenth-Century Childhoods and The Edinburgh History of Children's Periodicals.
The Secret Garden (page 70), Peter and Wendy (page 73), The Neverending Story (page 181)

MAUREEN SPELLER
Maureen Speller was a critic and reviewer of science fiction and fantasy, She was senior reviews editor at Strange Horizons and assistant editor of Foundation: The International Review of Science Fiction.
Inkheart (page 225)

BJÖRN SUNDMARK
Björn Sundmark is Professor of English literature at Malmö University, Sweden, and has published numerous books and articles on children's literature. He is also the co-editor of The Nation in Children's Literature (2013).
The Wonderful Adventures of Nils (page 60)

JOHN SUTHERLAND
John Sutherland is an English Academic, columnist and author, and is Emeritus Lord Northcliffe Professor of Modern English Literature at University College London. He is the author of many books including How to Read a Novel: A User's Guide (2006) and Curiosities of Literature: A Feast for Book Lovers (2008). He writes regularly for The Times, The Guardian and The New York Times among others.
Alice's Adventures in Wonderland (page 18), The Adventures of Tom Sawyer (page 32), Treasure Island (page 42), The Wonderful Wizard of Oz (page 50)

JOHN STEPHENS
John Stephens is Emeritus Professor at Macquarie University, Australia. He was Editor of International Research in Children's Literature from 2007-2016. In 2007 he received the 11th International Brothers Grimm Award and in 2014 the Ann Devereaux Jordan Award, in recognition of his contribution to research in children's literature.
The Arrival (page 234)

FRANCESCA TANCINI
Francesca Tancini is art and illustration historian with postdoctoral fellowships at Harvard, Oxford, Princeton and Yale. Librarian and curator, she has been Marie Skłodowska-Curie Fellow at Newcastle University with a project on picturebooks in partnership with the Victoria and Albert Museum and Seven Stories, the National Centre for Children's Books.
Telephone Tales (page 144)

PHOEBE TAPLIN
Phoebe Taplin is a freelance journalist and writer based in the U.K. She specializes in culture and travel and has written several guidebooks about walking, film locations, and literary explorations in Britain and beyond. Her work has appeared in The Guardian, Country Walking, Sunday Times Travel Magazine, amongst others.
The Tale of Peter Rabbit (page 56), The Room on the Roof (page 124)

JAMES THURGILL
James Thurgill is Associate Professor by Special Appointment at The University of Tokyo, Japan. He is the co-author of A Todai Philosophical Walk (2021) and co-editor of the University of Wales Press' Literary Geography: Theory and Practice book series.
Night on the Galactic Railroad (page 88)

ANJA TRÖGER
Dr Anja Tröger is Lecturer in Scandinavian Studies at the University of Edinburgh, Scotland. Her research focuses on contemporary Scandinavian literature and she also teaches Norwegian language.
Pippi Longstocking (page 111)

NICHOLAS TUCKER
Nicholas Tucker was formerly Senior Lecturer in Cultural Studies at the University of Sussex. He has also been a teacher and an educational psychologist. He is the author of books about childhood and reading, and has also written six books for children.
Black Beauty (page 32), *Five Children and It* (page 54), *The Faraway Tree* (page 106), *Charlie and the Chocolate Factory* (page 151), *The Mouse and His Child* (page 158)

LISA TUTTLE
Lisa Tuttle is an award-winning author of fantasy, horror and science fiction. She also reviews for *The Guardian*.
A Dog of Flanders (page 28)

KIERA VACLAVIK
Kiera Vaclavik is Professor of Children's Literature and Childhood Culture at Queen Mary University of London.
Nobody's Boy (page 34), *The Sheep-Pig* (page 188)

DERONG XU
Derong Xu is Professor of English Language and Literature at Ocean University of China, Qingdao. His research interests include children's literature and translation studies.
Bronze and Sunflower (page 230)

INDEX

101 Dalmatians (Smith), 128–9

Adams, Richard, 172–5
Adelaide, 132
adolescence, 126, 171, 245
Adventures of Pinocchio, The (Collodi), 42–3, 110
Adventures of Tintin, The (Hergé), 104–7
Adventures of Tom Sawyer, The (Twain), 15, 32–3
Aeschylus, 172
Africa, 14, 110
Aiken, Joan, 15, 152–4
Alcott, Louisa May, 11, 14, 26–9,
Alice's Adventures in Wonderland (Carroll), 10, 21–5, 78, 126, 215, 232
allegory, 123, 137, 200
American Civil War, 26, 32
Amis, Kingsley, 158
Andersen, Hans Christian, 18–20,78, 146, 168, 178, 192, 230
anime, 36, 56, 62, 93, 193, 240
Anne of Green Gables (Montgomery), 64–7

Are You There God? It's Me, Margaret (Blume), 170–1
Arrival, The (Tan), 234–5
Arthurian legend, 103, 118, 144, 176
Asterix the Gaul (Goscinny and Uderzo), 15, 136–7
Auckland, 181–3, 198
Australia, 47–9, 78, 94, 132–3, 228, 232, 234

Bad Beginning, The (Snicket), 218–9
Ballet Shoes (Streatfeild), 97–8
ballet, 61, 97–8
Barrie, J. M., 44, 75–9
Barthes, Roland, 227
Baum, L. Frank, 15, 52–5
Bear Called Paddington, A (Bond, M.), 130–1
Belgium, 30–1, 104
Berlin, 14, 84–5
Bildungsroman, 62
Black Beauty (Sewell), 30, 34–5
Blackadder, 137
Blackman, Malorie, 216–7
Blume, Judy, 14, 170–1

Blyton, Enid, 85, 108–9
Bonaparte, Napoleon, 173
Bond, Michael, 130–1
Bond, Ruskin, 126–7
Book Thief, The (Zusak), 228, 232–3
bourgeois society, 38, 100, 114
Brazil, 192, 228
British Empire, 50, 152
Bronze and Sunflower (Cao), 230–1
Brussels, 104
Buddhism, 90–3, 240
Bunyan, John, 139, 173
Burnett, Frances Hodgson, 72–4
butterfly, 220

California, U. S. A., 44
Camazotz, 142–3
Canada, 64–7, 152
Cao Wenxuan, 230–1
Carnegie Medal, 178 216, 222
Carroll, Lewis (Charles Lutwidge Dodgson), 21–5, 78, 89, 189, 214
Cat Who Came in off the Roof, The (Schmidt), 168–9

Cattish, 168–9
Charlie and the Chocolate Factory (Dahl), 115, 155–9, 124–5, 188
Cheshire Cat, the, 21, 24–5
China, 27, 230–1
Christianity, 18–20, 90–2, 112, 118, 142, 170
Clemens, Samuel Langhorne (Mark Twain), 15, 32–3
climate change, 220–1
Collodi, Carlo, 42–3
Colombia, 244
Cooper, Susan, 176–7, 183
Count Olaf, 218–9
countryside, 56, 61, 68, 102, 108, 129, 131, 150, 172, 187, 194, 222, 230–1
  see also rural life
Cruella de Vil, 128–9
Cultural Revolution, 230

Dahl, Roald, 89, 115, 155–9, 168, 180,
Dark is Rising, The (Cooper), 176–7, 183
death, 27, 30, 33, 39, 44, 46, 64, 68, 72, 90, 100, 113, 124–5, 133, 136, 159, 161, 188, 202, 216, 228–9, 232–3, 240–1, 242–3
detective genre, 84–5, 106, 162–3
Detective Nosegoode and the Music Box Mystery (Orłoń), 162–3
Devon, England, 186–7
Dickens, Charles, 20, 33, 152, 213, 222
Disney, 42–3, 50–1, 80, 94, 120–1, 128–9, 143
Döblin, Alfred, 85
Dodgson, Charles Lutwidge (Lewis Carroll), 21–5, 78, 89, 189, 214
Dog of Flanders, A (Ouida), 30–1
Dostoevsky, Fyodor, 173
Dover, England, 152
Dowd, Siobhan, 242
Dr. Who, 181
Dragt, Tonke, 14, 144–5
dream, 29, 30, 52–5, 56, 74, 94, 108, 128, 165, 170, 203, 208, 214–5, 220
Dumas, Alexandre, 36
dwarf, 52, 99–100, 118–9

Earthsea, 164–5
Edinburgh, 44
Edwardian period, 50, 60, 72, 78
Eeyore, 80
elf, 62, 99–100
Emerald City, The, 52–5
Emil and the Detectives (Kästner), 84–5
empathy, 68, 183, 229, 237
Enchanted Wood, 10, 108
Ende, Michael, 14, 184–5
England, 15, 21, 51, 58–61, 68, 70, 72, 100, 150, 152, 172, 177, 186, 204, 208, 222
English Caravan Club, 71
Enzensberger, Hans Magnus, 214–5

fable, 18, 58, 173
fairy, 43, 56–7, 108
fairy tale, 18–20, 62, 78, 90, 99, 144, 146, 152, 194, 200, 221
Fantastica, 184–5
fantasy, 14–5, 27, 42–3, 78, 96, 145, 152, 164–5, 181, 184, 194–5, 204, 224, 241, 242
  adventure, 42, 62
  novel, 152, 178, 240
  nonsense fantasy, 21
  world, 10, 75, 90, 99–100, 184, 194, 240, 242
Fattypuffs and Thinifers (Maurois), 88–9
Five Children and It (Nesbit), 50, 56–7
Flanders, 30–1
France, 15, 36, 110, 136–7
Franco-Prussian War, 36, 88
friendship, 75, 78, 102, 124, 126, 136, 150, 152, 163, 170, 192–3, 217, 220, 228–9
Funke, Cornelia, 15, 225–7

Gandalf, 99
Garibaldi, Giuseppe, 42
Gaul, 15, 136–7
Gee, Maurice, 181–3
genie, 200
Germany, 20, 84–5, 88, 136, 184, 186, 214, 225, 232–3
ghost, 154, 240–1
Gleitzman, Morris, 228–9
God, 20, 39–41, 118, 170–1, 204
Golden Compass, The (Pullman), 204–5
Gollum, 99–101

Goscinny, René, 136–7
Grahame, Kenneth, 68–71, 156
graphic novel (*bande-dessinée*), 104, 136, 142, 234
Great Piratical Rumbustification, The (Mahy), 178–80
grief, 39, 74, 218, 238, 242–3

Hamburg, Germany, 206
Handler, Daniel (Lemony Snicket), 218–9
Haroun and the Sea of Stories (Rushdie), 15, 200–3
Harry Potter, 85, 208–13
Harry Potter and the Sorcerer's Stone (Rowling), 208–13
Heidi (Spyri), 39–41
Hergé (George Remi), 104–7, 136
Himalayas, the, 106, 126
Hitler, Adolf, 233
Hoban, Russell, 160–1
Hobbit, The (Tolkien), 99–101
Hogwarts, 10, 208–13
Hollywood, 31, 52
horses, 18, 34–5, 45, 68, 113, 119, 145, 186–7
Howl's Moving Castle (Jones), 194–5
Huckleberry Finn, 32–3
Hugo, Victor, 36, 164

Iceland, 220–1
Ihimaera, Witi, 198–9
immigrant experience, 236–7, 244
India, 50–1, 72, 126–7
Indigenous Australians, 49, 132–3
Indonesia, 144
Inkheart (Funke), 225–7
Ireland, 118
Islam, 202
Italy, 36, 42–3, 136, 146–7

Jansson, Tove, 115–7
Japan, 14, 31, 36, 56, 62, 90, 144, 192–3, 239–40
Jerome, Jerome K., 71
Jones, Diana Wynne, 194–5
Judaism, 88, 131, 170, 228, 232
  persecution of Jews, 131, 228–9, 232–3
Jungle Book, The (Kipling), 50–1, 62, 78
Juster, Norton, 15, 138–41

Kadono, Eiko, 192–3
Kashiwaba, Sachiko, 239–40
Kästner, Erich, 14, 84–5
Kiki's Delivery Service (Kadono), 192–3
King Arthur, 102–3
see also Arthurian legend
King James III, 15, 152
King-Smith, Dick, 188–9
King, Clive, 150–151
Kingsley, Charles, 18–20, 21
Kipling, Rudyard, 50–1, 62, 150

L'Engle, Madeleine, 14, 142–3
Lagerlöf, Selma, 62–3,
Lang, Fritz, 85
Latin, 24, 125, 136,
Le Guin, Ursula K., 15, 164–167
Letter for the King, The (Dragt), 144–5
Lewis, C. S., 118–23, 176, 181, 194, 204, 240
Lindgren, Astrid, 113–4, 168, 236
Lion, the Witch, and the Wardrobe, The (Lewis), 118–23
Little Mermaid, The (Andersen), 18–20
Little Prince, The (Saint-Exupéry), 42, 110–2
Little Women (Alcott), 11, 26–9
London, 18, 27, 34, 36, 46, 58, 75, 78, 80, 94, 90, 126, 129, 131, 132, 152, 177, 186–7, 200, 204, 213, 222–4
Long John Silver, 44
Lord of the Rings, The (Tolkien), 100–1
loyalty, 10, 49, 106, 124, 217

MacDonald, George, 21, 100
Mad Hatter, the, 21, 23
Magic Faraway Tree, The (Blyton), 108–9
magic, 11, 52, 62, 65–67, 74, 78, 92–3, 94–6, 108–9, 118–9, 138–9, 146, 162, 164–5, 176, 192–3, 194–5, 200, 203, 208–213, 220
  of books, 236–8
  of childhood, 78
  of numbers, 138
magical realism, 203, 239
Magnason, Andri Snær, 220–1
Mahy, Margaret, 178–80
Malot, Hector, 36–8
Māori, 181, 198–9

Marshall, James Vance (Donald Gordon Payne), 132–3
Mary Poppins (Travers), 11, 94–6
Massachusetts, U. S. A, 26–27
Maurois, André, 88–9
Mexico, 238
Middle-earth, 99–101, 165, 181
migration, 234–5
  see also refugee
Milan, Italy, 147
Milne, A. A., 15, 80–3
minotaur, 119
Missouri, U. S. A., 32
Miyazaki, Hayao, 192–3, 194, 239
Miyazawa, Kenji, 90–3
Monster Calls, A (Ness), 241–3
Montgomery, Lucy Maud, 14, 64–7
Moomins and the Great Flood, The (Jansson), 115–7
moon, 104, 106, 108, 184, 240–1
Morpurgo, Michael, 186–7
Morris, William, 100
Mortal Engines (Reeve), 222–4
Mount Vernon, 124
Mouse and His Child, The (Hoban), 160–1
mythology, 68, 96, 100, 144, 176, 221, 241
  Greek, 56
  Norse, 99–100, 108–9, 118

Narnia, 10, 118–23, 181, 204, 213
Nazis, 84, 89, 137, 228, 232–3
Nesbit, E., 56–7
Ness, Patrick, 241–3
Netherlands, the, 144, 168
Neverending Story, The (Ende), 184–5
Neverland, 10, 65, 75–79
New Jersey, U. S. A., 170
New York City, 27, 80, 170, 199, 192–3, 200, 244
New York Times, The, 170, 225
New Yorker, The, 81, 124, 139
New Zealand, 178, 181–3, 198–9
Night on the Galactic Railroad (Miyazawa), 90–3
nightmare, 13, 49, 55, 241
Nobel Prize, 51, 62, 146
Nobody's Boy (Malot), 36–8
North Pole, 94
Number Devil, The (Enzensberger), 214–5

Oliver Twist, 20, 33

Once (Gleitzman), 228–9
Orientalism, 173
Orłoń, Marian, 162–3
orphan, 30, 36, 39, 50, 52, 64, 67, 72, 152, 218–9, 228
Orwell, George, 188
Ouida (Marie Louise de la Ramé), 30–1
Oxford, University of, 21, 99, 101, 118, 176, 181, 194, 204

Paddington Bear, 130–1
Palacio, R. J., 13, 244–5
paradise, 215
Paris, 27, 36, 208, 236
Payne, Donald Gordon (James Vance Marshall), 132–3
Peru, 130
Peter and Wendy (Barrie), 44, 75–9
Peter Pan, 75–9
Peter Rabbit, 58–61
Phantom Tollbooth, The (Juster), 14–5, 138–41
Pig-Heart Boy (Blackman), 216–7
Pinocchio, 42–3, 62, 110
Pippi Longstocking (Lindgren), 113–4
pirate, 33, 44–5, 65, 75, 78, 104, 178–80,
Platform 9¾, 10, 208, 212
Poland, 162–3, 228
pollution, 200, 207
Pooh, 80–3
Potter, Beatrix, 58–61, 156
Pratchett, Terry, 232
Primrose Hill, 129
Prince Edward Island, Canada, 14, 64–7
Princeton University, 89
Pullman, Philip, 10, 204–5

Queen Elizabeth II, 130

rabbits, 21–24, 58–61, 80, 172–5
rabbit hole, 10, 58
Reeve, Philip, 14, 222–4
refugee, 131, 222, 232
  see also migration
religion, 143, 162, 170–1
  critique of, 204
Remi, George (Hergé), 104–7, 136
Robin Hood, 33, 102
Rodari, Gianni, 14, 146–149

Roman Empire, 137
Room on the Roof, The (Bond, R.), 126–7
Rousseau, Jean-Jacques, 37
Rowling, J. K., 208–13, 225
Rubens, Peter Paul, 30
rural life, 30, 49, 55, 102, 173, 177, 189, 230–1
  see also countryside
Rushdie, Salman, 15, 200–3

Saint-Exupéry, Antoine de, 42, 110–2
satire, 70, 161, 188
Scandinavia, 115–7
Schmidt, Annie M. G., 14, 168–9
science, 18, 143, 216–7, 221
science fiction, 89, 217
Scotland, 58, 68, 128
Secret Garden, The (Burnett), 72–4
Sepúlveda, Luis, 206–7
Series of Unfortunate Events, A (Snicket), 218–9
Seven Little Australians (Turner), 47–9
Sewell, Anna, 30, 34–5
Shakespeare, William, 94, 97, 173
Sheep-Pig, The (King-Smith), 15, 188–9
Smith, Dodie, 128–9
Snicket, Lemony (Daniel Handler), 218–9
social norms, 10, 234
sorcerer, 164, 202, 208–13
Sorcerer's Stone, 208–13
South Carolina, U. S. A., 132
Spenser, Edmund, 118
Spielberg, Steven, 104, 106, 186–7
Spyri, Johanna, 39–41
Stevenson, Robert Louis, 44–6
Stig of the Dump (King), 150–151
Stockholm, 193
Stone Age, 150–1
Story of a Seagull and the Cat Who Taught Her to Fly, The (Sepúlveda), 206–7
Story of the Blue Planet, The (Magnason), 220–1
Stranger Things, 85
Streatfeild, Noel, 97–8
Studio Ghibli, 192–3, 194–5, 240
Surrealism, 146, 184–5
Sweden, 62–3, 113–4, 115, 168, 193
Swift, Jonathan, 89
Swiss Alps, 39

Switzerland, 36, 39
Sword in the Stone, The (White, T.), 15, 102–3

Tale of Peter Rabbit, The (Potter), 58–61
Tan, Shaun, 234–5
Taoism, 164–5
Telephone Tales (Rodari), 146–149
Temple Alley Summer (Kashiwaba), 240–1
Texas, U. S. A., 35
Thames Valley, 176
Thatcher, Margaret, 181
Tinker Bell, 75
Tintin, 14, 104–7
tipuna (ancestor), 198
Tolkien, J. R. R., 15, 99–101, 118, 176, 181, 194
Travers, P. L., 11, 94–6
Treasure Island (Stevenson), 44–6, 227
Turner, Ethel, 47–9
Twain, Mark (Samuel Langhorne Clemens), 15, 32–3

Uderzo, Albert, 136–7
Under the Mountain (Gee), 181–3
United Kingdom, 57, 97, 145, 155, 168, 241
United States, 55, 72, 97, 142, 147, 152, 155, 204, 241

Verne, Jules, 36
Victorian period, 49, 50, 58, 152, 194, 222
  childhood 20, 46, 218
  literature, 18, 72, 78,
Villoro, Juan, 236–8
Voldemort, 208

Wales, 59, 194
Walkabout (Marshall), 132–3
War Horse (Morpurgo), 186–7
Warsaw, 229
Water-Babies, The (Kingsley), 18–20, 21
Watership Down (Adams), 172–5
Weimar Republic, 84
werewolf, 119, 184
Whale Rider, The (Ihimaera), 198–9
whales, 198–9
Where the Wild Things Are, 13
White, E. B., 124–5

White, T. H., 15, 102–3
Wild Book, The (Villoro), 236–8
Wilde, Oscar, 70
Willy Wonka, 155–9
Wind in the Willows, The (Grahame), 50, 68–71
Winnie-the-Pooh (Milne), 80–3
witch, 55, 102, 118–23, 164, 192–3, 194–5, 204, 213, 239
witchcraft, 193, 212
Wizard of Earthsea, A (Le Guin), 164–7
wizard, 52–5, 99–100, 164–5, 181, 185, 194, 208–13
Wolves of Willoughby Chase, The (Aiken), 15, 152–4
Wonder (Palacio) 13, 244–5
Wonderful Adventures of Nils, The (Lagerlöf), 62–3
Wonderful Wizard of Oz, The (Baum), 15, 52–5, 185,
World War I, 44, 88, 186
World War II, 89, 97, 110, 124, 131, 137, 144, 187, 188, 195, 228
Wrinkle in Time, A (L'Engle), 142–3

Yorkshire, England, 47, 72

Zusak, Markus, 228, 232–3

PICTURE CREDITS

Alamy Stock Photo:
© AF Fotografie, 25. © AJ Pics, 219. © Alamy Cinematic Collection, 106. © Alamy Stock Photo Album, 111, 185. © Allstar Picture Library Ltd., 51, 129. © Chronicle, 177. © ClassicStock, 4-5. © Entertainment Pictures, 171. © Everett Collection Inc., 193. © The Granger Collection, 33. © GRANGER Historical Picture Archive, 69, 125. © Keith Corrigan, 71. © Lebrecht Music & Arts, 28, 45, 73. © Maximum Film, 196-197, 205. © Moviestore Collection Ltd, 133, 143. © Pictorial Press Ltd, 24, 53, 137, 187. © PictureLux / The Hollywood Archive, 199. © Pauline Baynes, 119. © Screenprod / Protononstop, 43. © TCD/Prod.DB, 190-191. © United Archives GmbH, 114. © Weinstein Company, 86-87. © ZUMA Press, Inc., 212.

© Alexis Deacon, 2024, 4-5. © Alice Cao, 2023, 227. © Aslaug Jonsdottir, 2015, 221. © Auckland Libraries Heritage Collections, 182. © Boston Public Library, 12. © The British Library, 31. © California Public Libraries, 19. © Camilla Cerea, 2020, 207. © Changjiang Literature Press, 2013, 229. © Cornelia Funke, 2005, 226. © Curtis Brown Group Ltd., 71 81, 82-83, 95. © David Lupton, 2015, 166, 167. © David Wyatt, 2009, 223. © Edward Ardizzone, used by permission of David Higham Associates, 151. © Frederick Warne & Co. Ltd., 59, 60. © French National Library, 37, 38. © Gabriel Martinez Meave, 2008, 239. © Group TAC Co., Ltd., 93. © HarperCollins Children's Books., 131. © ImagoAnimae, via The Commons, 147. © Janelle Carbajal, 2019, 195. © Jerzy Flisak, with permission by Wydawnictwo Dwie Siostry,, 163. ©Jim Kay, 209, 210-211, 243. © Joe Winter Blog, 89. © Jules Feiffer, used by permission of Random House Children's Books, 139, 140-141. © Kodansha, 2011, 241. © Maastricht University Library, 22, 23. © Macmillan 1997, 215. © Martin Rowson, 201, 203. © Mary Rayner Estate, 189. © Meilo So, 2015, 231. © Moomin Characters, 116, 117. © Natulive Canada, via The Commons, 67. © Orion Publishing Group, 1936, 98. © Paolo D'Altan, 2008, 174-175. © Parol-Sha Publishing, 2008, 91. © Penguin Random House, 1956, 127. © Penguin Random House, 1976, 161. © Penguin Random House, 2025, 217. © Quentin Blake, used by permission of United Agents Ltd., 157, 158-159, 179. © Rauner Special Collections Library, 74. © Rohan Eason, 2012, 153. © Saint-Exupéry Estate, 112. © Shaun Tan, 2006, 237. Shutterstock: © Neftali, 131. © Singel Uitgeverijen, 1971, 169. © Tintinimaginatio S.A., 105. © Tolkien Estate, via the Bodleian Library, 101, 246-247. © Twentieth Century Fox, 2013, 233. © Uitgeverij Leopold, 1962, 134-135, 145. © Ursula K. Le Guin, 2001, 165. © Victoria & Albert Museum, 76-77. © Valerio Vidali, 2020, 147, 148-149. © Zuma Press, Inc., 2017, 245.

Images in public domain:
Arthur Rackham, 16-17. Attilio Mussino, 43. Cecil Alden, 35. Emil Johann Lauffer, 103. Francis Donkin Bedford, 79. Frank T. Merrill, 27. John Fleming Cullen MacFarlane, 48. Mary Hamilton Frye, 63. M.A. and W.A.J Claus, 65. Oluf Bagge, 109. Walter Trier, 85. William Wallace Denslow, 54, 55, 57.